# How Congress Evolves

## By Nelson W. Polsby

*Community Power and Political Theory*
(1963, 1980)

*Politics and Social Life*
(Edited, with Robert A. Dentler and Paul A. Smith, 1963)

*New Perspectives on the House of Representatives*
(Edited, with Robert L. Peabody, 1963, 1969, 1977, 1992)

*Congress and the Presidency*
(1964, 1971, 1976, 1986)

*Presidential Elections*
(with Aaron Wildavsky, 1964, 1968, 1971, 1976, 1980, 1984, 1988, 1991, 1996, 2000)

*Reapportionment in the 1970s*
(Edited, 1971)

*Political Promises*
(1974)

*Handbook of Political Science*
(Edited, with Fred I. Greenstein, 1975)

*British Government and Its Discontents*
(with Geoffrey Smith, 1981)

*What if? Explorations in Social Science Fiction*
(Edited, 1982)

*Consequences of Party Reform*
(1983)

*Political Innovation in America: The Politics of Policy Initiation*
(1984)

*Media and Momentum*
(Edited, with Gary Orren, 1987)

*New Federalist Papers*
(with Alan Brinkley and Kathleen Sullivan, 1997)

# How Congress Evolves

*Social Bases of Institutional Change*

Nelson W. Polsby

OXFORD
UNIVERSITY PRESS

# OXFORD
UNIVERSITY PRESS

Oxford University Press, Inc., publishes works that further
Oxford University's objective of excellence
in research, scholarship, and education.

Oxford    New York
Auckland    Cape Town    Dar es Salaam    Hong Kong    Karachi
Kuala Lumpur    Madrid    Melbourne    Mexico City    Nairobi
New Delhi    Shanghai    Taipei    Toronto

With offices in
Argentina    Austria    Brazil    Chile    Czech Republic    France    Greece
Guatemala    Hungary    Italy    Japan    Poland    Portugal    Singapore
South Korea    Switzerland    Thailand    Turkey    Ukraine    Vietnam

Copyright © 2004 by Oxford University Press, Inc.

First published in 2004 by Oxford University Press, Inc.
198 Madison Avenue, New York, New York 10016

www.oup.com

First issued as an Oxford University Press paperback, 2005

Oxford is a registered trademark of Oxford University Press

Library of Congress Cataloging-in-Publication Data
Polsby, Nelson W.
How Congress evolves : social bases of institutional change /
by Nelson W. Polsby.
p. cm.
Includes bibliographical references and index.
ISBN-13 978-0-19-516195-3; 978-0-19-518296-5 (pbk.)
ISBN 0-19-516195-5; 0-19-518296-0 (pbk.)
1. United States. Congress. House—History—20th century. I. Title.
JK1319 .P64 2004
328.73'072—dc21    2003002296

3 5 7 9 8 6 4 2

Printed in the United States of America
on acid-free paper

For my colleagues at the Institute of Governmental Studies, 1988–1999
and especially for A

# PREFACE

This is not the first time I have attempted to write at length about what seemed to contemporary observers to be fundamental changes in the American political system. Thirty years ago, in a pair of long articles, I focused on trends in the House of Representatives that in the early years of the twentieth century produced the main features of the institutional structure we see today.[1] Twenty years ago I wrote a book surveying the principal consequences of the reforms in the late 1960s that transformed the presidential nominating process.[2] The intended contribution of this book is roughly similar to those earlier efforts. It revisits the House of Representatives and seeks to account for the most important recent changes in the way this body functions in the overall scheme of American politics.

Careful readers of the daily newspapers are perfectly well aware that, pursuant to the commands of the U.S. Constitution, the United States Congress embraces two co-equal chambers, the House and the Senate. But even they may not grasp one implication of this fact that professional observers of Congress, and the people who work there, confront every day: the two bodies are for many purposes quite separate institutions. Each has its own peculiarities of design, its own inner politics, and its own organizational history. On the whole the Senate—or at least senators—are better known to the general public; and this, among other things, made the House more attractive to my generation of congressional scholars, and to many of our students. For most of our lives, this lesser-known House of Representatives constituted a black hole into which dropped, never to re-emerge, the proposals and programs of liberal presidents from Franklin Roosevelt onward. In more recent times, the House, while still largely unfamiliar to casual observers of Congress, became less reliably hostile to liberal initiatives. And more recently still, the House went through a series of changes that for a while were seriously being characterized as a "revolution." The historical narrative undertaken in this book attempts to describe what happened by showing how the ways in which certain broad changes in American politics came to have an impact on the composition of the House (for convenience also called here Congress as it frequently is in popular discourse) and on the organization of the House, on its informal atmosphere, and, ultimately, also on its work product.

Scholarship in political science is most useful, I believe, when it sticks closely to ascertainable facts and provides orientation to readers who are curious about the world immediately around them. Occasionally, to the polite disapproval of our colleagues in the history department, we political scientists indulge a tendency to rummage through the recent past looking for ways of understanding the present and—sometimes—for ways of sustaining informed guesses about where events are taking us.[3] We write not for the ages but for our own generation, and create what I would describe as applied knowledge, rather than knowledge unconstrained by time and place. Since most of our fellow creatures live in particular times and places, we can aspire to discover for them a few things they may find it informative and possibly useful to know.

This particular project has absorbed a fair amount of the time that I have devoted to scholarship since I began to practice my trade over 40 years ago. I suppose it is inevitable that a research project stretching over most of a professional lifetime would involve debts to individuals no longer able to receive the heartfelt thanks of a grateful author. It is a privilege to remember but a sadness to record the names of colleagues and benefactors now deceased who along the way offered extraordinary professional courtesy and on occasion much-valued friendship. I remember with affection political scientists Doug Price, Ralph Huitt, Evron M. Kirkpatrick, Mark Ferber, Nick Masters, Lewis Anthony Dexter, Clem Vose, and Aaron Wildavsky; members of Congress Charles A. Mosher, Carl Elliott, Morris Udall, Bill St. Onge, Frank Thompson, and James G. O'Hara; congressional staff members Walter Kravitz, D. B. Hardeman, and Richard P. Conlon; two extraordinary journalists: John Jacobs, who wrote his wonderful biography of Representative Phillip Burton at the Institute of Governmental Studies here in Berkeley, and Howard Simons of the *Washington Post*, who shared his vast knowledge of Washington with great generosity, as did my wise and witty friends the economists Herb Stein and Joe Pechman and the remarkable all-around political guru George Agree.

Because this project has taken a very long time to complete, I am not sure that the records I can now lay my hands on fully reflect my indebtedness to the research assistants and student collaborators who have contributed to the final product. I list here the names I see in my papers, some of which go back many years, plus those of recent vintage whom I remember more clearly, but I ask forgiveness of those whom I have overlooked. I thank, in particular, Keith W. Smith and Casey B. K. Dominguez, two gifted Berkeley graduate students who involved themselves in an especially enthusiastic, skilled, and thoughtful way at a stage when the project needed to be completed, and who helped get it done. I also thank Paul D. O'Brien, Robert vom Eigen, Barry Spencer Rundquist, Miriam Gallaher, Michael Leiserson, Bob Geddes, Kathy Underwood, Matt Jarvis, Sharon Kaye Pinkerton, Dalia Dassa Kaye, Jonathan Bernstein, David Hopkins, Mark Oleszek, Dorothy Apollonio, Allison Wegner Leof, Russ Paulsen, Rebecca Noah, Nathaniel Persily, Thomas Burke, Douglas Strand, Matthew Pinkus, Michael Goldstein, Shai Feldman, Thad Kousser, Phil Wilson, Pev Squire, Caren Oto, John Gilmour, John Zaller, Beth Capell, Mark Westlye, Joel Budgor, and David Flanders.

As the dedication indicates, my work and I personally have benefited greatly from an association with the Institute of Governmental Studies of the University of California, Berkeley, where I have maintained an office since 1988. A lot of the pleasure of working at IGS derived from collaboration with Adrienne Jamieson, the administrative genius who served as assistant director from 1988 to 1994. Since 1999, when I stopped being director, I have received the hospitality and support of my successor, Bruce Cain, for which I am grateful. My colleagues in the IGS library, especially Terry Dean, Ron Heckart, and Diana Neves, have been enormously helpful, and no words of mine can fully convey what friendship with Jerry Lubenow, the IGS publications director, has brought to me and to this project all these years.

While incubating this book I had the pleasure of a delightful year (1985–86) at the Center for Advanced Study in the Behavioral Sciences, during which I was in daily contact with two superb historians of Congress, Allan G. Bogue and Joel Silbey, and my brilliant friend David Brady. The four of us made a study group that as I recall provided a fair amount of entertainment to the staff and some of the other fellows, who reciprocated with enthusiasm. I thank, in particular, the management, Gardner Lindzey and Robert Scott, and my classmates Bob Bates, Otis Graham, Peter Eisinger, Joe Gusfield, Erica Goode, Lance Davis, John Darley, Paul Joskow, Paul Rozin, Rick Shweder, and the late Gerald Lieberman, who kibbitzed constructively and often.

I have a lot of debts to acknowledge for help over the years in navigating through the Washington and the Capitol Hill communities: many thanks to Norman Ornstein and Judy Harris, Tom and Sheilah Mann, Micah and Beth Naftalin, Douglas and Suzy Bennet, Norman and Virginia Sherman, John and Nancy Stewart, Chris Demuth, Haynes Johnson, David and Ann Broder, Philip Kaiser, Andy Glass, Don Bacon, Neil MacNeil, Len Downie, Cathy Rudder, Alan Ehrenhalt, David and Carla Cohen, Elizabeth Drew, Edith Carper, Mark Furstenberg, Judith and Robert Martin, Mike Gillette, Kenneth Kato, John Hoving, Les Francis, Clark Hoyt and Linda Kauss, Steve Ebbin, Stanley Bach, Walter Oleszek, Bob Peabody, Milt Cummings, Adam Clymer, Michael Barone, Janet Brown and Michael Brewer, and Allen I. and Gail K. Polsby. The friendly folks at Stanford in Washington were especially nice: Kiki Setterlund, Catherine Cook-Graves, Suzanne Miller, Patrick Chamorel, and Adrienne Jamieson; so were my friends at the long-gone Roosevelt Center; at Brookings; at the American Enterprise Institute; at the University of California's Washington program, especially Scott Brickner, Larry Berman, Catherine Boyd, and Jim Desveaux; and at the American Political Science Association.

It has been intellectually rewarding and fun to have been a Congress-watcher for so many years in the company of Dick Fenno, Chuck Jones, Jim Thurber, John Manley, David Mayhew, Sam Kernell, Roger Davidson, Mo Fiorina, Joe Cooper, and a number of those Washingtonians already named. Members of Congress and former members who have been particularly forthcoming include Lamar Smith, Abner Sibal, Tom Foley, Bob Giaimo, Bob Matsui, Norman Mineta, Dick Cheney, Bob Kastenmeier, Emilio Daddario, John Brademas, David Price, Mickey Edwards, and the late Richard Bolling. Congressional staff who went out of their way to help include Bette Welch, Steve Strickland, Jack Golodner, Timothy Smith, Richard Edwards, Mary Allen, Bill Phillips, Eileen Nixon, Don Baker, Tom Keena, Charles Ward, and Jerry Horton.

Berkeley colleagues who have been a source of day to day inspiration and encouragement include Ray Wolfinger, Eric Schickler, Terri Bimes, Herb McClosky, Hal Wilensky, Sandy Kadish, the late John Harsanyi, Sheldon Rothblatt, Martin Trow, John Ellwood, Gene Smolensky, Tom Goldstein, Joe Tussman, Austin Ranney, Phil Siegelman, Susan Rasky, and Bob Kagan. Readers of a draft of the book who kindly offered reactions and corrections include Robin Einhorn, Morton Keller, Michael Barone, Bruce Cain, Linda O. Polsby, Jeff Biggs, Al Bogue, Julian Zelizer, Juliet Eilperin, Stanley Bach, David Cohen, Richard Fenno, Alan Ware, Barbara Sinclair, Eric Schickler, Sam Schickler, Robert Dahl, Philip Kaiser, Tom Mann, Adam Sheingate, Daniel R. Polsby, Daniel D. Polsby, John M. Barry, Thad Kousser, Gary Hymel, Chuck Jones, Jack Pitney, Walter Oleszek, Joe Cooper, John Gilmour, Austin Ranney, Allen I. Polsby, Marty Nolan, Lamar Smith, Mo Fiorina,

Ron Elving, Byron Shafer, and Arthur Burris. I thank them for their generosity.

I am indebted, as always, to my amazing family for their affection and support: Linda O. Polsby, Lisa Polsby, Eric, Benjamin, and Edward Stern, Emily Polsby and Daniel R. Polsby. None of them, nor any of those mentioned previously, necessarily agrees with what I have written here or, in the case of my wife, a fastidious editor, with how I have punctuated it.

I am unsure of the exact origins of the cover photograph, but I believe it is an official portrait of the House Rules Committee just after it was packed in 1961. In the foreground sits the chairman, Howard W. Smith of Virginia. To his right sit Democrats, in descending order of seniority: William Colmer of Mississippi, Ray Madden of Indiana, James Delaney of New York, James Trimble of Arkansas, Homer Thornberry of Texas, Richard Bolling of Missouri, and Thomas P. O'Neill of Massachusetts. On the left side, in descending order along the table are, Clarence Brown of Ohio, Katharine St. George of New York, H. Allen Smith of California, Elmer Hoffman of Illinois, and William Avery of Kansas, all Republicans. The last two seats on the Republican side are occupied by Democrats who were new appointments to the Committee: B. F. Sisk of California and Carl Elliott of Alabama.

# CONTENTS

# How Congress Evolves

# INTRODUCTION

---

Once upon a time, not so long ago, it was fairly common for political observers in the United States to complain that Congress never changed. Eighteenth-century machinery was found wanting as it confronted twentieth-century problems. Many of the complaints, to be sure, were politically motivated, based as they were upon quite accurate perceptions over long stretches of time that Congress could not be expected to enact proposals put forward by liberal presidents advocating public policies, which, arguably, majorities of Americans favored. The House of Representatives, in particular, was commonly identified as the great bottleneck.

Now Americans live in a different era, in which presidents are not necessarily liberal and the House of Representatives is not necessarily the graveyard of presidential proposals. What happened? Among other things, Congress changed. This essay describes the part of this story that involves the House of Representatives. Its central argument can be stated succinctly: changes that occurred in the political structure and functioning of the U.S. House of Representatives during the 1970s, 1980s, and 1990s can be traced back to certain changes that affected the political parties out in the country. These were caused by changes in the demographic profiles of the several states during the 1950s and 1960s and before that by certain changes in technology that took place in the 1940s and 1950s. In an oversimplified sentence, I shall argue that air conditioning (plus other things) caused the population of the southern states to change; that change in the population of the South changed the political parties of the South; these changed the composition and in due course the performance of the U.S. House of Representatives leading first to its liberalization and later to its transformation into an arena of sharp partisanship, visible among both Democrats and Republicans.

This essay thus consists in large part of narrative history, but it aspires to social science. There is a fair amount of exposition of events in their chronological order, but mainly in behalf of an interpretation that purports to explain why events unfolded as they did. The overall moral of the story is that understanding how institutions function requires understanding the social contexts in which they are embedded. Off and on in recent years we have heard complaints about how badly the American political system is performing. A sustained look at one institution, such as will be attempted here, may help us understand a little better why political outcomes have sorted themselves out as they have. The design of new institutions is liable, also, to be affected by our understanding of currently operating institutions. There is no need to kick aimlessly at the casing of the mysterious big black boxes that produce political outcomes in any society, when, conceivably, comparable effort expended in finding out how things work could make a difference.

In the life of a robust human institution, which Congress undoubtedly is, 60 years does not seem such a long time. Yet in the United States, 60 years marks off over a quarter of the history of our nation under the Constitution, itself one of the longer lasting political orders in recorded history. Congress 60 years ago sits just on the receding horizon of living memory, and it is at this horizon that I begin this account, starting at the effective end of the New Deal, roughly in 1937. The evolutionary sequence to be studied here has to do with the fate in the House during these three-score years of the major policy initiatives that were in one fashion or another funneled through Congress.

The story unfolds in three stages, beginning with a long period of political stalemate, continuing with a period of liberalization, and concluding with a dramatic reaction in which partisan lines were sharpened and clarified and which many participants and observers described as a revolution. For most of this period I shall be tracing events during which the House was transformed from a policy-making body highly resistant to proposals of the liberal presidents who dominated the era—Roosevelt, Truman, Kennedy—into an entity responsive to the largely liberal political priorities of the mainstream of the Democratic Party. There then followed a vigorous Republican reaction built upon the model of party responsibility that had been put in place by the Democrats.

Looking at this sequence of events thus traces those organizational influences in the House that operated to produce the major policy outcomes defined by large forces at work nationally in the American political system.

TABLE I.1  Party Balance in the House, 1932–2000

| After election of | President | Congress | Democratic seats | Republican seats | Other |
|---|---|---|---|---|---|
| 1932 | Roosevelt | 73th | 310 | 117 | 5 |
| 1934 | | 74th | 319 | 103 | 10 |
| 1936 | | 75th | 331 | 89 | 13 |
| 1938 | | 76th | 261 | 164 | 4 |
| 1940 | | 77th | 268 | 162 | 5 |
| 1942 | | 78th | 218 | 208 | 4 |
| 1944 | | 79th | 242 | 190 | 2 |
| 1946 | Truman | 80th[a] | 188 | 245 | 1 |
| 1948 | | 81st | 263 | 171 | 1 |
| 1950 | | 82nd | 234 | 199 | 1 |
| 1952 | Eisenhower | 83rd[a] | 211 | 221 | 1 |
| 1954 | | 84th | 232 | 203 | — |
| 1956 | | 85th | 233 | 200 | — |
| 1958 | | 86th | 283 | 153 | — |
| 1960 | Kennedy | 87th | 263 | 174 | — |
| 1962 | | 88th | 258 | 177 | — |
| 1964 | Johnson | 89th | 295 | 140 | — |
| 1966 | | 90th | 247 | 187 | — |
| 1968 | Nixon | 91st | 243 | 192 | — |
| 1970 | | 92nd | 254 | 180 | — |
| 1972 | | 93rd | 239 | 192 | 1 |
| 1974 | Ford | 94th | 291 | 144 | — |
| 1976 | Carter | 95th | 292 | 143 | — |
| 1978 | | 96th | 276 | 157 | — |
| 1980 | Reagan | 97th | 242 | 189 | — |
| 1982 | | 98th | 269 | 165 | — |
| 1984 | | 99th | 252 | 182 | — |
| 1986 | | 100th | 258 | 177 | — |
| 1988 | GHW Bush | 101st | 259 | 174 | — |
| 1990 | | 102nd | 267 | 167 | 1 |
| 1992 | Clinton | 103rd | 258 | 176 | 1 |
| 1994 | | 104th[a] | 204 | 230 | 1 |
| 1996 | | 105th[a] | 207 | 227 | 1 |
| 1998 | | 106th[a] | 211 | 222 | 2 |
| 2000 | GW Bush | 107th[a] | 211 | 221 | 3 |
| Total (% of major party seats) | | | 8,889 (59%) | 6,241 (41%) | 57 (0%) |

[a]Republican majorities

Note: Figures are for the beginning of the first session of each Congress.

Sources: *Congress and the Nation*, vol. 7, *Congressional Quarterly*, 1990; *Congressional Quarterly Almanac*, 1990, 1992, and 1994; *Congress A to Z Congressional Quarterly*, 1999.

This is one way of writing a history of the House of Representatives in our time, tracking changes in the role of the House in national policy-making. It is not the only such history that might be written,[1] but it does attempt to capture central historical trends determining the contributions of the House of Representatives to legislative outcomes—accomplishments and failures—that absorbed most of the attention and most of the political energy of national policy-makers from the New Deal to the present day.

Throughout most of the recent half century, with only fleeting fluctuations, it has been the Democratic Party, nationwide, that has supplied to the House the vast bulk of its members—almost three-fifths—as table I.1 makes clear. Thus, one method of following the emergence of the House from stalemate to liberalization—the first two stages of our story—and beyond is by tracing the declining fortunes over time of the main policy rival to the Democratic mainstream, a conservative coalition or voting alliance of Republicans and southern Democrats, and the uneven but roughly corresponding rise of the main institutional instrument through which Democratic mainstream sentiment came to be embodied and expressed in the House of Representatives—namely the House Democratic caucus. No competent observer doubts that this sequence of events took place, and so it is not the purpose of my narrative to lead to a surprise ending. The idea, rather, is to gather up the strands of a story that can shed light on important issues of process: how fundamental change takes place in the modern United States as reflected in the politics of one of its central institutions. But in order to explore the roots of institutional change, one must first establish that change of sufficient magnitude to warrant an observer's attention has in fact occurred. That is the immediate goal of the narrative that follows.

# 1

# THE HOUSE IN SAM
# RAYBURN'S TIME

## A Conservative House: 1937–57

Roughly six decades ago, in 1940, Sam Rayburn of Texas became Speaker of the House of Representatives. By the time he died 20 years later, still Speaker, he was widely recognized as one of the all-time great figures in congressional history. A strong regular Democrat from a poor rural district, Rayburn, as chairman of the Committee on Interstate and Foreign Commerce, had skillfully managed a large number of key New Deal bills through the House before becoming majority leader in 1937. He was a bachelor with no interests outside the House. His unpretentious manners, sturdy party loyalty, and industrious work habits promised an era of stable leadership after the rapid turnovers occasioned by the unexpected deaths of his three immediate predecessors, Henry Rainey of Illinois (Speaker, 1933–34), Joseph Byrns of Tennessee (1935–36), and William B. Bankhead of Alabama (1936–39).[1]

But Rayburn, hard-working, skilled, and devoted as he was, never had smooth sailing as Speaker. There is a general consensus among observers that by 1940 and for the previous few years the House had been in the grip of a conservative, anti–New Deal alliance of southern Democrats and Republicans who constituted the real majority of the House, notwithstanding the nominal Democratic majorities that elected the Speaker and determined that Democrats would chair committees.[2]

This consensus says that the first appearance of the conservative coalition was in 1937, on a piece of legislation called the Fair Labor Standards Act. From Franklin Roosevelt's 100 days (March–June 1933) until 1937, the conventional wisdom of historians and contemporary news coverage identify Congress as highly acquiescent to the enactment of the presidential legislative program known then and now as the New Deal. Of the 100 days, the historian William Leuchtenburg says: "When Congress adjourned . . . one hundred days after the special session opened, [in March 1933] it had written into the laws of the land the most extraordinary series of reforms in the nation's history. . . . Roosevelt . . . had sent fifteen messages up to the hill, seen fifteen historic laws to final passage."[3] Pendleton Herring, a shrewd contemporary observer, documents the speed with which Congress enacted emergency legislation during that special session in a revealing table (table 1.1).

It was, as James T. Patterson put it, "a tractable Congress."[4] Overwhelmingly Democratic majorities, elected in the 1932 landslide and, remarkably, sustained in the mid-term election of 1934—the only mid-term election since 1838 to increase the size of a sitting president's House majority—set a standard for presidential–congressional relations that has reverberated ever since in the memories and expectations of analysts and observers.[5]

A turning point came after the election of 1936—absent the power of the New Deal to capture the imagination one might even call it a reversion to normal form. The Democrats had gained 11 seats in the House, to reach their all-time high of 333. The Republicans, at 89 seats, were just one away from their all-time low (which had come after the election of 1890). But as Jerry Voorhis of California, Richard Nixon's hapless victim of a decade later, who entered the House of Representatives in that 1936 flood tide of Democrats, wrote in his 1947 book, "The huge Democratic majority was far from a unified group. . . . Even in the Seventy-Fifth Congress [elected in 1936], there was but a bare majority of progressive-minded members. In all subsequent Congresses, the conservatives were actually in the majority."[6]

Conservatives in the House balked over legislation that eventually became the Fair Labor Standards Act of 1938 and over President Roosevelt's proposal to pack the Supreme Court. "There is no question," said Arthur Krock in the *New York Times* in August 1937, "that a large majority in the House wants to act favorably on the Wages and Hours Bill."[7] But they were prevented from acting. Economists Paul Douglas and Joseph Hackman explain:

> The Rules Committee, consisting of five northern Democrats, five southern Democrats and four Republicans, refused to permit the bill to be brought out onto the floor. What had happened was a combination of

TABLE 1.1. Legislation during FDR's 100 Days, 1933

| Bill number | Title | Proposed by president | Passed House | Passed Senate | Date approved | Number of law or resolution | Hours of general debate in House |
|---|---|---|---|---|---|---|---|
| H.R. 1491 | Emergency banking relief | Mar. 9 | Mar. 9 | Mar. 9 | Mar. 9 | 1 | 0.66 |
| H.R. 2820 | Maintenance of government's credit (economy bill) | Mar. 10 | Mar. 11 | Mar. 15 | Mar. 20 | 2 | 2.0 |
| H.R. 3341 | Permit and tax beer | Mar. 13 | Mar. 14 | Mar. 16 | Mar. 22 | 3 | 3.0 |
| H.R. 3835 | Emergency agriculture relief; farm mortgage; currency issuance and regulation | Mar. 16 | Mar. 22 | Apr. 28 | May 12 | 10 | 5.5 |
| S. 598 | Unemployment relief (reforestation) | Mar. 21 | Mar. 29 | Mar. 28 | Mar. 31 | 5 | 5.0 |
| H.R. 4606 | Federal emergency relief | Mar. 21 | Apr. 21 | May 1 | May 12 | 15 | 2.0 |
| H.R. 5980 | Supervision of traffic in securities | Mar. 29 | May 5 | May 8 | May 17 | 22 | 5.0 |
| H.R. 5081 | Muscle Shoals and Tennessee Valley Authority | Apr. 10 | Apr. 25 | May 3 | May 18 | 17 | 6.0 |
| H.R. 5240 | Relief of small home owners | Apr. 13 | Apr. 28 | June 5 | June 13 | 43 | 1.5 |
| S. 1580 | Railroad reorganization and relief | May 4 | June 5 | May 25 | June 16 | 68 | 3.0 |
| H.R. 5575 | Industrial recovery; public construction and taxation | May 17 | May 26 | June 9 | June 16 | 67 | 6.0 |

Source: E. Pendleton Herring, *Presidential Leadership* (New York: Farrar and Rinehart, 1940), p. 44.

the five southern Democrats and the four Republicans against the bill in order to prevent the members from having the chance to vote on it. In order to obtain action, a group of 88 Democratic members therefore signed a petition demanding a party caucus to consider the matter. When the caucus met on the 19th of August, however, enough Democrats, chiefly from the South, either stayed away or refused to answer to their names when called, so that no quorum could be obtained. Action was thus prevented at this session.[8]

Court-packing, the second issue that divided the Democratic Party, died in the Senate and never received full House consideration. The strong opposition of Hatton Sumners of Texas, chairman of the House Judiciary Committee, made the project so precarious in the House it seemed sensible to try the more hospitable arena of the Senate first.[9]

Thus, by 1937, most of the elements of conservative coalition power that became familiar over the next two decades had emerged: (1) entrenchment of the coalition in the House Rules Committee, which provided an all-important strategic bottleneck;[10] (2) the enfeeblement of the caucus as a device to mobilize the majority of the majority party; and (3) the cloak of seniority that protected conservative committee chairmen (like Hatton Sumners) who opposed New Deal programs.

John Manley's authoritative roll-call figures show the two decades from 1937 to 1958 to have been particularly successful years for the conservative coalition. For most of the period a conservative voting alliance emerged on over a fifth of all recorded contested votes in the House, with victory rates averaging well above 80 percent (fig. 1.1, table 1.2).[11]

Participants and observers have sometimes worried over whether the conservative voting bloc properly deserved the term "coalition," since from time to time leaders of the southern Democrats and the Republicans in the House went out of their way to deny that elaborate consultations regularly took place and without consultation they argued there could be no coalition. When uttered by politicians this was a smokescreen. Whether or not there was elaborate consultation, or formal staff work, as evidently there usually was not, stable and long-lasting agreement between Republicans and a sizable group of Democrats on many public policy issues is plainly visible in the record.[12] Joe Martin of Massachusetts, Republican leader of the House for most of the period (1939–59), got around in his 1960 memoirs to explaining how the coalition worked:

> when an issue of spending or of new powers for the President came
> along, I would go to Representative Howard W. Smith of Virginia, for

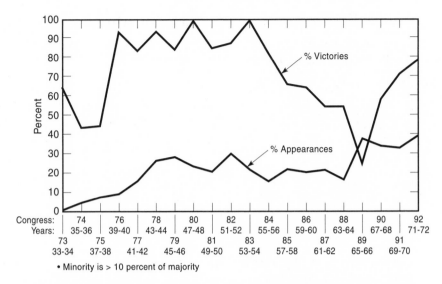

Figure 1.1: Percentage of All Contested House Roll Calls on Which the Conservative Coalition Appeared, and Won, 73rd–92nd Congress (1933–72). Source: John F. Manley, "Conservative Coalition in Congress," *American Behavioral Scientist* 17 (1973) p. 236.

example, and say, "Howard, see if you can't get me a few Democratic votes here." Or I would seek out Representative Eugene Cox of Georgia, and ask, "Gene, why don't you and John Rankin and some of your men get me some votes on this?" . . . [13] His opposition to the New Deal was much more ingrown than mine, and he was ready to fight to any lengths to keep further power out of the hands of Franklin Roosevelt. In these circumstances, therefore, it was unnecessary for me to offer any *quid quo pro* for conservative southern support. It was simply a matter of finding issues on which we saw alike.

Sometimes I discovered—not only in the case of the southerners but with conservative northern Democrats as well—the best way to combat the New Dealers was to put willing Democrats up to making the moves and delivering the speeches while we waited in silence to hand them our 169 votes on the roll call. We won a number of victories by this device, proving that wavering Democrats would often support a measure offered by one of their own party whereas they would balk if it was sponsored by a Republican.

By the end of the session we had succeeded, with the aid of the Democratic conservatives, in making substantial reductions in Roosevelt's appropriation bills.[14]

TABLE I.2. Conservative Coalition (CC) Appearances and Success, 1933–68

| Year | Total votes[a] | CC votes | % appears | CC wins | CC losses | Win % 1 (W/L) | Win % 2 (W/TV) |
|------|------|------|------|------|------|------|------|
| 1933 | 56 | 0 | 0 | 0 | 0 | 0 | 0 |
| 1934 | 77 | 3 | 4 | 2 | 1 | 67 | 3 |
| 1935 | 123 | 9 | 7 | 4 | 5 | 44 | 3 |
| 1936 | 70 | 0 | 0 | 0 | 0 | 0 | 0 |
| 1937 | 89 | 11 | 12 | 5 | 6 | 45 | 6 |
| 1938 | 57 | 0 | 0 | 0 | 0 | 0 | 0 |
| 1939 | 83 | 6 | 7 | 6 | 0 | 100 | 7 |
| 1940 | 119 | 15 | 13 | 14 | 1 | 93 | 12 |
| 1941 | 67 | 9 | 13 | 8 | 1 | 89 | 12 |
| 1942 | 51 | 10 | 20 | 9 | 1 | 90 | 18 |
| 1943 | 74 | 16 | 22 | 16 | 0 | 100 | 22 |
| 1944 | 52 | 18 | 35 | 17 | 1 | 94 | 33 |
| 1945 | 76 | 12 | 16 | 9 | 3 | 75 | 12 |
| 1946 | 101 | 39 | 39 | 37 | 2 | 95 | 37 |
| 1947 | 67 | 15 | 22 | 15 | 0 | 100 | 22 |
| 1948 | 64 | 17 | 27 | 17 | 0 | 100 | 27 |
| 1949 | 96 | 25 | 26 | 21 | 4 | 84 | 22 |
| 1950 | 121 | 21 | 17 | 18 | 3 | 86 | 15 |
| 1951 | 91 | 25 | 27 | 22 | 3 | 88 | 24 |
| 1952 | 59 | 21 | 36 | 18 | 3 | 86 | 31 |
| 1953 | 56 | 17 | 30 | 17 | 0 | 100 | 30 |
| 1954 | 52 | 8 | 15 | 8 | 0 | 100 | 15 |
| 1955 | 57 | 9 | 16 | 9 | 0 | 100 | 16 |
| 1956 | 52 | 6 | 12 | 4 | 2 | 67 | 8 |
| 1957 | 90 | 16 | 18 | 13 | 3 | 81 | 14 |
| 1958 | 67 | 18 | 27 | 9 | 9 | 50 | 13 |
| 1959 | 76 | 11 | 14 | 10 | 1 | 91 | 13 |
| 1960 | 74 | 21 | 28 | 8 | 13 | 38 | 11 |
| 1961 | 90 | 22 | 24 | 15 | 7 | 68 | 17 |
| 1962 | 86 | 17 | 20 | 8 | 9 | 47 | 9 |
| 1963 | 90 | 15 | 17 | 11 | 4 | 73 | 12 |
| 1964 | 84 | 14 | 17 | 6 | 4 | 43 | 7 |
| 1965 | 147 | 61 | 41 | 14 | 47 | 23 | 10 |
| 1966 | 119 | 41 | 34 | 10 | 31 | 24 | 8 |
| 1967 | 159 | 57 | 36 | 39 | 18 | 68 | 25 |
| 1968 | 155 | 50 | 32 | 25 | 25 | 50 | 16 |

[a]Votes include only those in which minority is > 10 percent of majority

% appears is percentage of votes in which the coalition appears; i.e., majority of southern Democrats and a majority of Republicans oppose a majority of non-southern Democrats.

Win % 1 is percentage of coalition votes in which the coalition wins.

Win % 2 is coalition wins as a percentage of all votes.

Source: John F. Manley, "Conservative Coalition in Congress," *American Behavioral Scientist* 17 (1973), p. 236.

As John Manley succinctly summarized in 1973: "The Conservative Coalition is an informal, bipartisan bloc of conservatives with leaders who jointly discuss strategy and line up votes."[15] The coalition obviously could not have worked at all during these years without a persistent split in the House Democratic Party.[16] But there were plenty of conservative Democrats. Table 1.3 shows roll-call numbers taken from the first-ever *Congressional Quarterly* (*CQ*) tabulation of conservative coalition activity for an entire session of Congress, in 1959, the year after a historic Democratic landslide. It shows that southern Democrats supplied one-third of the conservative coalition's hard-core members and just over 40 percent of the coalition at least half of the time. Southern historian Dewey Grantham writes,

> Southern leadership was a dominant feature of Congress between 1941 and 1945. During the war years, southern Democrats constituted the largest regional representation of their party in Congress, and they tended to display greater coherence in their votes than any other group in the two houses. The congressional elections of 1942, which increased Republican strength and brought the defeat of many northern and western Democrats, enhanced the southern position in Congress. In the Seventy-eighth Congress (1943–1944), southern Democrats outnumbered non-southern Democrats in the House and held just under 44 percent of the party's seats in the Senate. More importantly, the seniority rule had enabled the southerners to assume the chairmanships and ranking positions of the most powerful committees in the two chambers. The southerners' mastery of parliamentary procedure and legislative de-

TABLE 1.3. Conservative Coalition in the U.S. House, 1959

| Party | Number of members with 100% conservative coalition score | Number of members with 50% plus conservative coalition score | Total number of members |
|---|---|---|---|
| Northern Democrats | 2 | 13 | 170 |
| Southern Democrats | 31 | 103 | 110 |
| Republicans | 61 | 135 | 153 |
| Total Size | 94 | 251 | 433 |

Note: Speaker Sam Rayburn (TX, not voting) and Rep. Daniel Inouye (HI, not yet eligible to vote) are not included in *Congressional Quarterly*'s analysis.

Source: Data come from *Congressional Quarterly Almanac* 86th Congress, 1st Session, 1959, vol. 15, pp. 141–45.

tail gave them a decided advantage and frequently made it possible for them to provide the "know-how" in disposing of congressional issues. . . . Most of the southern congressmen viewed the federal government as an indispensable instrument in the economic development of the South, but they wanted such assistance without any strings attached. They opposed extensive changes in the southern social order or the region's power structure or its politics. Their dissatisfaction with the course of the national Democratic party, and their willingness to cooperate with congressional Republicans, as well as their deepening alarm over changes taking place in race relations, new national labor standards, and increasing federal intrusion, contributed to the rise of conservatism and greater resistance to Roosevelt's programs in Congress while preparing the way for later developments in regional and national politics.[17]

Carl Albert of Oklahoma was appointed Democratic whip by Sam Rayburn and John McCormack in 1955. His view of the southern bloc was that

most . . . southern Democrats represented a powerful establishment, an interlocking network of landowners, financiers, industrialists, and professionals, all men of power, all men of white flesh. Over generations, that establishment had learned to pick outstanding young men of talent, men imbued with the establishment's views, and send them to Congress. It kept sending them back and watched them grow old as they voted the establishment's way and expressed the establishment's opinion. . . . Its highest priority was to maintain that establishment. This meant to discourage voting by blacks and poor whites through poll taxes, literacy tests, and stiff registration laws. It meant maintaining states' rights to keep the federal bureaucracy out of Dixie. It meant minimal welfare laws to turn back the carpetbaggers. It meant harsh antilabor statutes to cast out union organizers. It meant miserly educational programs to ward off alien ideas. Most of all it meant white supremacy.[18]

The conservative coalition was mostly obstructionist in character, preventing action on a variety of issues. The list of liberal complaints from 1937 to 1957 was very long. One bill of particulars listing issues on which the conservative coalition was activated and covering most of the period was compiled by Representative Frank Thompson, Democrat of New Jersey, and published in 1960. It included anti-union bills passed and welfare, housing, civil rights, and economic redistribution bills defeated. In addition, mainstream Democrats were arrayed against the conservative coalition on procedural matters, in which the coalition sought to protect the capacity of the Rules Committee to act as a bottleneck.[19]

In short, after 1937, the House of Representatives became an increasingly high hurdle for the domestic programs of Democratic presidents to clear. Extensive lists of complaints such as Representative Thompson's did not tell the whole story. Reliable quantitative measures of the phenomenon of House resistance did not include the expectations about House action that have always entered the calculations of presidents, of Senate majority leaders, and of the Speaker. All of these leaders, having multiple goals, were reluctant to press difficult matters to the point where they would suffer a countable defeat. As Representative Clem Miller (D-Calif.) observed in just this connection: "They lead, but they lead only because they win. If they cannot be certain of winning, they don't want to go. Latent power, negative power, is so much better than power committed that lacks victory as a capstone."[20]

Thus, we must rely in part on the folklore that built up in the House after 1937 about lost opportunities, bills withdrawn or modified, watered down or defeated on account of insuperable obstacles somewhere in the organizational structure of the House. Library of Congress expert George Galloway says:

> During the decade 1937–1946. . . . The Rules Committee repeatedly framed rules designed to facilitate its own views of public policy rather than those of the House leadership and the Roosevelt Administration by including special provisions in its resolutions granting a green light for bills for the floor . . . [T]he coalition . . . repeatedly used its powers to obstruct and dilute important measures.[21]

In this period (1939–46, 1949–52), the chairman of the committee was Adolph Sabath of Chicago, Illinois, an elderly New Deal liberal who was no match for the coalition on the committee of Republicans and Dixiecrats led by Eugene Cox of Georgia.[22] Part of Cox's considerable influence as a broker of southern interests on the committee came through his close friendship with Sam Rayburn, who after 1940 was Speaker.[23] Sabath, by all accounts, was simply ineffective, bypassed and frequently outvoted.

For two years (1953–55), Republicans controlled the committee. After the election of 1954, the chair passed to the wily Howard W. (Judge) Smith of Virginia, who presided for over a decade. Carl Albert says,

> With the possible exception of Sam Rayburn, Howard Smith was the smartest man and the most able legislator that I ever saw in Congress.[24] . . . Smith always had the easy option of a six-to-six vote on sending a bill to the full house. . . . Even without employing that weapon, the mere

threat of it could be enough to compel his foes to accept his views, in effect to surrender the substance of the fight just to get the bill out of committee. During my first term as whip [1955–56] Howard Smith did exactly that with bills regarding housing, absentee voting, the doctor's draft, and the distribution of polio vaccine.[25]

Richard Bolling, Sam Rayburn's protege on the House Rules Committee, gives a similar account of Judge Smith's tactical acumen:

> When Smith's position in committee is occasionally imperiled, he resorts to various devices to preserve it. He will let a backlog of needed domestic legislation he opposes accumulate. Then he will let supporters of the accumulated bills know directly or indirectly that they are going to have to choose two or three preferred bills from the backlog for clearance to the floor.[26]

The difficulty for the majority of the Democrats was not confined to the Rules Committee. The Legislative Reorganization Act of 1946 consolidated and reorganized the committee system reducing the number of standing committees from 48 to 19, and, as Library of Congress expert Walter Kravitz pointed out, this "vastly expanded the range of policy areas controlled by many committees. These larger jurisdictions, in turn, magnified the influence of the chairs and made their abuses of power more intolerable. Moreover, the fewer the chair positions, the longer a member could expect to wait before succeeding to one under the seniority system."[27] Often, the problem was that a bill's sponsors believed that they could not get a majority of votes on the floor; but on numerous other occasions, the fact that a substantive committee was stacked the wrong way, or headed by a chairman unsympathetic to the bill, was the apparent cause of failure. For example, Representative Bolling wrote, "Legislation providing for Home Rule for the District of Columbia has not been debated in modern times by the House of Representatives simply because the House Committee on the District of Columbia has been stacked with Democratic members who oppose the legislation and will not report such a bill to the floor for debate."[28]

Accounts in this era written from the perspective of the mainstream of the Democratic Party abound in stories of this sort, giving an overall picture of a House of Representatives not unlike Jurassic Park, filled with very large, threatening, carnivorous committee chairmen who liked to dine on liberal legislation. Here is an example from the memoirs of a southern liberal, Carl Elliott (D-Ala.), in 1951 a junior member of the Committee on Education and Labor:

At the time I joined, and during the decade I spent on that committee, the member who meant the most to any plans I had in terms of building a bill was the chairman, Graham A. Barden of North Carolina. . . . Barden treated my education bills at best with amused humor and at worst with complete scorn. He was not about to let any bill like the ones I had in mind to get out of his committee. . . . [T]he chairman of the Education and Labor Committee was a man as anti-labor and anti-education as could be imagined. . . .

Once he became chairman in 1951, Barden could effectively choke any legislation that had a liberal smell to it. He called committee meetings . . . arbitrarily and often without warning. He adjourned them when he wished—often suddenly if they took a turn he didn't like. If an aid-to-education bill seemed to be gathering some momentum, he would call in a dozen Chamber of Commerce witnesses to kill it with a filibuster. If, on the other hand, witnesses appeared from a group he didn't particularly care for, like the AFL-CIO, he would chide, interrupt and verbally abuse them.

He was a rough, tough son of a bitch . . . [29]

Barden's House Committee on Education and Labor posed an especially acute problem for the Democratic Party, with its close ties to the labor movement and the broad sympathy within the party toward federal aid to education. Richard Fenno says as of 1961:

The Committee, activated in 1947, cut its legislative teeth on the Taft-Hartley Bill and has been a domestic political battleground ever since. In 1961, two out of President Kennedy's five major domestic programs came before it. All members agreed with two of their colleagues—the first a Republican, the second a Democrat . . . :

"This is where the basic philosophies of the two parties really come out strongly. It's a clash of philosophies. You don't get that on Merchant Marine and Fisheries. Oh, what battles! You should see the battles we have in executive session."

"This is probably the most partisan Committee in the House, because this is where the fundamental philosophical battles are fought. . . . The things that identify the administration's domestic program come out of our Committee. You take minimum wage. That's a black and white proposition there. And all of our issues are fundamental, philosophical questions. You don't get that on Space or Foreign Affairs."[30]

Fenno comments:

Nearly all of its members agree that it is probably the most difficult House committee in which to achieve a consensus and the easiest in which to promote and prolong conflict. In the words of a leading Democratic proponent of federal aid, "It's a very discouraging committee. You can't get a resolution praising God through that Committee without having a three day battle over it. . . . It's about the most difficult committee around."[31]

Environmentalists were similarly frustrated by Wayne Aspinall of Colorado of the Interior Committee (chairman, 1959–72). John Jacobs writes:

> Aspinall, a hated foe of environmentalists, ran the Committee on Interior and Insular Affairs with a rigid hand. Fifty-two when he entered Congress in 1949 for the first of twelve terms, Aspinall moved quickly up the seniority ladder, becoming chairman a decade later.
>
> A former teacher, peach farmer, and speaker of the Colorado legislature, Aspinall took attendance, required absolute decorum, and sat next to his subcommittee chairmen, no matter how senior, as they conducted hearings he scheduled. He decided who served on which subcommittee and where each bill went. If his colleagues deviated from script, he rebuked them like errant children. He controlled their budgets, staff and travel, and until his secretaries convinced him otherwise, he scheduled appointments in two minute allotments. He created a subcommittee on the environment that [committee member] Tom Foley later recalled was a "place of detention for bills he did not wish to move. Once committed, a bill was in for twenty, if not life." Environmentalist and longtime adversary David Brower told the *Wall Street Journal*, "We have seen dream after dream dashed on the stony countenance of Wayne Aspinall."[32]

Aspinall was not, however, a partisan chairman. Richard Fenno quotes a western Democrat:

> If you check his record in the House, I think you'll find he's a good Democrat. But when he gets over here in Committee, politics is adjourned and he thinks in terms of what's good for the West—for miners, for cattlemen, for sheep raisers, and farmers. He has to. He has more Republicans in his district than Democrats. The fact that he's re-elected and re-elected and re-elected is a tribute to Wayne Aspinall the man, not to any excess of Democrats. He can't afford to alienate all those Republicans.[33]

Another committee member said, "He dominates the Committee in a fair way. . . . We are the best-run committee, from a parliamentary standpoint, in the House. Everything is done according to the book. Aspinall is fairness personified. He bends over backwards to be fair."[34]

Fenno describes Aspinall as a meticulous manager:

He fixes priorities, fixes subcommittee agendas and decides when a bill shall move from the hearings phase into the decision phase. In a situation where traffic control is an absolute necessity, he acts as chief controller, coordinating the work of his subcommittees and regulating the flow of legislation. . . . Conservation-minded officials do not always appreciate the Aspinall slowdown—especially when subsequent Committee decisions tilt toward user interests. But they recognize the effective leadership he displays. One remarked: "If we can get by Aspinall we are in good shape. . . . He is very sensitive to the interests of the people who live in his district—to the cattlemen, for instance, and mining. We've had some classic battles with him over grazing policy. He prides himself on running a model committee, and he does. He's a fine chairman—one of the best. All our problems boil down to getting along with the chairman."[35]

Another famously recalcitrant committee chairman from the standpoint of liberal and mainstream Democrats was Clarence Cannon of Missouri. At his death in 1964 the *New York Times* commented:

As chairman of the appropriations committee, he enhanced his power by shuffling and reshuffling sub-committees, sitting and voting as an ex-officio member on all of them, and presiding over the one that doled out funds for public works projects. He was then in a position to wield great influence not only in the important 50-member committee but also among scores of House members who looked to him for money to finance projects in their home districts.[36]

Committee chairmen did not always rule with a light touch. Tom Foley, later a committee chairman and Speaker, recalls his introduction to the Agriculture Committee:

On the first day in the Agriculture Committee . . . [t]he chairman [Harold Cooley of North Carolina] . . . strode out, took his chair at the head of the dais, rapped the gavel several times, and announced that he wanted to say a few words to the new members. "I hate and detest, hate and detest, to hear senior members of this committee, of either party, interrupted by junior members of this committee, of either party," he said. "You new members in particular will find that you will require some time, some of you months, others of you regrettably probably

years, before you develop sufficient knowledge and experience to con-
tribute constructively to our work. In the meantime, silence and attention," rapping the gavel for emphasis, "silence and attention is the rule
for new members of this committee." . . .

Cooley . . . once described a junior member as being dead. He said,
"You can come and sit in your chair. You can attend the meetings, but
I'm not going to recognize you to speak. And you won't be able to amend
any bills in the committee. On the floor you won't be given any time to
speak in general debate, and I'll oppose any amendment you offer. And
you won't be allowed to travel anywhere. And nothing you want to do
for your district will come out of this committee. Soon as I find out it's
you who wants it, it will be stopped. Let me give you some advice. Get
off the committee. You're a zombie on this committee. You're a walking,
living, dead man."[37]

Thus, as far as "liberal," "activist" presidents (Roosevelt and Truman)
and their allies among interest groups and members of Congress were
concerned, the House was from the enactment of the first New Deal onward an increasingly difficult place to do business, as the coalition between
Republicans and southern Democrats solidified on a wide variety of domestic programs.[38]

On a few occasions, liberals were able to score important, temporary
gains—notably in 1949 when they forced through an amendment to the
rules making it possible to dislodge bills stuck in the coalition-dominated
Rules Committee after 21 days. In that Congress, bills were brought to the
floor under the 21-day rule and enacted establishing the National Science
Foundation, statehood for Hawaii and Alaska, and a few other matters.[39]
But this reform was only temporary; in the election of 1950 the Democratic
majority was reduced by 29 seats. None of the loss was sustained among
southern seats. Thus, the conservative coalition was able without difficulty
in 1951 to abolish the 21-day rule at the opening of Congress. Frustrating
as this was to committed liberals within Congress, it reflected genuine
majority sentiment in the House at the time. It thus established a sort of
equilibrium during the Eisenhower era, even in the face of growing Democratic majorities, since presidential initiatives would be in Republican
hands, and the enactment of a program sharply at variance with the president's (as Eisenhower occasionally intimated) would call forth a veto.[40]

## After the 1958 Election: Frustration

But by the opening of the 86th Congress, in January 1959, change was in
the air. The signs were plentiful. Eisenhower had failed to carry Republi-

cans into a congressional majority since his initial election in 1952. All the public opinion polls were proclaiming what the evidence of the elections had also shown: that the country was predominantly Democratic.[41] In 1960, just two years away, a presidential election would be held in which Eisenhower—most likely the only Republican who could win—could not, under the newly activated 22nd Amendment to the Constitution, be a candidate.[42] And in the 1958 congressional election itself, the country had produced a massive Democratic landslide.

In January of 1959, there were 82 new faces in the House of Representatives and there were 50 more Democrats and 47 fewer Republicans than in the previous Congress. Thus, the overall party ratio was 283 Democrats to 153 Republicans. Democrats gained seats in 23 states and scored massively in Connecticut and Indiana, where six seats turned over, in California, Illinois, Maryland, Ohio, and Pennsylvania, where Democrats gained three seats per state, and in such unaccustomed places for Democrats as Maine, Utah, Vermont, and Iowa.

In the aftermath of the election, it is not surprising that sentiment was strong among many Democratic congressmen for some sort of procedural changes that would make the passage of a Democratic program possible. Eisenhower vetoes—if they occurred—would set the stage dramatically for the 1960 campaign. Leaders of the Democratic Study Group (DSG)—a newly formed, loosely organized information-exchange group operated by northern liberal and moderate Democratic congressmen—called on the Speaker and asked him to move against the Rules Committee.[43]

The membership of the Rules Committee at the end of the 85th Congress had stood as shown in table 1.4

The two senior Democrats were as a matter of course voting with four Republicans and defeating by a tie vote resolutions to send bills they op-

TABLE 1.4. The Rules Committee, 85th Congress, 1958

| Democrats | Republicans |
| --- | --- |
| Howard W. Smith (VA), Chairman | Leo E. Allen (IL) |
| William S. Colmer (MS) | Clarence J. Brown (OH) |
| Ray J. Madden (IN) | Henry J. Latham (NY) |
| James J. Delaney (NY) | Hugh D. Scott (PA) |
| James W. Trimble (AR) | |
| Homer Thornberry (TX) | |
| Richard Bolling (MO) | |
| Thomas P. O'Neill, Jr. (MA) | |

Source: *Congressional Quarterly Almanac*, 1959, p. 47.

posed to the floor. Two solutions to the problem were possible. A change in the ratio of the committee—adding a Democrat and subtracting a Republican—would reflect the ratio of Democrats to Republicans in the House as a whole. Or, restoration of the 21-day rule would provide a means within the rules to move legislation stalled inside the committee.

Apparently Democratic Study Group leaders broached both alternatives to Speaker Rayburn, but on January 3, 1959, failed to win his support for either.[44] The 21-day rule gave control of the legislative program over to the chairmen of substantive committees. Rayburn pointed out that he had been able to work out a *modus vivendi* with Joe Martin, the Republican leader, so that bills he deemed really essential could be sprung loose from the Rules Committee with the aid of one or two compliant Republican votes (usually Henry Latham or Hugh Scott).[45] The two-to-one party ratio in the committee, Rayburn explained, "had been decided back in 1944 with Joe Martin, and I'm not about to go back on my word to Joe."[46] In the end, the delegation of liberal Democrats received only the assurance "that legislation which has been duly considered and reported by legislative committees will be brought before the House for consideration within a reasonable period of time."[47] The Speaker's closest ally on the committee, Richard Bolling, brought the subject up separately with the Speaker at the same time and was also rebuffed.[48]

But later that month, Rayburn's bargain of 1944 with Joe Martin fell to pieces. At the opening of the 86th Congress the Republicans deposed Joe Martin as their leader and replaced him with Charles Halleck of Indiana, whose mandate and whose inclinations were to be less cooperative with Rayburn. There were two Republican vacancies on the Rules Committee: Henry Latham retired and Hugh Scott moved to the Senate. They were replaced later in January, 1959, by strong conservatives: Hamer H. Budge (Idaho) and B. Carroll Reece (Tenn).[49]

The legislative results of the 86th Congress rubbed salt into the wounds of the 130-member Democratic majority. As the *Economist* (London) said:

> A Congress dominated by the Democrats more fully than any Congress since 1938 has itself been dominated by a Republican President in the twilight of his official life. The chief work of the men elected last November in what was thought to be a liberal-labour triumph at the polls, is a highly conservative piece of legislation [the Landrum-Griffin Bill] constraining the trade unions.[50]

"By the fall of 1959," Richard Bolling recalled, "the most liberal House in two decades had produced no legislative record of any high accomplishment. With the presidential elections of 1960 in sight, some strategy had to be developed to provide a Democratic presidential candidate with a party record to run on."[51] But this proved difficult to manage; "The Housing Bill died in Rules. The Minimum Wage Bill was pried from Rules by making concessions."[52]

> the area redevelopment bill passed the Senate in 1959, but the [Rules] Committee refused to report the House version. Through the almost forgotten procedures of Calendar Wednesday, the bill finally reached the floor in May, 1960, and passed after many procedural roll calls. In June, 1960, a discharge petition was used to circumvent the Committee and bring the Federal pay-raise bill to the floor for approval. . . . The threat of a discharge petition finally forced committee action on the 1960 civil rights bill. The threat of Calendar Wednesday prodded the Committee into clearing the school construction bill, although the Republican–Southern Democratic alliance within the Committee ultimately blocked the bill by refusing to report a resolution sending it to conference.[53]

Meetings with the Speaker continued as liberals persisted in voicing complaints. Representative Clem Miller of California describes one such visit:

> The Speaker is very friendly. The mouth, so down-curved for public ceremony, turns up readily and warmly in private. We range ourselves on the edges of chairs and sofas. The conversation begins, all brisk and rapid fire, about this and that and the other. . . . Finally a senior member of the group says, "Now Mr. Speaker, about the Depressed Areas Bill."
>
> The joviality evaporates. But just as easily as before, the Speaker responds. "When are you boys going to do something about them upstairs?" He gestures toward the ceiling, above which the Rules Committee has its rooms. . . .
>
> And what could we do, we asked? We were asking the help of the Speaker with the gentlemen upstairs.[54]

Certainly not all bills were obstructed by the Rules Committee, or even most major bills. As James A. Robinson shows, failure by the committee to grant a rule was a most uncommon event.[55] Judge Smith himself noted the same thing in remarks on the floor:

> The Committee has had 140 requests for rules on bills. Of these 8 were passed on suspension and the Committee held hearings on 121 bills. They granted rules on 107 of those 121. You never hear anything about

that. They denied five rules and laid four bills on the table. Nine bills did not get rules out of the 107. That is a record of over 90 per cent. And, if there is any other committee of this House that has a record of 90 per cent favorable reports on bills referred to it, I have not heard about it yet.[56]

But it was on measures that were regarded by liberal Democrats in the House as at the leading edge of their own attempts to put together a program for 1960 that the committee stalled or prevented action. These were by no means all civil rights bills.

Although the most important issue to the southerners in the conservative coalition was no doubt civil rights, it was not the only issue around which they united.[57] Some southerners who voted with the coalition on civil rights, like Bob Jones and Carl Elliott of Alabama or James Trimble of Arkansas, voted with mainstream Democrats on virtually all other issues; and a small group of Republicans deserted the coalition on civil rights. As one liberal freshman, Gerald Flynn of Wisconsin, said:

> It may be that only 7 to 10 per cent of the bills coming before the Rules Committee are denied a hearing on the floor of the House of Representatives, but it is in this 10 per cent area that the important bills affecting the public and the people of this country lie. . . . What are you going to do to curb two Southern Democrats and four Republicans on the Rules Committee for combining, to thwart the will of the entire House of Representatives and Senate of the United States by holding the bill enabling the Federal Government to aid in building classrooms for the school children of our Nation, after such a bill has been passed in both the House and Senate. . . . Now, what has happened to the housing bill? Why did they hold up the housing bill in committee, a bill of equal importance to the American people, and refuse to let it come down to the floor of the House? . . . Yes, and how about the depressed area bill?[58]

The 86th Congress was not one of unrelieved frustration for liberal Democrats: but it was hard sledding all the way. The Democrats managed to place five liberal freshmen on the Education and Labor Committee, giving a boost to their allies in the trade unions.[59] But it was not enough to prevent legislation hostile to labor. The Landrum-Griffin labor bill found the liberals split, unorganized, working at cross-purposes, and unlucky.[60] Civil rights and depressed area bills were enacted only through extraordinary exertion and maneuvering. A housing act was vetoed twice by Eisenhower. An education bill was passed by both House and Senate, but the Rules Committee prevented it from going to conference.[61]

If there was any lesson to be learned from all this difficult experience, it was, surely, that a healthy Democratic majority was simply not enough to enact Democratic-sponsored bills. What the Rules Committee could not contain, the president could veto. The Landrum-Griffin bill showed that a disorganized majority was no match for an organized minority. Indeed, some liberals were ready to argue that on some key issues the Democratic majority was no majority at all.

Toward the end of the period, Clem Miller echoed Jerry Voorhis's words of a decade earlier almost exactly:

> the combination of Southern Democrats and Northern Republicans can always squeak out a majority when they want to, and they want to on a great number of significant issues.
>
> There are 283 Democrats in Congress. There are 160 Northern Democrats and roughly 99 Southern Democrats. (This includes Texas but does not include the border states of Maryland, West Virginia, Kentucky, and Missouri, which generally cancel each other out. Maryland votes against us, West Virginia with us, Missouri cancels itself out, half liberal, half southern and Kentucky, ambivalent, sometimes with us and sometimes against us.) There were 63 new Democratic congressmen elected last November [1958]. Thirteen replaced Democrats who were retiring for one reason or another and 50 replaced Republicans. Actually, the Democratic party as northerners define it is a minority in the House.[62]

And Frank Thompson said, "On the basis of three key roll call votes in the first session [86th Congress] on which the conservative coalition achieved its maximum strength . . . the approximate real party alignment is [as shown in table 1.5]."

Thus, there was a significant conflict between two proximate influences upon political outcomes in the House of Representatives: those that re-

TABLE 1.5. Coalitions in the House, 86th Congress, after 1958 Election

| Coalition | | Liberals | |
|---|---|---|---|
| Southern Democrats | 80 | Southern Democrats | 20 |
| Border Democrats | 9 | Border Democrats | 15 |
| Northern and western Democrats | 6 | Northern and western Democrats | 143 |
| Republicans | 130 | Republicans | 1 |
| Total | 225 | | 196 |

Source: Frank Thompson, *Congressional Record* (perm.), p. 1441, Jan. 27, 1960.

sulted from compositional characteristics of the House and those that re-
sulted from organizational characteristics. The composition of the House
is determined by elections, by whoever is elected to the institution and
shows up to take the oath of office. This discloses a fair amount about
basic partisan and ideological characteristics of majorities. Expectations
about results change as the numbers in the head counts change. In consideration of the numbers given by Jerry Voorhis, Clem Miller, and Frank
Thompson, observers noted that the actual majority in the House was not
always with the majority party, but rather with the conservative cross-
party voting alliance, and the sovereign remedy from the standpoint of the
nominal Democratic majority would be to elect more non-southern Democrats or more mainstream Democrats from the South.[63]

Parties are features of House organization, as are committees. How
members are distributed across committees was the business of the party
organizations in Congress, constrained by the custom of seniority, which
entrenched members in their committee positions. Seniority is not a rule
of the House, but rather a customary practice of the two partisan caucuses
in making committee assignments. At the opening of each Congress the
caucuses present resolutions to the floor assigning all members to their
respective sides of each committee, from top to bottom.[64] The number of
slots available to each party on each committee is a matter of negotiation
between the leaders of the two parties at the opening of Congress and
ordinarily varies according to the party ratios established in the whole
House by the aggregate outcomes of the preceding election. Many customs
supplementary to seniority have grown up in connection with committee
assignments. State delegations, for example, especially large ones, frequently claim property rights to succeed to vacancies on desirable committees created by the departure of one of their members. The Rules Committee, as a committee having significant influence over the agenda, is by
custom constituted with a two to one ratio favoring the majority party no
matter what the ratio is in the whole House in a bow to principles (otherwise sparingly observed) of party responsibility. As we have seen this
could be frustrated by compositional effects (the existence of a large conservative minority in the majority party) and seniority.

Carl Albert observed:

> When I became whip [1955], New England, the North Atlantic, the
> Midwest, and the West all combined to provide chairmen of only five
> committees. . . . Everywhere else I looked—across fifteen committees—
> there ruled a solid phalanx of southern chairmen. . . . Surrounding them
> were the ranking members of the majority party. As heads of the chief

subcommittees, these men controlled many of the separate pieces of legislation. In full committee deliberations, their voices spoke louder than others in shaping those pieces into a whole. And because of the seniority system, those voices, too, usually had southern accents. Take, for example, my own committee, Agriculture. Ranking behind Chairman Cooley in order were the following in 1955: Bob Poage of Texas; George Grant of Alabama; E. C. Gathings of Arkansas; John McMillan of South Carolina; Tom Abernathy of Mississippi; myself of Oklahoma; Watkins Abbitt of Virginia. Altogether, then, the South not only held fourteen of the twenty-one Democratic seats on that committee, but southerners occupied all of the top eight positions. It was the South, then, not [Secretary of Agriculture] Ezra Taft Benson, not Dwight Eisenhower, not the Democratic National Committee, and not some outside advisory group, that wrote America's agricultural legislation. It was also southern committee chairmen, none of these others, who decided what the Democratic House of Representatives would do.[65]

As of 1959 southerners occupied most of the electorally safe seats held by Democrats and House seniority had entrenched them within the committee system as a whole, not just in the Rules Committee. (see table 1.6).[66] These southerners were for the most part strong supporters of the conservative coalition.

Thus, although the election of 1958 had greatly increased the number of liberal Democrats in the House, organizational factors had put into the leadership of most committees chairmen who did not necessarily reflect mainstream sentiment (see tables 1.7, 1.8, and 1.9).

Despite the large numbers of Democrats allied with the conservative coalition, a majority of Democrats were not coalition participants. This presumably meant that on issues brought before the caucus the majority of the majority could prevail, although according to rules adopted in 1909, and then still in effect, a two-thirds vote would be required to bind caucus

TABLE 1.6. Southern Committee Chairs, 1959

| | Number from southern states | Total number | % from southern states |
|---|---|---|---|
| Full committee chairs | 13 | 21 | 61.9 |
| Full committee and appropriations subcommittees chairs | 21 | 34 | 61.8 |
| Entire Democratic caucus | 110 | 280 | 39.3 |

Source: *Congressional Quarterly Almanac*, 1959, pp. 38–49.

TABLE 1.7. Conservative Coalition Scores of House Committee Chairs, 1959

| Committee | Chairman | CC score (percentage) |
|---|---|---|
| District of Columbia | John McMillan (SC) | 100 |
| Post Office and Civil Service | Tom Murray (TN) | 100 |
| Rules | Howard Smith (VA) | 100 |
| Armed Services | Carl Vinson (GA) | 91 |
| House Administration | Omar Burleson (TX) | 91 |
| Ways and Means | Wilbur Mills (AR) | 91 |
| Appropriations | Clarence Cannon (MO) | 83 |
| Education and Labor | Graham Barden (NC) | 83 |
| Interstate and Foreign Commerce | Oren Harris (AR) | 82 |
| Veterans' Affairs | Olin Teague (TX) | 82 |
| Agriculture | Harold Cooley (NC) | 73 |
| Merchant Marine and Fisheries | Herbert Bonner (NC) | 73 |
| Science and Astronautics | Overton Brooks (LA) | 73 |
| Select Small Business | Wright Patman (TX) | 73[a] |
| Interior and Insular Affairs | Wayne Aspinall (CO) | 45 |
| Un-American Activities | Francis Walter (PA) | 36 |
| Banking and Currency | Brent Spence (KY) | 27 |
| Foreign Affairs | Thomas Morgan (PA) | 0 |
| Government Operations | William Dawson (IL) | 0 |
| Judiciary | Emanuel Celler (NY) | 0 |
| Public Works | Charles Buckley (NY) | 0 |

[a]This was a wildly atypical number for Patman, whose median score from 1959 to 1975 was 30. See Appendix, table A.2.

Source: *Congressional Quarterly Almanac*, 1959, pp. 38–49 and 144–45.

members on the floor.[67] But this was simply not an option. As Speaker Rayburn's biographers explain:

> [H]e refused to convene Democratic caucuses where members might discuss and choose a party position on major issues . . . Members were free to vote largely as they wished . . . [Former speaker] John Garner once [in 1956] chided his old friend, "Why don't you take those fellows into caucus and bind 'em?"
>    Rayburn replied:
>    John, you haven't been around the House in twenty years. You don't know what the hell you're talking about. You can't do that any more. . . . You get in that caucus and a wild man from the North will get up and make a wild speech. Then someone from another section will answer him with a wild speech. First thing you know, you've got the Democratic Party so divided you can't pass anything.[68]

TABLE 1.8. Conservative Coalition Scores of House Appropriations Subcommittee Chairs, 1959

| Subcommittee | Chairman | CC score (percentage) |
|---|---|---|
| Agriculture | Jamie Whitten (MS) | 100 |
| Defense | George Mahon (TX) | 100 |
| Departments of Treasury and Post Office | Vaughan Gary (VA) | 100 |
| Foreign Operations | Otto Passman (LA) | 100 |
| Legislative | W.F. Norrell (AR) | 100 |
| General Government Matters | George Andrews (AL) | 91 |
| Public Works | Clarence Cannon (MO) | 83 |
| Commerce | Prince H. Preston (GA) | 82 |
| Independent Offices and Special Subcommittee on Deficiencies | Albert Thomas (TX) | 45 |
| Departments of Labor and Health, Education, and Welfare and Related Agencies | John Fogarty (RI) | 27 |
| Military Construction | Harry G. Sheppard (CA) | 27 |
| DC | Louis Rabaut (MI) | 18 |
| Department of Interior and Related Agencies | Mike Kirwan (OH) | 9 |
| Departments of State and Justice, The Judiciary and Related Agencies | John J. Rooney (NY) | 9 |

Rayburn never changed his mind about the caucus. A few years later, Lee Metcalf of Montana told *Time* correspondent Neil MacNeil: "The Speaker is against the caucus. Members ask around for a caucus and he talks them out of it. He says, 'I'll speak to. . . . ' The avoidance of open controversy is his genius."[69]

In practice, the composition of the Democratic Party in the House and Rayburn's strategic judgment caused the caucus to fall into disuse except to do pro-forma party business at the opening of Congress, nominating a candidate for Speaker. The caucus did not even ratify the resolution from the Committees on Committees appointing members to committees until

TABLE 1.9. Summary: Committee Chairs in the Conservative Coalition, 1959

| | Number in conservative coalition | Total number | % in conservative coalition |
|---|---|---|---|
| Full committee chairs | 14 | 21 | 66.7 |
| Full committee and appropriations subcommittees chairs | 21 | 34 | 61.8 |

1965. From 1940 onward, throughout the entire period Rayburn was leader of the Democratic Party in the House, according to a diligent search of the *New York Times*, the Democratic Party caucused biennially, to organize Congress, and that was all.[70]

## The Rump Session of 1960

As if the passage of Landrum-Griffin were not enough, one further indignity was heaped upon the liberal Democrats in the 86th Congress. Rather than adjourn Congress for the national party presidential nominating conventions of the summer of 1960, it was a part of Senate majority leader Lyndon Johnson's strategy for seeking the presidential nomination of his party to put Congress in recess, subject to recall after the conventions had done their work. This would emphasize to Democratic convention delegates and their leaders the extent to which the programmatic fortunes of the party were in Johnson's hands and would provide a potential source of leverage for Johnson at the convention.[71] Additionally, it was argued that the rump session might provide a showcase for the sharpening of partisan differences, at a time when Democrats had a commanding majority in both Houses and a solid lead in party identification among voters nationwide. As a loyal backer of his fellow Texan for the presidency, Speaker Rayburn went along with Johnson's strategy.

The result was something of a public relations disaster. Johnson received no boost to his presidential chances at the convention. True to form, the convention was notably insensitive to the realities of congressional power, and instead responded to the realities of the presidential nominating process. This produced a Democratic ticket headed by John Kennedy, a sitting U.S. Senator. Kennedy chose Johnson as his running mate, making a calculation that may have taken some account of Johnson's congressional influence, but which more likely took advantage of the fact that Johnson was an energetic campaigner and a Baptist from a large, southern state, which might neutralize the impact in the Bible Belt of Kennedy's Catholicism.[72]

After the convention, there was no way for Kennedy and Johnson to avoid showing up for the rump session, and no incentive at all for President Eisenhower to cooperate with them. The session lasted 25 days.[73] It was an exercise in futility. The Democrats identified six major bills that could dramatize their program and illustrate the sort of effectiveness they could promise to bring to government. None of them went anywhere.

The 86th Congress was, ultimately, less significant for the legislation that it passed than for the way it crystallized liberal Democratic sentiment. The frustrations of the liberals led to the further organization of the Democratic Study Group. What had been a tacit alliance consisting mostly of very junior parliamentary innocents and older lone wolves germinated into a mutual protective association that could organize itself around legislative priorities, think through and execute parliamentary strategies, arrange for relevant staff work, and seek information and support from friendly interest groups. On the civil rights and depressed areas bills the Democratic Study Group mobilized a whip system to supplement the regular Democratic whips—many of whom were out of sympathy with the legislation. They took care not to alienate the Speaker and majority leader, accepting their leadership in matters of legislative priority, and not pressing Rayburn too hard on structural and procedural reform.[74]

But when Senator Kennedy was elected President in 1960, the Speaker saw that he had to do something about the Rules Committee. As D. B. Hardeman, Rayburn's confidential assistant, says, "He realized something had to be done. He had been convinced by the deadlock between 1955 and 1961 that Howard Smith would, in order to get his way, block legislation even of a Democratic president."[75] The 86th Congress had demonstrated the need for action. Liberals within the House would demand it. Without some modification of the committee's situation, the House would be a most inhospitable place for the program of the new President—and Rayburn, as Speaker, would be responsible for the passage of the President's program in the House.

## Packing the Rules Committee by Avoiding the Democratic Caucus: 1961

In retrospect, it seems inevitable that something should have been done about the Rules Committee at the start of the 87th Congress in 1961. A new Democratic president, a healthy Democratic majority in both House and Senate, the frustrations of the two previous years, and a clearly identifiable policy bottleneck in the system all pointed in the direction of reform. Yet the issue was, for participants and observers at the time, uncertain. Speaker Rayburn had grown increasingly gruff, reluctant to waste his effort, out of touch with many of his colleagues, and possibly even more conservative as the weight of his 80 years at last began to tell on him physically.[76] Could he and would he rouse himself for the bruising,

TABLE I.IO. Diminished Democratic Success in 1960

| Democratic districts | Won in 1960 | Lost in 1960 |
|---|---|---|
| Lost in 1956 and won in 1958 | 26 | 23 |
| Lost in 1958 | 0 | |

Source: *Congressional Quarterly Almanac*, 1961.

divisive struggle that a fight over the Rules Committee would certainly entail? And if he did so, could he win? The election of 1960 had actually reduced the Democratic majority in the House. About half of the marginal districts that in 1958 had elected freshman Democrats reverted to Republican hands, with no new gains. Kennedy carried 28 districts in which the Democratic House candidate was defeated, while Nixon won a plurality in 81 districts where the GOP House candidate went down to defeat. Kennedy carried 178 districts where the Democratic House candidate won and Nixon carried 146 districts where the GOP House candidate was also victorious (see also table I.IO.).[77]

Table I.II shows the breakdown of congressional districts in which Kennedy and Nixon ran ahead or tied the percentage of the vote received by their party's 1960 House candidates.

It is easy, now, to forget how weak a candidate John F. Kennedy was in his one national election. While Democratic candidates for the House were receiving 35 million votes, Kennedy polled only 27 million—and he did particularly badly in marginal congressional districts. The Democratic majority in House seats declined from 283 to 263. If Democrats were to take seriously the arithmetic demonstrations that there was no real liberal majority in the 86th Congress, would it be worth even trying to do something about the Rules Committee in the more closely divided 87th Congress?

TABLE I.II. Presidential Coattails Presidential Vote by House Seats, 1960

| Presidential candidate | East | Midwest | South | West | Total seats |
|---|---|---|---|---|---|
| Kennedy ahead of Democrats | 60 | 48 | 7 | 19 | 134 |
| Nixon ahead of Republicans | 78 | 80 | 113 | 40 | 311 |

Source: *Congressional Quarterly Almanac*, 1961, pp. 1028–32.

Several possibilities suggested themselves as the 87th Congress opened. They were bruited about in the press and were the subject of negotiations between Rayburn and leaders of the Democratic Study Group. There was a clear majority in the Democratic caucus ready to back Rules Committee reform. The Speaker could keep the issue in the caucus if he chose, by fighting the battle on the matter of committee assignments, where traditionally the parties never interfere on the floor with one another. Rayburn could allow the caucus by majority vote to instruct the Democratic Committee on Committees, whose work would be voted upon by the caucus before it was reported to the floor, thus avoiding the need for the two-thirds caucus vote that it would take to bind all caucus members on the floor.[78]

The instruction could interfere with a member's customary entitlement to reappointment and reconstitute the Rules Committee. In theory, the entire Democratic membership of the committee could be changed in this way, but in practice the desired change in the ideological balance of the committee could be effected by simply purging one of the two conservative members. Representative William Colmer of Mississippi, the second ranking member, was the obvious choice. As chairman, Judge Smith had a certain immunity. He was also personally more popular than Colmer. Colmer had opposed the Democratic presidential ticket in the 1960 election. Thus, an excuse for the purge lay to hand, if Rayburn cared to use it. This despite the fact that, as Neil MacNeil describes it,

[T]he precedents for punishing Colmer were weak. The most recent example of such discipline that even the Democratic Study Group could cite had been in 1925. Then the Republican regulars, under Speaker Nicholas Longworth, had deprived thirteen Republicans of their committee posts for supporting Robert La Follette's Presidential candidacy. In 1948, thirty Southern Democratic Representatives had supported Strom Thurmond's Presidential candidacy. They had gone unpunished. So had the Southern Democrats who had bolted against Adlai Stevenson in 1952 and 1956. In 1956, Adam Clayton Powell of New York, a Democrat, had openly supported Dwight Eisenhower for President; and he had not been punished either. The failure to previously punish members for party disloyalty in effect had condoned their action. Besides, until now Rayburn had always taken the position that a Representative's party loyalty in the House of Representatives was determined solely by his vote in the House for the election of a Speaker. If he voted for the Democratic candidate for Speaker, he automatically was a Democrat. If he voted for the Republican candidate, he was a Republican. It did not matter what he had done or how he had been designated in the election campaign.[79]

Until the very last moment, it appeared nevertheless that Rayburn would reverse his long-standing position on party loyalty. Leaders of the Democratic Study Group, under a pledge of secrecy, received Rayburn's commitment to submit the purge of Colmer to the caucus of House Democrats.

And so they were surprised when Rayburn announced he would take the issue to the floor of the House instead and attempt to change the rules and add three members to the Committee: two Democrats and a Republican. This was the most moderate solution available. It would give the administration an expected working majority of exactly one vote—8 to 7. No one would suffer personally. The traditional two to one ratio of majority to minority would be maintained. The change would be temporary, for one Congress only. And Rayburn would not even ask the caucus for a two-thirds vote which, in theory, could bind all Democrats to vote for the measure on the floor. Rayburn also let it be known that one of his two new appointments would be a southerner, Carl Elliott of Alabama—thus presumably preserving southern strength on civil rights matters.[80]

The story of the fight that followed this announcement has been told and retold.[81] The brand-new Kennedy administration was plunged into its first crisis. Rayburn, administration Democrats, the liberals of the Democratic Study Group, and a small group of urban Republicans ranged themselves on one side. Judge Smith led a coalition of conservative southern Democrats and an almost solid phalanx of Republicans. Carl Elliott recalls, "Charlie Halleck started playing rough, announcing that he would not make committee assignments for Republicans until after the Rules Committee vote. . . . [A]s usual, lobbyists were swarming all over Capitol Hill. . . . In Congress the pressure is always on to some extent, but this was about the most intense I've ever seen."[82]

Smith did not get all the southern members. The Speaker's old friend Carl Vinson of Georgia, after Rayburn the most senior member of the House and Chairman of the Armed Services Committee, took a pro-Rayburn position and provided a little cover for the other mainstream southerners who wanted to back the expansion of the committee. B. F. Sisk, a transplanted Texan representing the central valley of California was one of the new members Rayburn planned to appoint to the Rules Committee. He says:

> It was my understanding that Carl Vinson . . . committed himself to go with Rayburn, although he was a vocal southerner and was greatly respected in the South. As a result, Vinson was bound to influence votes because he was a senior member of the House, carrying great weight and respect. However, a lot of Southerners resisted his position in this

fight. . . . Without Vinson's help, Rayburn would not have won, in my opinion.[83]

In the end, Rayburn won. The vote was 217–212; and the committee was expanded—for the life of the 87th Congress. The net effect of this change is hard to measure. The most meticulous study of the influence of the Rules Committee on legislation in the 87th Congress remarks that the committee "does not issue a calendar or summary of its activities, infrequently publishes hearings or reports, and conducts most of its significant business in executive session."[84] A statistical study comparing the committee's performance in 1961–63 with previous years would also be faced with the fact that "Following Chairman Smith's loss on the reorganization fight, he opened the floodgates on resolutions the Committee had never considered before, many of them strongly opposed by Rayburn, forcing the new pro-administration majority into the position of tabling them."[85]

But on the whole, the new majority on the committee worked well together. On most issues, they voted to back the administration. The only conspicuous exception was education legislation, which found Democrats in the House as well as on the committee split on the question of federal aid to parochial schools.[86] But the reform of 1961 was only a beginning. In order to keep the valve open, a pro-administration majority had to be maintained on the committee in the next Congress as well. Rayburn's strategy in 1961 bought time by postponing the problem. By asking for the very minimum that he needed, Rayburn made the strongest pitch he could for the support of Democratic moderates. Two years hence the 15-member committee would be hallowed by at least two years of "tradition" and could be justified to some members as a renewal of prior practice. The Kennedy administration, a bit easier in the saddle, would be a more formidable and more knowledgeable ally. And, in the interim, Father Time could do some work. In 1961, Rayburn's two Democratic antagonists were aged 79 (Smith) and 70 (Colmer). If either of them gave way to the erosion of the years, the Speaker would name his successor, and a 15-member committee would no longer be necessary. Ironically, it was Sam Rayburn, and not his Democratic opponents on the Rules Committee, who succumbed in the interim. On November 16, the Speaker died in Bonham, Texas, his hometown. The 1961 fight over the committee was Rayburn's last battle.

## 2

# TOWARD LIBERALIZATION

## Succession to Rayburn

When Speaker Rayburn took his final trip home to Texas at the tag end of the 87th Congress's first session, John W. McCormack of Massachusetts, the majority leader, was automatically elevated to Acting Speaker, and on January 9, 1962, the Democratic caucus of the House of Representatives elected McCormack as its candidate to be the 45th Speaker of the House. On the following day, the whole House ratified this choice with its customary party line vote. On the surface, the promotion of McCormack from his post as majority leader had the appearance of a routine matter. Of the 11 Speakers since 1899 only one (David B. Henderson), elected 63 years earlier, had no record of previous service as a party leader. Nonetheless, the selection of McCormack was not a foregone conclusion. There had been contests for the Speakership on several occasions before; Rayburn himself lost one such battle in 1935.[1] But in 1962 there was no contest, even though McCormack was widely reported to have been the private first choice of well under a majority of his Democratic colleagues. As *Newsweek* said, "Liberals pull back at McCormack's sometimes violent anti-Communism. Conservatives resent the liberal votes that have marked his 33 years in Congress. Protestants sometimes rankle at his pious Roman Catholicism."[2]

In covering the House, newspapers and periodicals often gravitate quickly to ideological explanations. In this instance, McCormack's alleged ideological differences with his Democratic colleagues in the House, aside from the conservative southerners, were exaggerated. More to the point was the fact that McCormack's background and old-fashioned, teetotaling, uxorious, formal style of behavior were very much of a different generation from, for example, his fellow Bostonian the president, or even from the president's successor in the Cambridge seat, Tip O'Neill, to whom McCormack was an odd duck. O'Neill's memoirs say:

> [McCormack] was a man of firmly fixed habits, especially around mealtimes. Every morning at exactly 8:25 he would arrive at his regular corner breakfast table in the House dining room, where they'd bring him a cup of coffee. (He had already eaten breakfast at home with his wife, Harriet.) He ordered the same lunch every day—a grilled cheese sandwich with a cup of tea and a dish of chocolate ice cream. He would ask for the dessert together with the sandwich, so that by the time he finished the sandwich, the ice cream would be melted, which was how he liked it. He ate supper with Harriet every night of their life.
>
> Although we knew each other for twenty-two years, he never called me Tip, because he disapproved of nicknames. No matter where we went, he would always introduce me in the same way: "This is Tom O'Neill. Tom was the speaker of the Massachusetts legislature. He's in Congress now, and I want you to keep your eye on him."[3]

Younger members seemed to have had a hard time relating to McCormack as a person and this bafflement was no doubt to a considerable extent mutual. No "liberal" member I interviewed made any allusion at all to McCormack's anti-Communism, but a fair number of his severe critics were liberal, anti-clerical Roman Catholics. They and others had misgivings of a non-ideological nature.[4]

The *Wall Street Journal*'s January 10 headline referred to a "Lack of Enthusiasm of Democrats," and the accompanying story sounded a major subtheme: "Certainly Mr. McCormack, who has never been noted as a master strategist, will not enjoy nearly the prestige that was Mr. Rayburn's and few feel he will display the Texan's skill at winning the crucial legislative battles."[5] The *New York Times*, which had editorially opposed McCormack's elevation to the Speakership, said, in a news story, "hardly anyone believes that Mr. McCormack will approach his predecessor . . . in power, prestige, or popularity," and cited "his relentless attacks on the opposition, sometimes quite harsh, usually loud, and occasionally personal [which] are credited with winning more arguments than votes."[6] Displaying nostalgia for his lost career as a sports writer, James Reston aptly summed up the innumerable invidious comparisons of McCormack with his predecessor by calling the change "the worst trade since the Kansas City Athletics sent Roger Maris to the New York Yankees."[7] *Time* magazine's slightly more cautious treatment of the same subject was as follows:

> There was no Democratic challenge to Majority Leader McCormack's more or less automatic succession to Rayburn's chair—nor was there any marked enthusiasm about it. Some liberal columnists and editorial writers grumbled, but the young liberals of the House . . . were much too prudent to voice their misgivings publicly. . . . Beyond these liberals there was general House concern about the capacity of John McCormack to achieve real stature in the Speaker's chair.[8]

And *Time's* able Capitol Hill reporter, Neil MacNeil, writing in *Fortune*, said, "Privately, House liberals accuse [McCormack] of 'double dealing', promising one thing but arranging for something else to happen . . . McCormack's Catholicism has also bothered some of the Southerners."[9]

These and similar sentiments were repeatedly echoed by members of Congress in private interviews. Several members told me that McCormack's major first choice strength lay with perhaps 20 or 25 of his coreligionists in the House who represented heavily Catholic, urban constituencies, but even a few leaders meeting this description were known to prefer other candidates for Speaker.

One Congressman from an eastern, urban area said, "I don't like the so-and-so [McCormack] any better than anybody else does around here, but you can't always pick the boss."

Morris Udall said:

> It's easy to see why he's so unpopular in spite of the fact that he has a progressive record, is fairly able, and works like hell. He's stand-offish, high-handed, not warm at all. He's blunt and brusque, doesn't mix with the boys or go out and get drunk with them. I suppose the main thing people have against him is his total lack of tact and finesse. Just about everybody I have talked with, especially among the younger men, said they'd have voted for *anybody* running against McCormack.[10]

A border state Congressman said, "He's not at all skillful. He was ready to settle for $100 million worth of foreign aid at the end of last session and it was the Republicans who took the credit for raising the total to $300 million. I've seen this sort of thing happen with him before. He has no feel at all for the House."

A midwesterner said, "He's terribly vain. He's not trusted. His word isn't regarded as good. . . . And he's regarded as an axe-grinder, especially on this religious issue."

A senior southerner said, "He very rarely wins votes when he speaks on the floor. Instead he alienates people. He's quite willing to help in debate, but on my bills I tell him no thanks."

And another Congressman said, in January 1962, "I doubt that anybody thought three months ago that McCormack would have made it."

Yet in spite of these widely (though not universally) held, serious misgivings, any reader of the newspapers could tell by the end of Sam Rayburn's lingering, last illness, that John McCormack had the Speakership entirely sewed up without a fight.[11] This was in part because no other Democrat was anywhere nearly as well positioned to move into the void at the point in time when 260 Democrats were required to fix upon a candidate to succeed Sam Rayburn.

Rayburn died on November 16, 1961, while the House stood in recess. "We were scattered far and wide, to the ends of the earth," one congressman said. Another, Clem Miller, from California, said:

It's a hell of a big state. When we're at home we [Democratic congressmen] never see each other. Some of the men, like John Moss and Bernie Sisk, have home bases, where they can be reached every day, but not me, or my good friend Bizz Johnson. The dean of our delegation, Harry Sheppard, is always very hard to get a hold of. Even when I'm in my district I might be traveling around and it might take two or three days to get a hold of me by telephone. But, as it happened, when the Speaker died and for quite a time thereafter, I was on vacation and entirely out of touch with the situation. And I know that was true of others. Cecil King was in Geneva, at an international meeting; Jeff Cohelan was touring army bases, and so on.[12]

Yet the Democrats had to have a candidate for Speaker within 55 days, and during none of them would the House be in session. McCormack, as one of the senior members of the House and as majority leader, was conspicuously on the map of alternatives obviously open to members. Precedent, and the fact that he had been Acting Speaker during Rayburn's absence made McCormack's position unique.[13] There were many committee chairmen, many deans of large delegations, many senior members, many centers of power in the House, but only one Acting Speaker. And from the standpoint of most of the powerful and well-known members of the House, McCormack was one of them, and surely entitled to recognition before a more junior member could be considered. He would also be much more dependent on them than Rayburn was. As one member put it: "I pity the guy who becomes the next Speaker. He will be in the same position as the early kings of England were vis-à-vis the dukes. He'll spend much of his time fighting the dukes, and will have to give away much of his power, at first, until he can pyramid it over time."

No clear alternative was ever open to Democrats because they were restrained by canons of good taste from milling about, negotiating, and reaching another solution while Speaker Rayburn still lived. By the time he had passed on, too much geography separated them. In settling upon McCormack, many Democrats had to stretch quite a distance. Judge Smith and the conservative southerners swiftly settled on McCormack as the best they could get under the circumstances. Despite his Catholicism and his progressive voting record, two things commended McCormack to the conservatives in the South. He was not regarded as an especially wily or subtle antagonist, and secondly, he regularly voted in favor of, and in debate supported, agriculture subsidies.

McCormack's southern support coupled with his first-choice strength among several urban delegations left only the programmatic liberals with no place to go, and McCormack himself had a liberal voting record. This fact would have made intervention by the Kennedy White House on grounds other than personal impossible. Hence, the McCormack coalition soon came to include liberal Democrats as well. As one of the more pragmatic among them said, "it is rather important in this institution to land on the raft and not in the water."

The main immediate consequence of the McCormack succession was to place the leadership of the Democratic Party in the control of a less imaginative and less sure-footed tactician than Sam Rayburn. It very soon transpired that Speaker McCormack's tactical judgment could not command the confidence of his colleagues.

## Conflict within the Caucus: Liberals against the Leadership, 1963

Outside observers may be puzzled that dramatic episodes of reform—when they occur at all—seem to take place at the openings of sessions of Congress. Like any organization, Congress moves the bulk of its activity through channels. But unlike most organizations, in the House the channels themselves must formally be re-established every two years. Every two years, a new Congress meets, elects party leaders and a Speaker, adopts rules, and constitutes committees. No pending business is left over; in principle, everything starts fresh.

To be sure, if this principle were literally followed in practice, life would be intolerably complicated for members. Many customs of the House therefore provide for continuity. The rules are commonly readopted without substantial change; and the precedents stand behind the rules. Congressional staff members, for the majority and the minority, in the 1960s and before had virtually lifetime tenure. And the seniority rule—actually a custom, not a rule—provided that members would always be reassigned to their previous committees, and ranked in order of consecutive years of service on the committee, by party. This left only a small area of discretion to would-be reformers. They might try to amend the rules at the time of adoption in some way, as Rayburn and his coalition did in 1961. Or they might attempt to alter the ideological balance of committees, by appointing freshmen or transferring veterans, to fill vacancies.[14] But this strategy could succeed only if vacancies existed. Only on the rarest of occasions could a sitting member be deposed. Normally, it was necessary to wait for vacancies to occur on key committees, and then fill them properly. And the time when most vacancies occur is at the opening of Congress.

By 1963, it was clear that the Ways and Means Committee had become the key committee in Congress as far as the program of the Kennedy administration was concerned. Once the bottleneck on the Rules Committee was broken, or at least stretched, the main legislative problems of the administration, and their hopes for a successful campaign in the 1964 presidential election, lodged in the Ways and Means Committee. Specifically, three bills of great complexity and enormous consequence were involved: Reciprocal Trade, a tax cut, and Medicare.

In the 87th Congress, the membership of the Committee had been as shown in table 2.1.

Two Democrats, neither mainstream liberals, dropped off the committee: James Frazier of Tennessee was beaten in a primary election and Burr Harrison of Virginia decided to retire. And so at the opening of the 88th Congress in 1963, the main issues that concerned the Democratic leadership, and the party in the House more generally, were three: replacement of Frazier on Ways and Means, replacement of Harrison, and the maintenance of the 10–5 partisan ratio on the Rules Committee.[15] This last matter arose because the committee-packing resolution on which Ray-

TABLE 2.1. Ways and Means Committee, 1962

| Democrats | | Republicans | |
| --- | --- | --- | --- |
| Member | CC score | Member | CC score |
| Wilbur D. Mills (AR), Chairman | 37 | Noah M. Mason (IL) | 50 |
| Cecil B. King (CA) | 0 | John W. Byrnes (WI) | 63 |
| Thomas J. O'Brien (IL) | 0 | Howard H. Baker (TN) | 69 |
| Hale Boggs (LA) | 12 | Thomas B. Curtis (MO) | 81 |
| Eugene J. Keogh (NY) | 0 | Victor A. Knox (MI) | 88 |
| Burr P. Harrison (VA) | 44 | James B. Utt (CA) | 75 |
| Frank M. Karsten (MO) | 0 | Jackson E. Betts (OH) | 100 |
| A. Sydney Herlong, Jr. (FL) | 69 | Bruce Alger (TX) | 94 |
| James B. Frazier, Jr. (TN) | 31 | Steven B. Derounian (NY) | 75 |
| William J. Green, Jr. (PA) | 6 | Herman T. Schneebelli (PA) | 75 |
| John C. Watts (KY) | 25 | | |
| Al Ullman (OR) | 12 | | |
| James A. Burke (MA) | 25 | | |
| Clarke W. Thompson (TX) | 19 | | |
| Martha W. Griffiths (MI) | 19 | | |

Source: *Congressional Quarterly Almanac*, 1962, p. 58.

burn won his famous fight was a temporary one, good only for the 88th Congress, and therefore had to be regularized as a permanent arrangement.

In preliminary skirmishing prior to the opening of Congress, it became apparent that soon-to-be Speaker McCormack, weighing most heavily the solidifying of the Rules Committee majority coalition, traded for the support of the 10-member Georgia delegation on that vote one of the vacancies on Ways and Means. Georgia's candidate was none other than Phil Landrum, of Landrum-Griffin bill fame.[16]

Landrum, an intelligent, hard-working conservative member (1962 conservative coalition score of 75), had the respect, but not the trust of his liberal colleagues in the Democratic caucus.[17] No doubt seeking to soften the impact of Landrum's candidacy, Speaker McCormack extracted from him a pledge to support two major Kennedy administration initiatives for the 87th Congress: the tax program and Medicare.[18]

But this served also to underscore to liberals who in the light of the Landrum-Griffin bill scarcely needed reminding that the Democratic leadership was asking them to place on a key committee a colleague with whom they had very little politically in common. The Democrats on Ways and Means after all were responsible not only for extremely important legislation but also were the party's Committee on Committees. A liberal member said to *Time Magazine*, "It's not just this year's bills . . . Landrum will be hitting us in the head for the next 20 years."[19]

There ensued an event of historic dimensions, though it was not much appreciated at the time, namely a revolt in the caucus against the leadership. Pat Jennings of Virginia, the only member from Virginia to vote with Rayburn on the expansion of the Rules Committee (despite a conservative coalition score of 69), was induced by liberals to stand for one of the Ways and Means vacancies.[20] This was a shrewd choice. The preservation of Harrison's seat for the state delegation of Virginia might have an appeal to Virginians that could cut across ideological loyalties. The third candidate was Ross Bass of Tennessee (conservative coalition score of six), a liberal running with leadership support.

In a secret ballot in the caucus, Bass and Jennings prevailed. Jennings got 161 votes to Landrum's 126, and Bass received 169 votes.[21] Analysis showed a number of unexpected crosscurrents. Out of 228 valid ballots cast, there were 102 Bass–Jennings, 67 Bass–Landrum, and 59 Jennings–Landrum.[22] Howard Smith led the Virginia delegation in voting against Landrum presumably in part to preserve the seat for Virginia, but also to pay back the leader of the Georgia delegation, Carl Vinson, for his support of Rayburn in the 1961 Rules fight, and for his mobilization of the entire Georgia delegation in 1963 in favor of making the packing of the Rules Committee permanent.[23]

Liberal success in packing the Ways and Means Committee had substantial further effects. This was true not only with respect to legislative matters deemed important by the Kennedy administration, but also by virtue of the status of committee members on the Democratic side of the committee as the House Democratic Party's Committee on Committees. This was the arena in which the assignment of members to committees takes place, all of which occur at the opening of each Congress. Ordinarily, these assignments follow the rule that each member is entitled to reappointment to whatever assignment he or she has had in the past, and as vacancies occur, members move up the ladder of seniority in their committees. Once in a while, members ask or are asked by the party leadership to transfer from one committee to another, in which case they go on their new committee roster ranked below members already on board, and await their turn, years away, to chair subcommittees or, eventually, if they last that long, the full committee. Newly elected members are added to fill vacancies on the bottom of the roster. Elections in which there is heavy turnover of members provide opportunities for the leadership—the Committee on Committees willing—to modify the ideological cast of a committee. One such opportunity presented itself after the 1962 election.

## Incremental Committee Packing:
## Appropriations, 1963

Committee packing, the incremental transformation of the ideological and programmatic orientations of congressional committees, has been a major source of institutional change in Congress since Congress became a well-bounded, stable body in the early years of the twentieth century.[24] And as the composition of Congress changes continually—shedding members at a rate of between 10 and 20 percent in every two-year cycle[25]—the task of replenishing committees and adjusting their compatibility with party and factional and interest group goals (depending upon who is doing the monitoring) is never-ending. In 1950, for example, Appropriations Committee Chairman Clarence Cannon succeeded in reporting a single consolidated omnibus bill, dramatizing the sheer size of the federal budget. An unamused Speaker Rayburn said, "I can't do anything with Cannon." The next year, the committee reverted to its customary 13 separate appropriations bills. Cannon said, "Sam packed the committee against me."[26] In 1963, following the revolt in the Democratic caucus that changed the composition of the Ways and Means Committee, the Democratic leadership began once again the slow but significant task of moving the House Appropriations Committee toward the Democratic mainstream.

The Appropriations Committee is the third of the triumvirate of committees—Rules and Ways and Means are the others—that observers invariably identify as dominating the business of the House of Representatives. The committee's appropriations of money—always done on an annual basis—give practical effect to authorizations made by all other standing committees of Congress. The subcommittees of Appropriations are where all the detailed work of sorting out budget priorities is done. Control of these subcommittees by members opposed to presidential programs and entrenched by the protections of the seniority system constituted a continuing annoyance to the House leadership and to the mainstream liberal bloc. The case of the Foreign Operations Subcommittee led by Otto Passman of Louisiana, scourge of foreign aid (his unofficial title), from 1955 to 1977 was no doubt the most publicized example of this.[27] Another was John Rooney's (N.Y.) mistrustful handling of the State Department. Not all other Appropriations subcommittees were particularly ideologically offensive to liberals, but they were all quite programmatically influential, even when their cognate substantive committees were well run.[28] In turn the subcommittees' recommendations customarily sailed through the full committee and were usually accepted *in toto* on the floor of the House. In 1963, this is the way it worked:

Most sessions of the 50-member Committee are as ritualistic and meaningless as a gathering of the Supreme Soviet in Moscow. A subcommittee's report isn't even seen by the full committee until members file into the meeting room. Before they have a chance to glance at the report, Cannon gavels the bill through. The entire process takes about five minutes.[29]

Richard Fenno's famous tabulation of the reception of all subcommittee appropriations bills dealing with domestic subjects for a 16-year period (1947–62) shows that the House amended committee reports only 10 percent of the time.[30] In all other cases the recommendations of the subcommittees were accepted to the last dollar.

Although new members of the Appropriations Committee were formally chosen by Committees on Committees, the best study of committee assignments in this era reports that in practice it was unusual for a member of this committee to be assigned without the leadership's stamp of approval.[31] Five vacancies existed on the Appropriations Committee's Democratic side after the election of 1962. Three of the seats had been held by northern liberals. Following the customary (but not mandatory) rule of thumb awarding rights of succession to state delegations, liberal congressmen from New York, Illinois, and Washington replaced departed colleagues from these three states. The other two seats had been held by southern conservatives (Dale Alford of Arkansas and Hugh Alexander of North Carolina). Both of these seats had been held by southerners for an extended period of time, but they were replaced by northern liberals, Robert N. Giaimo of Connecticut and Charles Joelson of New Jersey. Speaker McCormack asked one member at the meeting when the assignments were announced, "Did you get a look at Cannon's face? . . . May he rest in peace" (see table 2.2).[32]

Substantial though these changes were, they could not altogether overturn the extraordinary stability of the committee. From the 80th to 87th Congress (1947 to 1962), 35.7 percent of the committee remained constant.[33] The next most stable committee, Agriculture, retained only 26.7 percent of its membership from the 80th Congress to the 87th. On the Democratic side, 10 members (out of 18 in the Democratic minority) who were on the Appropriations Committee in 1947 were still there in 1963. From 1947 to 1963, only two members left the Appropriations Committee for another committee (excepting those temporarily forced to leave when the control of Congress, and hence party ratios, changed).[34] This continuity of membership made packing of this committee a slow and difficult process.

Stability of committee membership also contributed to resistance to

TABLE 2.2. "Liberalism" of "Old" vs. "New" Democratic Members of the House Appropriations Committee, 1962–63

| Retiring members, 1962 | Score | New members, 1963 | Score |
|---|---|---|---|
| Sidney Yates (IL) | 81 | Edward R. Finnegan (IL) | 87 |
| Alfred Santangelo (NY) | 76 | Robert N. Giaimo (CT) | 76 |
| Don Magnuson (WA) | 75 | Charles S. Joelson (NJ) | 76 |
| Hugh Alexander (NC) | 14 | Julia Butler Hansen (WA) | 74 |
| Dale Alford (AR) | −2 | Joseph P. Addabbo (NY) | 73 |
| Average | 49 | Average | 77 |

Note: A member's liberalism score is the average of a member's presidential domestic support indices from 1961 to 1962 minus the average of the 1961–62 presidential domestic opposition indices.

Source: *Congressional Quarterly.*

change by helping to maintain an integrated social system with recognized norms. Richard Fenno's classic study, *The Power of the Purse,* established that the committee had constructed an internal culture in which they claimed to deal not with programmatic questions but with "dollars and cents," that theirs was a "business" rather than a "policy" committee.[35] They maintained a consensus on the proposition, soon accepted by new members, that the executive departments were interested in the expansion of their particular programs, and that, therefore, each budget request asks for more money than is really needed in order to run an adequate program. The committee members saw it as their function, therefore, to cut whatever budget estimates were submitted.[36] Even the newly appointed liberal members readily differentiated themselves from the "wild-eyed spenders." One liberal member told Richard Fenno, "Some of these guys would spend you through the roof."[37] Another northern liberal on the committee expressed the committee creed: "Yes, it's true. I can see it myself. I suppose I came here a flaming liberal; but as the years go by I get more conservative. You just hate like hell to spend all this money. . . . You come to the point where you say, 'By God, this is enough.' "[38] Not all the northern liberals succumbed. John Fogarty of Rhode Island, for example, ran a much more generous subcommittee on Heath, Education, and Welfare than was the overall norm. But there was no doubt the general tendency on the committee was less indulgent of mainstream Democratic values than the average member of the caucus. Before the 1963 packing, the Democrats on the Appropriations Committee had a mean liberalism score of 53.[39] The score of all Democratic congressmen in the House was 56. After the packing, the mean score of the Democratic members of the committee was 58.

Cannon fought back using his powers to appoint to subcommittees and assign subcommittee jurisdictions. One of the new members, Charles Joelson of New Jersey commented, "They're trying to pack Appropriations, but the way Cannon runs it, it will take forever. You saw what he did. Giaimo and Finnegan got D.C. Addabbo got Agriculture. I have Legislative. Liberals don't have any influence in committee."[40] Senior conservative members were assigned to two or three important subcommittees, while younger liberals served on only one, usually unimportant, subcommittee. In 1963, Cannon organized 13 subcommittees. The Democratic membership of five of these subcommittees was substantially more conservative than the Democratic membership of the full committee or the House. These five subcommittees handled 76.6 percent of the total national budget for the fiscal year 1963. The Democratic membership of seven of the subcommittees scored more liberal than the full committee or the House. These subcommittees, however, processed only 22.4 percent of the total budget. And of this sum, more than half, or 13.1 percent of the total budget, was appropriated by one subcommittee, on Independent Offices. Three of the four Democratic members on this subcommittee, Albert Thomas of Texas, Joe Evins of Tennessee, and George Shipley of Illinois, were veteran members of the Appropriations Committee who earned the reputation in committee as "fiscal conservatives," even though they had liberal voting records on the House floor. Such important subcommittees as Agriculture, Foreign Operations (which handled foreign aid), Treasury and Post Office, and Public Works were firmly controlled by the more conservative members. The only subcommittee handling controversial appropriations controlled by more liberally oriented Democrats was John Fogarty's Subcommittee on the Departments of Labor and Health, Education, and Welfare. And the Democratic composition of all subcommittees became more conservative when Clarence Cannon exercised his privilege as an *ex officio* voting member of all subcommittees.

The newly appointed liberal members in 1963 found themselves serving on such subcommittees as District of Columbia, which handled 0.003 percent of the federal budget, and Legislative Expenses, which deliberated over 0.12 percent of the budget. As noted, New York City freshman Joseph Addabbo was assigned to the Agriculture subcommittee. Another member chuckled, "[T]here's not even a flower pot in his district."[41] Charles Joelson described his responsibilities as a new member of the Legislative or "housekeeping" subcommittee:

The subcommittee really doesn't have much to do. We haven't
had more than a week of meetings. All we decide is whether the
Library of Congress should have copper plumbing. I can't even object
to the [new congressional] swimming pool. By the time I got over
here, they'd already dug the hole. All I could do was to tell them,
"Don't put in the water."[42]

In addition to appointing the new members to relatively insignificant
subcommittees, Cannon realigned some of the other subcommittees
slightly. He reshuffled them so that despite the addition of two liberals and
the loss of two conservatives, all the subcommittees but three had the same
policy orientation as they had had in the previous Congress. Of the three
that changed, two, Legislative and District of Columbia, became more liberal. But between them they handled less than 1 percent of the budget.
One subcommittee, Agriculture, became more conservative. That subcommittee handled 6.7 percent of the budget in fiscal year 1963 (see table 2.3).

Cannon also changed the jurisdictions of his subcommittees for policy
purposes. In 1956 he reorganized the subcommittees in order to prevent
Vaughn Gary (Va.), a moderate supporter of foreign aid, from controlling
the relevant subcommittee.[43] In 1962 he plucked the civil defense program
out of the Department of Defense budget—which had been placed there
in order to avoid this fate—and assigned it to a subcommittee whose chairman opposed the program. In 1964 he abolished the Deficiencies subcommittee, one of the most liberal of the subcommittees, and distributed its
jurisdiction among the other subcommittees. Previously executive agencies
had sought supplemental appropriations from Deficiencies after absorbing
cuts by other subcommittees.

Despite his agile maneuvers, Cannon's control over his committee was
not absolute. In 1956, when he reorganized his subcommittees, he was
prevented by the full committee, led by the subcommittee chairmen, from
making an even more drastic reorganization. By 1962 the 85-year-old Cannon was in a bad mood, feuding with Carl Hayden, his opposite number
in the Senate, and calling McCormack's leadership "biased and inept" in
a speech on the House floor.[44]

From the time of the Court Packing Bill in 1937 right on through to
the abrupt and traumatic conclusion of the Kennedy presidency in November 1963, life in the House of Representatives for liberal and mainstream
Democrats was, as Clem Miller aptly described it, "World War I warfare":
a trench operation, with progress made inch-by-inch over hostile terrain,
a matter of two steps forward and one step back.[45] Liberal advocates of
party responsibility in the population at large tore their hair over the

TABLE 2.3. Liberalism of Democratic Subcommittee Members of the House Appropriations Committee, 1962–63

| Subcommittee | Mean liberalism score | | Processed % of 1963 budget |
|---|---|---|---|
| | 1962 | 1963 | |
| Department of Defense | 40 | 40 | 50.20 |
| Independent Offices | 76 | 72 | 13.10 |
| Foreign Operations | 42 | 44 | 7.69 |
| Department of Agriculture and Related Agencies | 43 | 36 | 6.67 |
| Departments of Treasury, Post Office, and Executive Office | 27 | 31 | 6.65 |
| Departments of Labor and Health, Education, and Welfare and Related Agencies | 62 | 67 | 5.54 |
| Public Works | 53 | 49 | 5.37 |
| Departments of State, Justice, and Commerce, the Judiciary and Related Agencies | 67 | 68 | 2.10 |
| Military Construction | 57 | 57 | 1.78 |
| Department of Interior and Related Agencies | 72 | 72 | 0.98 |
| Deficiencies[a] | 84 | 84 | 0.59 |
| Legislative | 45 | 71 | 0.12 |
| District of Columbia | 67 | 75 | 0.003 |

[a]The Deficiencies Committee was abolished by Cannon in early 1964.

Notes: The mean liberalism score for the Democratic membership of the full committee was 53 in 1962 and 58 in 1963. The score for all Democrats in the House was 56.

Sources: Analysis by Paul D. O'Brien, "Party Leadership and the Committee Selection Process in the House of Representatives," Honors College, Wesleyan University (June 1964), table 3–4. Data from *Congressional Quarterly Almanacs*, 1962, 1963.

"deadlock of democracy," the inability of Democratic presidents to redeem their campaign promises in an arena—the House of Representatives—nominally controlled by Democrats.[46]

During this era the separation of powers itself took a beating from liberal critics. Defenders of Congress, not all of them reactionaries, pointed out that the Constitution was, after all, designed to provide members of Congress with constituents of their own, that a geographically expansive, heterogeneous society like the United States could scarcely be expected to produce a spontaneous nationwide uniformity in policy preferences, that the legitimacy of public policy and possibly the long-term viability of the regime depended heavily on the genuine, uncoerced consent of the governed and their representatives.

Both the New Deal and the centralizing measures of World War II[47] showed that the American political system could in fact grant legitimacy to something other than deadlock when the will was widespread enough. All the rest of the experience of contemporary commentators attested to the fact that widespread agreement to liberal legislation could not regularly be counted upon. Therefore the advocacy of a liberal agenda in the House required prudent management as of a slow-growing garden, the preparation of soil, the nurturing of tender shoots, patient cultivation, and waiting for an eventual, occasional harvest. This is what committee packing was all about: the clearing of channels through which—later on—proposals could move without excessive hindrance.

### Republican Committee Packing: Maintaining the Party Mainstream, 1961–63

While the Democrats were working toward change in the ideological balance of the Rules, Ways and Means, Education and Labor, and Appropriations Committees, Republicans were making similar moves. Soon after he succeeded Joe Martin as Republican leader in 1959, Charles Halleck was faced with a series of losses on the Rules Committee as Leo Allen of Illinois retired in 1960. Hugh Scott of Pennsylvania went off to the Senate, and Henry Latham left Congress to become a New York state judge. To succeed them, he appointed a series of staunch conservatives, keeping the Republican contingent on the Rules Committee securely to the right (see table 2.4.

TABLE 2.4. House Republicans Appointed to the Rules Committee, 1959–61

| Member (appointed) | 86th Congress (1959–60) conservative coalition score |
|---|---|
| Budge, ID (1959) | 93 |
| Reece, TN (1959) | 87 |
| St. George, NY (1961) | 90 |
| Smith, CA (1961) | 97 |
| Hoffman, IL (1961) | 97 |
| Avery, KS (1961) | 100 |
| Average of all Republican members | 75 |

Source: *Congressional Quarterly Almanac*, 1960.

Republican appointments were made by vote of the Republican conference on recommendation of its Committee on Committees. This committee was composed of one member from each state delegation having a Republican representative. Each state delegation picked its representative to the committee, and each representative had as many votes on committee business as there were Republicans in their state delegation. The composition of the committee in the 86th Congress is given in table 2.5.

Power in this committee was concentrated in a subcommittee appointed by the party leader consisting primarily of senior representatives of the large state delegations. In the 86th Congress this subcommittee was constituted as in table 2.6.

It will be noted that there was a considerable overlap between influential members of the Republican Committee on Committees and Republican holdovers and appointees to the Rules Committee. In an interview we asked Clarence Brown about his new Rules Committee colleagues. "Picked 'em all," he said, based on his personal knowledge of them, their reliability on party matters. He wanted, he said, "team players. Very able, every one." "Also, you look at the type of district. Can they take the heat?"[48]

In 1963, six Republican vacancies popped up on the Foreign Affairs Committee (out of 13 slots). During the eight years of the Eisenhower administration (1953–61), the Republican leadership had gone along with the president and appointed supporters of foreign aid, the main business of the committee. Alvin O'Konski of Wisconsin said that in these years, "I was vetoed . . . because I was a strong critic of foreign aid." He went on to say that, "on important things . . . the leadership tells [the Republican Committee on Committees] who it wants."[49] But in 1963, with Ike out of the White House, different criteria prevailed, and five out of six vacancies were filled with members who, as the *Washington Post* reported, "opposed all major foreign policy bills that year."[50] They were conservative, too, and much higher in party unity on average than the members they replaced (see tables 2.7 and 2.8).

The new members were quite conscious that they were bringing change to the committee. E. Y. Berry of South Dakota said: "When what's-his-name from New Hampshire [Chester Merrow] announced for the Senate . . . a year and a half ago I went up to Charlie Halleck the next day, and told him I could be a ballast, a balance on Foreign Affairs, for some of the liberal and internationalist sentiment on the other side of the table."[51]

Vernon Thomson of Wisconsin complained about the holdover Republicans: "You talk about being out of line. Nearly every Republican [on the committee] voted the same way as the Democrats. They talk about being bipartisan. I guess that means voting with your opponents."[52] H. R. Gross

TABLE 2.5. House Republican Committee on Committees, 86th Congress, 1959–60

| State | Member | Votes | State | Member | Votes |
|-------|--------|-------|-------|--------|-------|
| Arizona | John J. Rhodes | 1 | New Jersey | Frank C. Osmers | 9 |
| California | James Utt | 14 | New York | Katharine St. George | 24 |
| Colorado | J. Edgar Chenoweth | 1 | | | |
| Florida | William C. Cramer | 1 | North Carolina | Charles R. Jonas | 1 |
| Idaho | Hamer Budge | 1 | North Dakota | Don L. Short | 1 |
| Illinois | Leo E. Allen | 11 | Ohio | Clarence J. Brown | 14 |
| Indiana | E. Ross Adair | 3 | Oklahoma | Page Belcher | 1 |
| Iowa | Charles B. Hoeven | 4 | Oregon | Walter Norblad | 1 |
| Kansas | Edward H. Rees | 3 | Pennsylvania | Richard Simpson | 14 |
| Kentucky | Eugene Siler | 1 | South Dakota | E. Y. Berry | 1 |
| Maine | Clifford G. McIntire | 1 | Tennessee | Howard H. Baker | 2 |
| Massachusetts | William H. Bates | 6 | Texas | Bruce Alger | 1 |
| Michigan | Clare E. Hoffman | 11 | Utah | Henry A. Dixon | 1 |
| Minnesota | H. Carl Anderson | 5 | Virginia | Joel T. Broyhill | 2 |
| Missouri | Thomas B. Curtis | 1 | Washington | Jack Westland | 6 |
| Nebraska | Phil Weaver | 2 | West Virginia | Arch A. Moore | 1 |
| New Hampshire | Perkins Bass | 2 | Wisconsin | John W. Byrnes | 5 |
| | | | Wyoming | E. Keith Thomson | 1 |

Source: Nicholas A. Masters, "Committee Assignments in the House of Representatives," *American Political Science Review* 55 (June 1961), p. 349.

TABLE 2.6. House Republican Subcommittee on Committees, 86th Congress

| State | Member | Votes | Seniority |
|-------|--------|-------|-----------|
| California | James Utt | 14 | 4 consecutive terms |
| Idaho | Hamer H. Budge | 1 | 5 consecutive terms |
| Illinois | Leo E. Allen | 11 | 14 consecutive terms |
| Michigan | Clare E. Hoffman | 11 | 13 consecutive terms |
| New Jersey | Frank C. Osmers | 9 | 7 non-consecutive terms |
| New York | Katharine St. George | 24 | 7 consecutive terms |
| North Carolina | Charles Raper Jonas | 1 | 4 consecutive terms |
| Ohio | Clarence J. Brown | 14 | 11 consecutive terms |
| Pennsylvania | Richard M. Simpson | 14 | 7 consecutive terms |

Source: Nicholas A. Masters, "Committee Assignments in the House of Representatives," *American Political Science Review* 55 (June 1961), p. 349.

TABLE 2.7. Republicans on the Foreign Affairs Committee, 1963

| Departures | | Holdovers | | New appointees | |
|---|---|---|---|---|---|
| Member | Party unity | Member | Party unity | Member | Party unity |
| Robert Chiperfield (IL) | 70 | Frances P. Bolton (OH) | 73 | H. R. Gross (IA) | 93 |
| Chester E. Merrow (NH) | 24 | E. Ross Adair (IN) | 82 | E. Y. Berry (SD) | 75 |
| Walter H. Judd (MN) | 58 | William S. Mailliard (CA) | 52 | Edward J. Derwinski (IL) | 77 |
| Marguerite Stitt Church (IL) | 89 | Peter Frelinghuysen (NJ) | 60 | F. Bradford Morse (MA) | 63 |
| Laurence Curtis (MA) | 47 | William H. Broomfield (MI) | 70 | James F. Battin (MT) | 73 |
| Horace Seely-Brown (CT) | 59 | Robert R. Barry (NY) | 64 | Vernon W. Thomson (WI) | 86 |
| | | J. Irving Whalley (PA) | 63 | | |
| Average party unity | 57.8 | | 66.2 | | 77.8 |

Source: Party unity scores are for the 87th Congress, from the *Congressional Quarterly Almanac*, 1961 and 1963.

TABLE 2.8. Support of Bipartisan Foreign Policy, Republican Members of the House, 1963

| Departures | | Holdovers | | New appointees | |
|---|---|---|---|---|---|
| Member | Mean B-P score | Member | Mean B-P score | Member | Mean B-P score |
| Robert Chiperfield (IL) | 44 | Frances P. Bolton (OH) | 58 | H. R. Gross (IA) | -82 |
| Chester E. Merrow (NH) | 72 | E. Ross Adair (IN) | -44 | E. Y. Berry (SD) | -56 |
| Walter H. Judd (MN) | 85 | William S. Mailliard (CA) | 81 | Edward J. Derwinski (IL) | -41 |
| Marguerite Stitt Church (IL) | -27 | Peter Frelinghuysen (NJ) | 80 | F. Bradford Morse (MA) | 91 |
| Laurence Curtis (MA) | 62 | William H. Broomfield (MI) | 68 | James F. Battin (MT) | -57 |
| Horace Seely-Brown (CT) | 65 | Robert R. Barry (NY) | 70 | Vernon W. Thomson (WI) | -42 |
| | | J. Irving Whalley (PA) | 40 | | |
| Average bipartisan foreign policy score | 50 | | 50 | | -31 |

Note: Bipartisanship scores were calculated by subtracting members' administration opposition scores on foreign policy from their administration support scores, as calculated by *Congressional Quarterly*.

Source: Paul D. O'Brien, "Party Leadership and the Committee Selection Process in the House of Representatives," Honors thesis, Wesleyan University (1964), tables 4–8 and 4–9; data from the *Congressional Quarterly Almanac*, 1961 and 1963, pp. 624–25, pp. 720–21.

of Iowa said that the reason he applied for the committee was to "help save the taxpayers some money."[53] Gross was a conspicuous gadfly, identifying himself as an all-out foe of the foreign aid "give-away program."[54] His moderate Republican colleague from Iowa, Fred Schwengel, commented, "I don't know why they let him on Foreign Affairs. Why he's against even having a foreign policy, not only against foreign aid."[55]

Halleck and the Republican Committee on Committees, even before the new Congress convened, had decided to change the composition of the Republican side of the Foreign Affairs Committee. It was well known by January 1963, as Brad Morse put it, that "[Clarence] Brown [Chairman of the Republican Committee on Committees] and Halleck had decided . . . that they would let just one liberal on the committee, in order to make Foreign Affairs more representative of the whole party." James Utt of California said: "We've been tired of these East Coast internationalists dominating the thing. So when we came up with six vacancies, we made an agreement that we were going to put on five Midwesterners and only one internationalist. We weren't even getting a minority report. And of course the internationalists are still in the majority."[56] Republican whip Les Arends (Ill.) said: "The Committee was clearly out of balance. We never get facts. Most of the old people believed whatever the State Department said and never would challenge anything. This is the first time we got balance on the Committee."[57] James Battin of Montana agreed:

We were accused of stacking the committee. Actually, we unstacked it by allowing for a divergence of opinion. Most committee members are still for foreign aid. But if you put foreign aid on a national referendum, there's no question that it would be trounced. To get it through, it has to be put on an emotional basis, i.e., that the world would go bankrupt without it. That just isn't true.[58]

The one internationalist assigned to the committee was Bradford Morse, who took the Massachusetts seat formerly held by Laurence Curtis. John Lindsay of New York City's "silk stocking" east side—then still a Republican—was turned down for a seat on the committee. He said:

Without question, one [factor] was my known commitment to the principle of foreign aid. They were tired of people who went along, you know, "me-tooers." Look at the people who make the selections. . . . They were a pretty strong group. They were opposed; they are a group of long-range isolationists. Clarence Brown was sincerely committed to see that the spirit of the Committee, our side of it, was changed.[59]

With the addition of the five conservatives, the House Committee on Foreign Affairs became solidly representative of the Republicans in the House. The six newly assigned members had an average bipartisanship score of −31. This reduced the mean score for the Republican side of the committee to slightly less than 13 (down from 51) or almost equal to the mean of all GOP congressmen, 13.[60]

Although both Democrats and Republicans sought to pack committees to reflect central tendencies in party sentiment, Republicans had a much easier time of it during the 1960s and thereafter. Their deviant liberals were a smaller and less resourceful crew than conservative southern Democrats were in the Democratic caucus, and the Republican mainstream position was correspondingly easier to sustain. The comparative unity of Republicans in the House thus presented Democrats with an ongoing strategic problem that greatly exacerbated the Democrats' inability to agree among themselves about policy and priorities.

## The Landslide: 1964

Once Democrats regained the presidency after eight years of Dwight Eisenhower, it took time for them to resume forward motion on the unfinished business of the New Deal. This meant chiefly moving toward the installation of a welfare state providing services roughly comparable to those available in virtually all other western democracies, especially in the areas of old-age assistance and health care, and also, even more important, dealing with civil rights.

Civil rights was a problem of great complexity owing to the way in which its origins were embedded in American history and geography. At the end of World War II, what was arguably the world's most remarkably successful democratic nation was, intolerably, running a racially divided caste system in a large part of its territory. The coercive power of the state was enlisted in preventing a substantial part of its population from enjoying routine access to public facilities of all sorts and from exercising the elementary rights of citizenship.[61]

In a halting but meaningful way the national Democratic Party had begun to address this festering sore with its famous battle over the party's platform in 1948. It was a Democratic Party struggle because virtually all of the South was run by Democratic politicians, not by the party of Lincoln. So the struggle over civil rights, when it was eventually joined, pitted national against southern regional Democrats, with Republicans mostly in secondary roles and frequently content to seize local partisan advantage from the intra-party warfare of the Democrats.[62]

John Kennedy's assassination was not the sole cause of the Democratic landslide in the election of 1964. The ineptitude of Nelson Rockefeller as a presidential hopeful on the Republican side more or less guaranteed the nomination of Barry Goldwater, an amateurish campaigner who shared the common view that the Republican nomination in the wake of Kennedy's death was, as John Lindsay put it, "a ticket on the Titanic."[63]

Indeed, so it proved to be: Lyndon Johnson won by a margin of 486 to 52 electoral votes, with a 61.1–38.5 percent edge in popular support. He brought in with him 295 Democrats (a net gain of 37 seats), more than the 283 Democrats elected in the flood year of 1958 (a 49-seat gain). And they would not only be serving with a Democratic president, but with an obsessively driven Democratic president fixated on legislative results as the most significant measure of his own success.

In the aftermath of the 1958 election, Democrats learned that sheer numbers of votes, or potential votes, on the floor of the House were not sufficient to enact a liberal or even a Democratic mainstream legislative program. Seven times since 1932 the Democrats have sent more than 280 (out of 435) members to the House of Representatives (see table 2.9.). The Republicans have never done this well; their high water mark was 245 members elected to Harry Truman's punching bag 80th Congress (1946). There are at least two other factors, organizational factors, which we can now see are necessary to produce legislative results. The system of committees and subcommittees must be favorably aligned and the president must not only be favorably disposed, but active in the legislative process.

Something like this liberal alignment finally did occur after the 1964 election. In part this was the product of virtually unpublicized committee packing in the previous few years, and in part it was due to the 1964 electoral results. Republicans, disappointed at these results, replaced Charles Halleck as their leader with Gerald Ford,[64] and new party ratios on committees were negotiated, reflecting the size of the Democratic landslide. At the opening of Congress, the Democratic Study Group (DSG) took the lead in proposing rules changes in the Democratic caucus and in pressing the claim of party loyalty on its members. The DSG initiated discipline of two southern members of the caucus who had supported Barry Goldwater for president, a distinct departure from Rayburn's and from Demo-

TABLE 2.9. Democratic Landslides in House Elections, 1932–80 (over 280 seats to winning party)

| Election year (Congress) | Democratic edge in seats after election | President | Net gain in Democratic seats | Domestic policy outcome |
|---|---|---|---|---|
| 1932 (73rd) | 313–117 | Roosevelt (D) | 97 | 100 Days |
| 1934 (74th) | 322–103 | | 9 | New Deal |
| 1936 (75th) | 333–89 | | 11 | Court packing stalemate |
| 1958 (86th) | 283–154 | Eisenhower (R) | 49 | Landrum–Griffin stalemate |
| 1964 (89th) | 295–140 | Johnson (D) | 37 | Great Society |
| 1974 (94th) | 291–144 | Ford (R) | 48 | Procedural reforms |
| 1976 (95th) | 292–143 | Carter (D) | 1 | |

Source: Harold Stanley and Richard Niemi, *Vital Statistics on American Politics, 1999– 2000* (Washington, D.C.: CQ Press Inc., 2000), pp. 36–37.

cratic Party practice.[65] John Bell Williams of Mississippi was deprived of his position as second-ranked member on the Commerce Committee and fifth-ranked Democrat on the District of Columbia Committee; Albert Watson of South Carolina, a member only since 1963, had less seniority to lose on the Post Office and Civil Service Committee, but both were, by a 157–115 vote of the caucus, sent to the bottom of the seniority lists of their respective committees. This sanction was less severe than the original DSG proposal to deprive these members of their membership in the caucus, which would have required them to seek committee assignments from the Republican Party.[66] Ten days later Watson declared himself a Republican anyway. He resigned his seat and ran as a Republican to succeed himself and was elected in the South Carolina special election that followed. He served until January 3, 1971. In 1970 he ran unsuccessfully for governor of South Carolina.

In addition, the caucus voted 189–71 to move to revise House rules.[67] The DSG proposed two of these changes with Speaker McCormack's approval, both aimed at the Rules Committee bottleneck. The first restored a version of the 21-day rule that had existed in the 81st Congress. This permitted the Speaker to recognize a member of a House committee for the purpose of bringing from that committee to the floor a measure that had been before the Rules Committee for 21 days without action moving it to the floor. The second allowed the Speaker to recognize a member offering a motion to send a bill to conference by majority vote, not, as before, by unanimous consent, or through the Rules Committee, or through suspension of the rules (two-thirds vote). As a result, no major administration bill was hung up in the Rules Committee in 1965.

The conservative coalition fought the rules changes on the floor, but lost 224–201 on a roll-call vote. On the key vote, to move the previous question, 123 Republicans, 75 southern Democrats, and 3 northern Democrats voted no, against 185 northern Democrats, 23 southern Democrats, and 16 Republicans.[68]

The legislative productivity of the 89th Congress was extraordinary. This was the Congress that in its first session (1965) enacted landmark Medicare, aid to education, and voting rights laws, and numerous other major measures dealing with such matters as air pollution and water pollution, regional development, poverty, housing, immigration, and so on. *CQ* commented: "The scope of the legislation was even more impressive than the number of new laws. Measures which, taken alone, would have crowned the achievements of any Congress, were enacted in a seemingly endless stream."[69]

The only slightly less impressive second session (1966), even in the face of an increased American commitment to the Vietnam War, "included strong auto and highway safety bills, a substantially higher minimum wage, new educational incentives, continuation of the war on poverty, a 'demonstration cities' plan to counter urban blight, bail reform, civil commitment for narcotic addicts and far-reaching anti-pollution measures."[70] In the spring of 1966, the Rules Committee's chairman, Judge Smith, lost his primary election. Redistricting had finally caught up with the 83-year-old leader of the southern conservatives. In the next Congress he was succeeded as Rules Committee chairman by his ally, William Colmer of Mississippi, next in seniority. Two liberals were appointed to the committee in 1967, Spark M. Matsunaga (D-Hawaii) and William R. Anderson (D-Tenn.).[71]

## The Democratic Study Group Uses the Caucus: 1967–72

The conservative coalition nevertheless had a successful year in 1967, aided by rising concerns over the Vietnam War and its costs, and the votes of 47 new Republicans who won House seats in the mid-term election of 1966. *Congressional Quarterly* (*CQ*) listed 54 roll-call votes on which the coalition appeared (out of 245 roll-call votes in 1967) with 38 victories.[72] John Manley's figures, calculated slightly differently, more or less agree (see table 1.2: in sheer numbers, the incidence of conservative coalition wins (39) reached an all-time high, even in the face of Republican leader Gerald Ford's denials that the alliance existed.[73]

Of the dozen votes listed by *CQ* as especially important, the coalition appeared on 10. They prevailed, in the House, on across-the-board budget cuts and temporarily on funding to aid localities in rent control and removed about half the authorization for the Office of Economic Opportunity.[74] The Democratic leadership plan to censure and fine Democratic Representative Adam Clayton Powell of New York for financial misbehavior was overturned by the House and instead Powell was excluded from the House in an action later deemed unconstitutional by the Supreme Court.[75] Norman Ornstein, a leading observer, says: "The period of 1967–1970 was one of maximum frustration, both substantive and procedural, for the Democratic liberals: Much was tried and little was accomplished."[76]

The Democratic House majority continued strong in the 1968 election, and throughout Richard Nixon's presidency, but from 1969 to 1976 presidential initiatives passed to the hands of Republicans. At the beginning of the 91st Congress (January 1969), Morris Udall, a popular liberal member from Arizona, challenged John McCormack as Democratic leader but lost overwhelmingly 178–58 in a secret ballot in the caucus.[77] McCormack's strategic leadership of the caucus had been shaky—illustrated in the fight over the composition of the Ways and Means Committee in 1963, in 1965 when the Democratic Study Group, not the Speaker, took the lead in the caucus to attack the Rules Committee bottleneck and also in the management of the Powell case.[78]

The caucus also penalized Representative John Rarick of Louisiana for supporting George Wallace for president in 1968 by depriving him of his seniority on the Agriculture Committee. This had little immediate effect on public policy—Rarick was very junior on the committee—but, consistent with the action against John Bell Williams and Albert Watson in 1965, it signaled that the caucus was beginning to move toward the development of precedents enforcing behavioral criteria for membership beyond the vote for Speaker, Rayburn's traditional benchmark.

By the end of 1972 the Democratic Party had been in the majority in the House for 18 consecutive years and with two brief interruptions for the 40 years since 1932. The episodic appearance of huge Democratic majorities had enabled the enactment of the first New Deal and Lyndon Johnson's Great Society legislation. However, the normal patterns of legislative output were not otherwise especially encouraging to mainstream Democrats. Some of them, notably members of the Democratic Study Group, liberals, and relatively new members of Congress, consequently became interested in "reform."[79] Complaints centered on the seniority system that tended to bring members to positions of organizational responsibility—committee chairmanships—regardless of their views on the substance of policy. Not all committee chairmen were antagonistic toward mainstream Democratic sentiment on the subject matter their committees dealt with, but some were, and over the most recent arc of time these had been disproportionately southern members.[80]

In his 1965 book, Richard Bolling had diagnosed the problem as the inability of the majority party—the Democrats—to mobilize effectively:

[T]he Democratic party has held a majority in the House in fifteen of the seventeen Congresses elected since 1930. In sixteen of the seventeen, the majority of Democrats in the House maintained liberal to moderate voting records on domestic and social welfare legislation. But the seniority system and the method of appointing standing committees, combined with the skill of conservatives and the ineptness of the liberals, have blunted this advantage.

In the Eighty-sixth Congress, for example, the Appropriations Committee was composed of fifty Members—thirty Democrats and twenty Republicans. But in terms of viewpoints of the Members there were thirty-two conservatives and eighteen liberal or moderate Members. This was the line-up on the purse-strings committee, during the most liberal House since 1938. Actually, the outlook of the committee, because of the custom of seniority, had been fixed years earlier. It is said that measures reported from conservative committees can be modified on the House floor to suit the majority views in the House. However, there is a strong habit of supporting committee recommendations that grows out of inertia, respect for the specialist, and fear of reprisal.

In 1964, an example was the deadlock on the King-Anderson hospital-benefits bill held in bondage by the Ways and Means Committee. It would provide hospital and nursing-home benefits for millions of Americans sixty-five years of age or more, to be financed by a slight increase in the social security tax. This is a perfectly sound, conservative method of financing. It is, in effect, a user's tax, as pointed out by Representative Hastings Keith of Massachusetts, an insurance man whose credentials as a traditional Republican conservative are unchallengeable.

A majority of Democrats in the House supported the measure when it was sent to Congress by President Kennedy in the 1961–1962, Eighty-seventh Congress. However, the bill never came to a vote because a majority of the Ways and Means Committee opposed it. The committee consists of fifteen Democrats and ten Republicans. On the basis of party label, this would seem to assure the bill a fair hearing and a pathway to the House floor. However, the seniority system with its conservative bias long ago assured that conservative Democrats outnumbered liberal Democrats, regardless of the liberal majority among the House Democrats. The ten Republicans, conservatives, needed only three of the fifteen Democrats to fashion a committee majority to keep the bill bottled up. The committee chairman, himself a southern Democrat, provided one of the three. The others were also easily rounded up. Again, the majority voice of the majority party was made ineffective.[81]

"The failure of the House," he concluded, "is the failure of the Democratic party. . . . Its responsibility cannot be evaded much longer without reducing the national assembly to impotence, which would mean a vital failure in the democratic process itself."[82]

Bolling's was an influential voice. Elected in 1948 from Harry Truman's congressional district in Missouri, by 1955 he had been placed on the Rules Committee where he was Sam Rayburn's principal watchdog and agent. With Frank Thompson of New Jersey and Bob Jones of Alabama, Bolling ran the Rayburn campaign to pack the Rules Committee in 1961 and he was widely understood to be a major Democratic leadership strategist in the House from the mid-1950s through the Kennedy years.[83] Although he was identified on the jacket of his book as a "principal mover" of the Democratic Study Group, the truth was more complicated. While he sympathized with many of the DSG's goals, he was not an early member and took pains to avoid collaborating with them openly, presumably in order to preserve his relationship with Speaker Rayburn. Clem Miller said in a 1960 interview: "He came to Democratic Study Group meetings but always identified himself as an observer, not as a participant. He came in a sense to lecture us like small children rather than lead us in our councils. There was a good deal of hostility toward him in the Study Group as a result of that."[84] Stewart Udall served in Congress from 1955 to 1961 and was a Bolling admirer. He said in an interview, "Some of my friends regard Dick as kind of a traitor to the cause, because he was part of Rayburn's apparatus. He would talk a great game but you could never get him to *do* anything. But he was a very wise and perceptive person [emphasis in original]."[85] Thus, so far as his colleagues in the party were concerned, Bolling was, in the words of his friend Jim O'Hara of Michigan, "aloof from the uprisings of the peasants."[86] This posture cost him support when he ran in 1961 for the majority leadership in the wake of Rayburn's death and John McCormack's ascent to the Speakership, and 15 years later when he ran for majority leader.[87]

In 1969, O'Hara and Don Fraser of Minnesota, who at the time led the Democratic Study Group, persuaded the Democratic leadership to enact a rule convening the largely moribund caucus on a monthly basis, primarily for discussion only. Norman Ornstein reports:

> In the first two and a half years of this practice (through June 1971) 27 nonorganizational caucuses were held: of these 19 were adjourned for lack of a quorum. But the other eight caucuses did meet and the most common topic on the agenda was House reform.[88]
>
> The caucus of April 1969 included the first attack on John McMillan [of South Carolina], chairman of the District of Columbia Committee. . . . The caucus of March 1970 set up the Hansen Committee [on Organization, Study, and Review of Seniority], and in the caucus of December 1970 the Hansen Committee reported back.[89]

Dick Conlon, the DSG's energetic staff director, called the Hansen Committee "an inoffensive way to maneuver for change in the seniority system."[90]

In the early 1970s, serious proposals for reform, and reforms themselves, began to arrive by the truckload on the agenda of the House. The Legislative Reorganization of 1970 made numerous amendments to the House Rules, including the adoption of electronic voting on the floor and the recording of teller votes.[91] Ornstein explains:

> The recorded teller reform made public previously unrecorded votes on amendments taken in the Committee of the Whole. . . . [T]urnout on these votes . . . jumped phenomenally, and some significant outcomes . . . changed as well. Recording these votes . . . also made it more difficult for committee chairmen to control events on the floor; their private bargaining must now be weighed by congressmen against perceived public pressure. One member noted simply, "It's more difficult for me to go along now."
>
> Electronic voting has shortened the time of roll call votes from 45 to 15 minutes. This has also had "spillover" effects. The normal practice of cue-taking has been changed somewhat. Examining other members' votes for clues on the "right" way to vote is easier with the large electronic screen and instant reporting featured in the new system; but asking other members for their advice is more difficult because of the time element. This also potentially hurts committee chairmen and senior members, whose expertise made them the prominent sources of information. Thus, these two reforms together, unintentionally perhaps, have diminished the powers of committee chairmen.[92]

Even more significant were the reforms developed in the Democratic caucus and instigated by the Democratic Study Group and the Hansen

Committee, a committee of the caucus. In 1971 and 1972 the caucus established a Steering and Policy Committee and expanded the Ways and Means-dominated Committee on Committees by adding the Speaker, the majority leader, and the chairman of the caucus. Subcommittee chairmanships were limited to one to a member, immediately expanding the number of members who could exert special influence on legislation, and each subcommittee chairman was given the right, subject to the approval of the full committee caucus, to hire one staff member. This marks the first appearance of the committee caucus—all Democrats on a standing committee—as a meaningful entity in House business.[93]

The rules of the caucus were changed so that, rather than voting on the entire slate of committee assignments in one motion, the Committee on Committees was required to make its recommendations to the organizational caucus meeting one committee at a time. Upon the demand of 10 or more members, nominations could be debated and voted on. Subcommittees got a bill of rights, fixing jurisdictions, providing for budgets and staffing, giving the committee caucus the right to vote on subcommittee chairmen and giving each member the right to choose at least one subcommittee. In the 93rd Congress the individual vote on committee chairmen became automatic. In the 94th Congress the nominations of subcommittee chairmen of the Appropriations Committee were also brought before the caucus, and the Speaker was given the power unilaterally to appoint members of the Rules Committee.

These changes pared away at the prerogatives and power of committee chairmen, who before these changes could rearrange subcommittees, hire and fire staff, and manage the committee's business pretty much as they pleased. As Jeffrey Biggs says:

> From the 1920s into the 1970s . . . the chairmen controlled the committee's agenda, organization, budget, and staff. The chair determined the committee's subcommittee structure and appointed its subcommittee chairs. Because committee chairmanships were attained purely on the basis of seniority, they were independent positions of influence. Neither the party leaders nor the members had any practical means of removing a chairman. Consequently, in the exercise of their powers, chairs were not constrained by a need to be responsive to any internal party constituency in order to retain their positions.[94]

In light of this long-standing concentration of powers in the hands of committee chairmen, the caucus reforms carried an enormous potential. As Norman Ornstein said, "Each chairman is now theoretically regularly accountable to the full Democratic caucus."[95] Ornstein points to the influx of 38 new Democratic members in the election of 1970 and 30 new members in the election of 1972 as on balance helpful to the cause of reform.[96] After the Watergate election of 1974, when 75 new Democrats were elected, 123 Democrats out of 291 in the House had served six years or less.

## Fallout from Watergate: The Caucus Puts Seniority under Siege

This giant freshman class of Democrats in the 94th Congress, 75 strong, constituted themselves in a novel way after the 1974 election. They organized into a separate entity, the "Class of the 94th." Michael Malbin says: "Rep. Tim Wirth of Colorado raised the money to pay for a staff of two and some office space, and the group immediately began to inform new members of issues likely to come up in the caucus."[97]

They elected as their temporary chairman Richard Ottinger of New York, "whose previous service" (1965–71), said Malbin, "was useful during the procedurally confusing early caucuses."

> The freshmen met frequently during caucus recesses and, while they did not take any votes, it generally appeared, Ottinger said, that the new members overwhelmingly supported . . . DSG proposals.
>
> Asked to compare the new group with his first freshman class, the large group elected in 1964, Ottinger said, "we had substantial numbers [in 1964] but we were not prepared and DSG was not prepared. Because everything has to happen on the first day [in an organizing caucus] if you are not prepared nothing happens.[98]

Rather than passively accepting, as heretofore, the decisions of the party Committee on Committees, they availed themselves of options created by changes in caucus rules providing for a secret ballot on individual committee chairmen. Norman Y. Mineta, (D-Calif.) a member of the Class of the 94th, reported:

> We collectively invited all Committee Chairmen and women to appear before us, so we could directly question their policies and records. We felt that this would enable us to cast better-informed votes, for or against the Chairmen or women, in the caucus.
>
> Our unprecedented action was greeted with much disdain by the

Committee Leaders. We began to receive notes from each of them explaining how their schedules were too busy and there was no way they could manage to fit in a meeting with us. We new Members met to determine our next course of action. It was agreed that we would vote as a block against any Committee Chairman or woman who refused to meet with us. Word got out to that effect. Suddenly, these same Chairmen and women began sending notes asking when it would be convenient to get together with us.[99]

Not all chairmen concealed their annoyance at this turn of events, and they did not interview well. Party loyalty was an issue, though not the only issue. Three chairmen were deposed and others threatened, a bloodletting quite without precedent in the memories of members.[100]

There was an accidental element about the purge. Political scientist Barbara Hinckley wrote that the tacit criteria making the purged chairmen vulnerable were advanced age, "southernness," and the presence of an acceptable challenger.[101] To journalists Rowland Evans and Robert Novak, the issues were less clear-cut: "a mishmash cross between college fraternity politics and a byzantine Kremlin struggle, lacking any serious yardstick" they opined.[102] The oldest committee chairman was the 83-year-old Ray Madden of Indiana, of the Rules Committee, conspicuously hard of hearing, but a mainstream liberal. Fellow liberals admitted, "His leadership is uneven."[103] The chairman most faithful to the conservative coalition in the last Congress was the dignified George Mahon of Texas, of the Appropriations Committee, age 75.[104] Both were left undisturbed. All three of the victims were elderly and southern, and undoubtedly all three interviewed poorly, but for all three there were also special circumstances. Edward Hebert of Louisiana, age 74, headed a committee—Armed Services—that dealt cooperatively with the executive branch. In the Vietnam era this was not, from the liberal perspective, an unalloyed virtue.[105] He also annoyed liberals on other grounds. Common Cause, a progressive lobbying group, issued a "Report on House Committee Chairmen" on January 13, 1975, timed to influence the caucus. In the Report Hebert received conspicuously low marks. "He violates the rules [the Report said], he treats members unfairly, and he abuses his powers as Chairman. He has denied subcommittee chairmen the right to hire their own staff, he harasses and discriminates against members who disagree with him, he creates 'special' subcommittees to evade caucus rules regarding subcommittee membership."[106] Hebert was replaced by the more agreeable Melvin Price of downstate Illinois, age 70, second in line. No doubt Hebert suffered most from the patronizing way he addressed the freshmen class. John Jacobs reports:

When . . . Hebert showed up, [a new member,] Gladys Spellman of Maryland, was prepared. The previous summer, Carl Albert had appointed Pat Schroeder his representative to a NATO meeting in Europe, the first woman to be so honored. Hebert tried to block her appointment, refusing to even sign her voucher to travel. "Mr. Chairman," Spellman said, "I'd like to ask you about your attempt to prevent Representative Schroeder from being the Speaker's representative to the NATO meeting."

At that point, [Rep.] Mineta said, "you could see the red flames" emerging. Hebert clearly didn't yet feel any heat but his own. With a condescending air, he stood up, leaned over and said, "Okay, boys and girls. Let me tell you what it's like around here." With that comment, Hebert was history.[107]

Bob Poage of Texas, age 76, an ebullient and mercurial man, though himself quite conservative was in fact not unpopular with the liberal members of the Agriculture Committee and was regarded as a fair-minded chairman. Norman Ornstein and David Rohde interviewed one liberal member, who said, "I supported Poage—he had always been very fair to me and a very fair chairman overall. He knew he wasn't stabbed in the back by liberals on the committee. I think all of us except the new members supported him."[108]

Democratic Study Group activist Tom Foley of Spokane, Washington, ranking member of the committee, and Poage's successor as chairman, spoke in favor of Poage to the freshmen caucus, and committee member Bob Bergland of Minnesota, later Jimmy Carter's Secretary of Agriculture, lobbied on Poage's behalf. Foley's evaluation was:

> Mr. Poage had been singled out by a number of activists on the nutrition and food stamp issues as being insensitive and hostile. While it's true he was a critic of nutrition programs, I always thought he was fair in permitting them to be debated and voted on by the committee. While Chairman Poage's manner was somewhat autocratic, he listened to opposing views and allowed amendments to be offered. I didn't think he was guilty of the kind of abuse that I'd seen in other committees.[109]

Common Cause, however, complained, "He has violated the letter and spirit of the caucus and committee rules by budgeting only a skeletal committee staff . . . cutting short debate and ruling motions out of order."[110]

In this era, Agriculture was primarily a committee that focused on aid to farmers and was dominated by its commodity subcommittees. As Unekis and Rieselbach say: "[It] has traditionally operated as a re-election (pork-barrel, constituency-oriented) panel. Its members, drawn disproportionately from farm districts, promote the crops that their constituents grow."[111] Only a token number of urban congressmen served on the committee in the 1970s; hence Poage's natural ties to the liberal freshmen were weak. Poage's colleagues on the committee immediately elected him vice chairman when the committee met in January. Poage also received the major subcommittee chairmanship he asked for, on Livestock and Grains.[112]

The third overthrown chairman was Wright Patman of Texas, age 82, for 12 years chairman of the Banking and Currency Committee and for 46 years a member of the House. Patman was a prairie populist devoted to soft money and the bashing of Wall Street. In the business before his committee, in other words, Patman was a liberal, though a maverick.[113] No doubt his grasp of the issues before his committee must have seemed out of date and doctrinaire. Speaker Carl Albert comments: "For twenty-three terms, Wright Patman had been a fighting Congressman, fighting for farmers and poor people and black people. His only sin was his age."[114] He was replaced by Henry Reuss of Wisconsin, the fourth ranking Democrat, quite a long reach by House standards. Reuss, scion of a Milwaukee banking family, was a liberal activist, more modern but scarcely more liberal than Patman.[115]

Arguably, then, of the three, only Hebert matched the stereotype of the chairman as ogre. Neither he nor Poage were especially out of step with liberals on most of the issues centrally occupying their committees, though Poage was clearly on the wrong side on nutrition issues, and bearing in mind that the Armed Services Committee was not, on the whole, the forum through which Democratic dissatisfactions with the Vietnam War would be expressed.

One genuine ogre, Wayne Hays of Ohio, was rejected by the Steering and Policy Committee as chairman of the House Administration Committee and replaced by DSG stalwart Frank Thompson of New Jersey.[116] Hays fought back in the caucus, capitalizing on his chairmanship of the Democratic Congressional Campaign Committee and an alliance with the ambitious liberal chairman of the caucus, Phillip Burton of California, and was restored by a vote of the caucus to his chairmanship.[117]

In addition, the Ways and Means Committee was deeply affected by caucus action. In a DSG-instigated move, it was deprived of its role as the Democratic Committee on Committees, a task that was assigned to the two-year-old Democratic Steering and Policy Committee. The Ways and Means Committee was expanded from 25 to 37 members; 13 incumbent Democratic members and 12 new appointees, for whom, said caucus chairman Phil Burton, the "litmus test" "will be to get a balanced membership on the committee to produce a decent and comprehensive health bill and tax reform."[118]

Under the capable and conservative leadership of the redoubtable Wilbur Mills of Arkansas, chairman since 1957, the Ways and Means Committee had never formed into subcommittees; hence pockets of expertise among members beyond Mills's purview never developed.[119] Carl Albert writes: "Every title, every section, every paragraph, and every line of every bill on every subject was worked out by . . . the entire committee, with Wilbur Mills presiding."[120] Changes in the House rules—aimed in part at Mills—requiring all committees to form subcommittees further diluted the power of the committee chairmen.

Mills himself suffered a series of personal misadventures that by 1974 required him to resign his chairmanship. He ran a tentative and unsuccessful campaign for the presidency in 1972 in the aftermath of which there were charges that he had received illegal campaign contributions.[121] His health faltered "in 1973 and early 1974 when back problems and surgery kept him away from the committee for long periods of time."[122] But there was worse to come. What looked like a belated mid-life crisis (he was 65-years-old) and was explained as the effects of pills and alcohol caused Mills to engage in two widely publicized episodes of unseemly behavior in late 1974 that shocked and embarrassed his colleagues.

> On October 7, 1974, the U.S. Park Police stopped Mills's 1973 Lincoln Continental, which was driving at "unreasonable speed with its lights off" near the Tidal Basin at 2 a.m. Mills, bleeding from the face and intoxicated, emerged from the vehicle. One of his fellow passengers, Annabel Battistella, a thirty-eight-year-old stripper, who performed locally as "Fannie Fox, the Argentine Firecracker," jumped out of the car and into the Tidal Basin. Battistella was taken to St. Elizabeths Hospital with two black eyes after a scuffle in which Mills tried to prevent her from leaving the car. A television cameraman arrived at the scene after hearing police reports, and captured the arrest on camera. Battistella later admitted that she was having an affair with Mills, who frequented the nightclub (the Silver Slipper) where she performed. After her romance with Mills began in the summer of 1973, Battistella stopped dancing and became his companion at the Silver Slipper. Battistella, who had immigrated to the United States from Argentina in 1965, lived next door to the Mills's in Arlington, Virginia.[123]

The bad publicity damaged Mills in Little Rock, where he won reelection with only 58 percent of the vote.[124] In late November came the last straw, as Albert Hunt reports:

Mr. Mills was televised on stage in Boston with his striptease friend and held an impromptu press conference in which he promised to get her into the movies. . . . The only committee Democrat willing to comment on Mr. Mills's declining fortunes was Rep. Charles Vanik of Ohio, who conceded he is giving "very serious thought" to voting against Mr. Mills as chairman. Given the present mood of the House, "they might take away everything from Ways and Means unless we do something," Rep. Vanik added.

Privately, other members were equally critical, some even suggesting the chairman is a "sick man." Mr. Mills attended the caucus meeting yesterday but reportedly hardly participated at all. Some committee members believe that his weekend publicity was a crucial factor in the 146-to-122 vote to take away the panel's committee-assignment responsibility.[125]

Although Mills's exit from congressional power differed from his colleagues on Agriculture, Banking and Currency, and Armed Services, the impact was the same or perhaps even more startling, since it coincided with a sharp reduction in the powers of the committee chairmen and of the committee. The Democratic Steering and Policy Committee—the new Committee on Committees—was more liberal in its makeup than the group of Democrats on the Ways and Means Committee, the old Democratic Committee on Committees. (see Tables 2.10 and 2.11)

In addition, as Mary Russell reported in the *Washington Post*:

On Appropriations, liberals who had been confined to one or two subcommittees became a major force on a number of subcommittees because of a new caucus rule that prevents senior Democrats from installing themselves on all the most important ones.

The Commerce Committee adopted rules which significantly democratized its operations—limiting the chairman's power to control budgets, setting ratios on subcommittees, and becoming the first committee to decide to elect its subcommittee chairmen by secret ballot among committee Democrats.

Russell continues, "The Rules changes were pushed by senior liberals . . . but the addition of 11 freshmen to the committee provided the balance of power to push them through."[126]

As a result of the changes in committee rules, two subcommittee chairs were unseated, including full committee chairman of the Commerce Committee Harley Staggers of West Virginia from the committee's Special Subcommittee on Investigations. Thirteen new members of the Banking and

TABLE 2.10. Democratic Committees on Committees, Party Unity Scores

| Steering and Policy Committee (94th) | | Ways and Means Committee (93rd) | |
|---|---|---|---|
| Member | Party unity score | Member | Party unity score |
| *Elected by the caucus* | | Wilbur Mills (AR) | 26 |
| Speaker Carl Albert (OK) | — | Al Ullman (OR) | 66 |
| Majority leader Thomas P. O'Neill, Jr. | | James A. Burke (MA) | 88 |
| (MA) | 83 | Martha W. Griffiths (MI) | 56 |
| Caucus chairman Phillip Burton (CA) | 80 | Dan Rostenkowski (IL) | 70 |
| | | Phil A. Landrum (GA) | 32 |
| *Elected by members from their region* | | Charles A. Vanik (OH) | 87 |
| John E. Moss (CA) | 79 | Richard Fulton (TN) | 71 |
| Morris K. Udall (AZ) | 80 | Omar Burleson (TX) | 26 |
| Henry S. Reuss (WI) | 86 | James C. Corman (CA) | 82 |
| Melvin Price (IL) | 91 | Willam J. Green (PA) | 88 |
| Richard Bolling (MO) | 67 | Sam Gibbons (FL) | 70 |
| Wright Patman (TX) | 51 | Hugh L. Carey (NY) | 47 |
| Tom Bevill (AL) | 47 | Joe D. Waggonner, Jr. (LA) | 26 |
| Robert G. Stephens (GA) | 45 | Joseph E. Karth (MN) | 84 |
| Frank Thompson (NJ) | 78 | | |
| John H. Dent (PA) | 72 | | |
| Jonathan B. Bingham (NY) | 86 | | |
| Robert N. Giaimo (CT) | 74 | | |
| *Appointed by the Speaker* | | | |
| John J. McFall (CA), majority whip | 80 | | |
| John Brademas (IN), chief deputy whip | 93 | | |
| Jim Wright (TX), deputy whip | 67 | | |
| Richard Fulton (TN), deputy whip | 71 | | |
| Spark M. Matsunaga (HI), deputy whip | 90 | | |
| Mendel Davis (SC), second and third term members | 51 | | |
| Ralph H. Metcalf (IL), black caucus | 80 | | |
| Barbara Jordan (TX), women members | 88 | | |
| William M. Brodhead (MI), first term members | — | | |

Note: Party unity scores are from the 93rd Congress. Party unity scores are the percentage of recorded votes in 1973–74 on which the representative voted "yea" or "nay" with a majority of his or her party.

Source: *Congressional Quarterly Almanac*, 1974, pp. 1004–5.

TABLE 2.11 Democratic Committees on Committees, Party Unity Scores, 93rd and 94th Congresses

| Steering and Policy | Party unity | Ways and Means |
|---|---|---|
| Brademas (IN) X | 95 | |
| Price (IL) X | | |
| Matsunaga (HI) X | 90 | |
| Jordan (TX) X | | XX Burke (MA), Green (PA) |
| | | X Vanik (OH) |
| Reuss (WI), Bingham (NY) XX | | |
| | 85 | |
| | | X Karth (MN) |
| O'Neill (MA) X | | |
| | | X Corman (CA) |
| Metcalf (IL), McFall (CA), Udall (AZ), | | |
| Burton (CA) XXXX | 80 | |
| Moss (CA) X | | |
| Thompson (NJ) X | | |
| | 75 | |
| Giaimo (CT) X | | |
| Dent (PA) X | | |
| Fulton (TN) X | | X Fulton (TN) |
| | 70 | XX Rostenkowski (IL), Gibbons (FL) |
| Bolling (MO) X | | |
| Wright (TX) X | | |
| | | X Ullman (OR) |
| | 65 | |
| | 60 | |
| | | X Griffiths (MI) |
| | 55 | |
| Davis (SC), Patman (TX) XX | | |
| | 50 | |
| | | X Carey (NY) |
| Bevill (AL) X | | |
| Stephens (GA) X | 45 | |

TABLE 2.11 *(continued)*

| | 35 | |
|---|---|---|
| | | X Landrum (GA) |
| | 30 | |
| | | XXX Mills (AR), Waggonner (LA), |
| | 25 | Burleson (TX) |

Source: See table 2.10.

Currency Committee tipped the balance against Leonor Sullivan of Missouri on the Consumer Affairs subcommittee. Neither of these reflected a clear ideological struggle. Sullivan was, however, pro-Patman in his losing fight to retain his chairmanship.[127]

## A Remodeled House

By the end of the decade of the 1970s, the power structure of the House of Representatives had been very substantially remodeled. Since the first election of Franklin Roosevelt the House had been dominated by Democrats, and so most of the change took place in the Democratic Party. The Rules Committee, for nearly half a century predominantly a force independent of the majority leadership, had been transformed into an arm of the leadership. The leadership itself had been greatly reinvigorated: the powers of the Speaker grew, a Steering and Policy Committee with real functions was established, and the whip system was expanded. The authority of committee chairmen shrank as powers were devolved to subcommittees and their chairmen, and committee chairmanships were no longer automatically allocated or sustained by the seniority system. Incentives to specialize in the substance of legislation and oversight were spread more broadly among the members as more opportunities for influence at the subcommittee level were created. This led to the taking of more initiatives at the subcommittee level and to more legislative activity among a larger proportion of Democratic members.[128]

The proximate causes of all these changes were actions taken by the Democratic caucus. The caucus had been largely moribund since Woodrow

Wilson's presidency and completely quiescent during the 20 years of Sam Rayburn's highly effective but highly personal Speakership. Only after Rayburn passed from the scene did the caucus become usable as an instrument for the assertion of mainstream Democratic policy. This occurred not as the result of initiatives by the elected leadership of the caucus but rather was pressed on the leadership in increments by the Democratic Study Group, an increasingly effective organization of liberal and mainstream Democratic members. The main condition of their effectiveness was changes in the composition of the House Democratic caucus.

# 3

## CAUSES OF LIBERALIZATION

The first two chapters have offered a selective historical narrative covering key events within the House of Representatives from the New Deal to the mid-1970s. This narrative shows how the House was transformed from an environment hostile to the programs and proposals of the liberal presidents who dominated the era and their congressional allies to a far more cooperative arena as far as mainstream Democrats were concerned. Now we turn to a closer examination of the trends that made this transformation possible, with special attention to the interesting issue of why it took so long in coming.

### The House Democratic Caucus

In tracking these changes in the role of the House of Representatives in the policy-making system of the United States over the middle years of the twentieth century, we have noted the importance of initiatives taken in the House Democratic caucus. So it makes sense to seek an explanation for the timing of these initiatives at least in part by looking at changes in the composition of the caucus from the late 1930s to the 1970s.

Sam Rayburn basically closed the caucus down as an instrument of party leadership during his 20-year-long briefly interrupted Speakership lasting from 1940 to 1961. It will be recalled that the reason he gave to John Nance Garner was sectional rivalry—southern members versus the rest. In Rayburn's era the southern component of the caucus was for a short time (1947–48) a majority, but for most of the period it approximated 40 percent (see table 3.1, and figure 3.1).

The gentle decline by between a fourth and a third in the southern share of the Democratic caucus after Rayburn died, from 1960 to 1980, while substantial, is not really enough to account for the growing effectiveness of the caucus as an instrument of mainstream Democratic leadership over the same period. Not all southerners voted consistently in op-

TABLE 3.1. The South in the Democratic Caucus, 1940–98

| | Southern members | Non-southern members | Total | % southern |
|---|---|---|---|---|
| *Rayburn era* | | | | |
| 1940 | 100 | 162 | 262 | 38 |
| 1942 | 100 | 167 | 267 | 37 |
| 1944 | 102 | 120 | 222 | 46 |
| 1946 | 103 | 139 | 242 | 43 |
| 1948 | 103 | 85 | 188 | 55 |
| 1950 | 103 | 160 | 263 | 39 |
| 1952 | 103 | 128 | 235 | 44 |
| 1954 | 102 | 111 | 213 | 48 |
| 1956 | 100 | 130 | 230 | 43 |
| 1958 | 99 | 135 | 234 | 42 |
| 1960 | 102 | 180 | 282 | 36 |
| *Post-Rayburn* | | | | |
| 1962 | 99 | 164 | 263 | 38 |
| 1964 | 95 | 160 | 255 | 37 |
| 1966 | 90 | 205 | 295 | 31 |
| 1968 | 84 | 161 | 245 | 34 |
| 1970 | 80 | 163 | 243 | 33 |
| 1972 | 79 | 175 | 254 | 31 |
| 1974 | 74 | 168 | 242 | 30 |
| 1976 | 78 | 208 | 286 | 27 |
| 1978 | 81 | 211 | 292 | 28 |
| 1980 | 78 | 199 | 277 | 28 |
| 1982 | 70 | 172 | 242 | 29 |
| 1984 | 80 | 186 | 266 | 30 |
| 1986 | 73 | 180 | 253 | 29 |
| 1988 | 77 | 178 | 255 | 30 |
| 1990 | 75 | 183 | 258 | 29 |
| 1992 | 77 | 189 | 266 | 29 |
| 1994 | 77 | 179 | 256 | 30 |
| 1996 | 56 | 142 | 198 | 28 |
| 1998 | 54 | 152 | 206 | 26 |

Source: *Congressional Quarterly Almanacs* 1948–98 and *Historical Maps of Congressional Districts for 1940–88.*

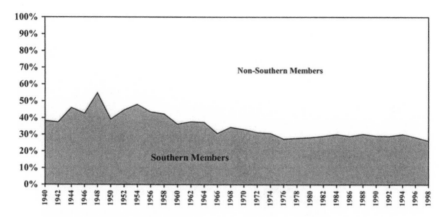

Figure 3.1: The Democratic Caucus, 1940–98

position to the rest of the Democrats in Congress. But those who did—Dixiecrats—declined more steeply over time, perhaps enough to change the character of the caucus (see table 3.2).[1]

As these numbers suggest, variation in the proportion of Dixiecrats occurred in part when non-southern constituencies elected more Democrats. Even more important is what happened in southern constituencies themselves where, starting in the late 1960s, many more Republicans, on the whole, were elected replacing Dixiecrats, but not, after the 1970s, replacing mainstream southern Democrats (see figure 3.2 and table 3.3). Republicans moved from fewer than 10 seats in 1958—and for many previous decades—to 30 seats in 1980 and 48 seats elected in 1994, a sevenfold gain in 30 years. Conservative Democrats—as measured by

TABLE 3.2. Dixiecrats in the Democratic Caucus, 1950–90

|  | 1950 | 1960 | 1970 | 1980 | 1990 |
|---|---|---|---|---|---|
| Caucus total | 259 | 282 | 245 | 277 | 258 |
| Non-South | 157 | 180 | 165 | 199 | 183 |
| South | 102 | 102 | 80 | 78 | 75 |
| Mainstream South | 55 | 40 | 15 | 34 | 63 |
| Dixiecrats | 45 | 62 | 65 | 44 | 12 |
| Non-South + Mainstream South | 212 | 220 | 180 | 233 | 246 |
| Dixiecrats % of caucus | 17 | 22 | 27 | 16 | 5 |

Source: *Congressional Quarterly Almanacs* 1950, 1960, 1970, 1980, 1990.

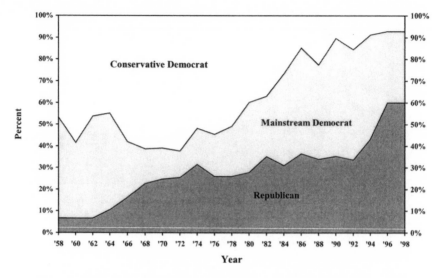

Figure 3.2: Distribution of Southern Seats. Note: A conservative Democrat has seat occupied by a member with a party support to party opposition ratio of less than 2:1. A mainstream Democrat has a party support to party opposition ratio of greater than 2:1. Party support and opposition scores come from the *Congressional Quarterly Almanacs* for the various years.

roll-call voting—were nearly wiped out, from 66 at peak strength to fewer than a score, while southern moderates gained from a low of 13 to the range of 40 to 60. Thus, a significant contribution to change in the Democratic caucus occurred through the subtraction of Dixiecrat members.

All through the postwar era, there was never for long any question of the South outnumbering the rest of the Democratic caucus overall. As mentioned, southern members outnumbered non-southerners only briefly, in the 80th Congress (1947–48). Otherwise even among Democrats the South was always in a minority. This sustains the view that Rayburn could have packed the Rules Committee in 1961 by using the caucus. Only two years later, after all, it was in the Democratic caucus where the South lost its attempt to put Phil Landrum on Ways and Means. Dixiecrat members continued in succeeding years to diminish from a large and influential fraction of the whole to a considerably smaller minority. This made much more feasible the employment of the caucus as a forum for the expression of mainstream policy.

TABLE 3.3. Partisan Distribution of Southern Seats, 1960–94

| Election in | All Southern Number | Republican Number | (%) | Mainstream Democrat Number | (%) | Dixiecrat Number | (%) |
|---|---|---|---|---|---|---|---|
| 1958[a] | 106 | 7 | (6.6) | 49[b] | (46.2) | 49 | (46.2) |
| 1960 | 106 | 7 | (6.6) | 37 | (34.9) | 62 | (58.5) |
| 1962 | 106 | 7 | (6.6) | 50 | (47.5) | 49 | (46.2) |
| 1964[a] | 106 | 11 | (10.4) | 47 | (44.3) | 47 | (44.3) |
| 1966[a] | 106 | 17 | (16.0) | 27 | (25.5) | 61 | (57.5) |
| 1968 | 106 | 24 | (22.6) | 17 | (16.0) | 65 | (61.3) |
| 1970[a] | 106 | 26 | (24.5) | 15 | (14.2) | 64 | (60.4) |
| 1972 | 106 | 27 | (25.5) | 13 | (12.3) | 66 | (62.3) |
| 1974 | 108 | 34 | (31.5) | 18 | (16.7) | 56 | (51.9) |
| 1976 | 108 | 28 | (25.9) | 21 | (19.4) | 59 | (54.6) |
| 1978 | 108 | 28 | (25.9) | 25 | (23.1) | 55 | (50.9) |
| 1980 | 108 | 30 | (27.8) | 35 | (32.4) | 43 | (39.8) |
| 1982 | 108 | 38 | (35.2) | 30 | (27.8) | 40 | (37.0) |
| 1984 | 116 | 36 | (31.0) | 49 | (42.2) | 31 | (26.7) |
| 1986[a] | 116 | 42 | (36.2) | 56 | (48.3) | 17 | (14.7) |
| 1988[a] | 116 | 39 | (33.6) | 50[c] | (42.2) | 26 | (22.4) |
| 1990 | 116 | 41 | (35.3) | 63 | (54.3) | 12 | (10.3) |
| 1992 | 116 | 39 | (33.6) | 59 | (50.9) | 18 | (15.5) |
| 1994 | 125 | 48 | (38.4) | 59 | (47.2) | 18 | (14.4) |
| 1996 | 125 | 75 | (60.0) | 41 | (32.8) | 9 | (7.2) |

[a]One vacancy in the year
[b]Includes Speaker Rayburn
[c]Includes Speaker Wright

Note: Entries in "Number" rows represent the number of seats held by the type of member. A mainstream Democrat has a party support to party opposition ratio greater than or equal to 2:1. A Dixiecrat has a party support to opposition ratio less than 2:1.

Source: *Congressional Quarterly Almanac*, various years, party unity–opposition scores.

It took time and trial and error for Democrats to rediscover the caucus as an instrument of mainstream policy-making and policy enforcement. Rayburn's successors in the leadership, Speakers John McCormack and Carl Albert, were hesitant and took few initiatives of their own, but did respond to initiatives by the Democratic Study Group.[2] The habits and practices of many years changed slowly. But, as we have seen, they did change.

Why did it take so long? It is frequently said that the House of Representatives, as a popular body, elected every two years, must in consequence respond to sentiments and opinions that exist at the grass roots, out in the country. Arguments of this sort are generally made in order to explain the results of national elections, as the fortunes of Democratic and Republican candidates for seats in Congress ebb and flow from election year to election year. Perhaps the same sort of argument can be pressed into service to explain a longer term trend resulting in something more institutionally enduring than momentary fluctuations in a partisan majority. Substantively, the argument would be that the invigoration of the House Democratic caucus had to await the decline in the numbers of its Dixiecrat members, and the decline of the Dixiecrats was caused by the rise of the Republican Party in the South.

## The Rise of the Two-Party South

Like most large social events, the causes of the liberalization of the U.S. House of Representatives are over-determined in that more than one plausible explanation to account for it can be imagined. Two features make an explanation plausible: (1) the explanation points to events occurring within an appropriate time frame that are more or less adequate in scale to produce the outcomes at the focus of inquiry; (2) it cannot be rejected on the basis of available evidence. Two such explanations will be explored in the pages that follow.

One takes note of the effects of the Civil Rights Act of 1964 and the Voting Rights Act of 1965, which dramatically increased the registration of voters in southern states. The registration of black voters strengthened the liberal factions of the Democratic parties in the several states and encouraged conservative voters and leaders to desert the Democrats and become Republicans. In addition, newly registered white voters—in many places these outnumbered new black voters—were less bound by habitual party loyalties to the Democratic Party and therefore were available to strengthen the ranks of the Republican Party. Thus, a Republican candidate for Congress might come to believe that he had some hope of winning. This attracted better candidates and more resources and in time led to a substantial number of Republican congressional victories (see tables 3.4 and 3.5).

The second explanation accounts for the rise of the Republican Party in southern states by calling attention to patterns of migration into the South. Northern retirees came to live in the South in large numbers after the introduction of residential air conditioning in the 1950s. A younger population of white-collar workers came to cities and created suburbs in the same period, also taking advantage of modern air-conditioned housing, office buildings, and factories. It makes sense to invoke air conditioning as

TABLE 3.4. Percent Registered to Vote Pre- and Post-VRA, by Race

| State | % registered pre-VRA 1965 | | % registered post-VRA 1967 | | % increase in registration | |
|---|---|---|---|---|---|---|
| | White | Black | White | Black | White | Black |
| Alabama | 69.2 | 19.3 | 89.6 | 51.6 | 29 | 167 |
| Arkansas | 65.5 | 40.4 | 72.4 | 62.8 | 11 | 55 |
| Florida | 74.8 | 51.2 | 81.4 | 63.6 | 9 | 24 |
| Georgia | 62.6 | 27.4 | 80.3 | 52.6 | 28 | 92 |
| Louisiana | 80.5 | 31.6 | 93.1 | 58.9 | 16 | 86 |
| Mississippi | 69.9 | 6.7 | 91.5 | 59.8 | 31 | 792 |
| North Carolina | 96.8 | 46.8 | 83.0 | 51.3 | −14 | 10 |
| South Carolina | 75.7 | 37.3 | 81.7 | 51.2 | 8 | 37 |
| Tennessee | 72.9 | 69.5 | 80.6 | 71.7 | 11 | 3 |
| Texas | n/a | n/a | 53.3 | 61.6 | n/a | n/a |
| Virginia | 61.1 | 38.3 | 63.4 | 55.6 | 4 | 45 |

Note: States reported registered voters as percentage of census-calculated voting age population.

Source: U.S. Commission on Civil Rights, *Political Participation* (Washington, D.C.: United States Commission on Civil Rights, 1968), appendix VII, table 1.

TABLE 3.5. Change in Registered Voters Post-VRA, by Race

| State | 1965–67 change in white voter registration | 1965–67 change in black voter registration | Difference (white − black) |
|---|---|---|---|
| Alabama | 276,622 | 155,695 | 120,927 |
| Arkansas | 60,056 | 43,286 | 16,770 |
| Florida | 172,606 | 58,417 | 114,189 |
| Georgia | 319,315 | 154,833 | 164,482 |
| Louisiana | 163,333 | 138,547 | 24,786 |
| Mississippi | 64,066 | 152,733 | −88,667 |
| North Carolina | −339,020 | 19,404 | −358,424 |
| South Carolina | 53,182 | 51,473 | 1,709 |
| Tennessee | 137,000 | 7,000 | 130,000 |
| Texas | n/a | n/a | n/a |
| Virginia | 69,832 | 98,741 | −28,909 |

Source: U.S. Commission on Civil Rights, *Political Participation* (Washington, D.C.: United States Commission on Civil Rights, 1968), appendix VII, table 1.

a major factor in stimulating the flow of northerners into what became known as the sunbelt (southern and southwestern states) because before air conditioning was available northerners who could afford to do so—many of them well-to-do Republicans—came south in the winter but did not, on the whole, settle permanently.

We need not choose between these explanations, since both converge to account for the rise of the Republican Party and the creation of a two-party South. Both focus on changes that took place in relatively recent times. For roughly a century after the Civil War (1861–65), the congressional politics of the South were dominated by the Democratic Party. Political scientists of an earlier generation, brought up on V. O. Key's remarkable book, *Southern Politics in State and Nation*, first published in 1949,[3] learned how political patterns established in the South at the time of the trauma of the Civil War persisted and persisted as the years and decades rolled by. Key and his co-workers argued that the South was by no means uniform, however. Variation was introduced by virtue of rural–urban differences, differences in the economic bases of different localities, and especially by the uneven distribution of African Americans, and therefore of white reactions to the presence of African Americans.[4]

There were even some Republicans, concentrated mostly in small clusters. A group of counties in the Texas hill country that voted Republican had large populations of German immigrants, but usually not enough to elect a Republican member of Congress.[5] And a larger group of Republican counties were located up along the ridge of the Appalachian mountains and in the Ozarks of northwest Arkansas.[6] These mountain counties had been populated by subsistence farmers who kept no slaves and raised no cash crops to speak of. They had voted against secession from the Union, and the Republican reconstruction affected them far less adversely than participants in the plantation economy of the lowlands. A full century after secession, the Appalachian ridge is where Republicans in Congress from the South still came from. V. O. Key called them mountain Republicans.[7] After World War II, mountain Republican voters supplied all of the handful of Republican members, out of the 100 or so southern members of Congress.

This is a picture of extraordinary political stability over a very long time. Yet we know that in its underlying demography the South experienced significant changes over at least the latter half of that period. Among these changes were (1) a movement of inhabitants away from farms, (2) many blacks heading north, (3) whites heading to southern cities, and (4) the expansion of cities and the creation of suburbs. The net effect has been that in the last few decades the South has at long last become much more like the rest of the country, its population more urban and suburban, less rural. Much of this is due to technological change, in the first instance to the widespread introduction of farm machinery, especially the gasoline-powered tractor, fertilizer, pesticides, and so on, which from the 1930s on began sharply to reduce the need for farm labor.[8]

The reduction of employment opportunities on farms brought people into town, off the farms and in some cases sent them north to work in factory jobs created by World War II.[9] In the movement toward urbanization the South lagged behind the rest of the country for most of the century, but by the time of the 1990 Census, less than 2 percent of the U.S. working population, southern and non-southern alike, worked in agriculture, fewer than 3 million people. They harvested, on the whole, more in the way of agricultural products than the 7 million American farmers who worked the land in 1950, when farmers constituted 11.6 percent of the national workforce. This major social transformation, which began at the end of the nineteenth century, was bound sooner or later to have an impact on the most rural section of the country. An enormous gap existed between the size of the rural population of the South and the rest of the country early in the twentieth century, but a significant movement toward convergence took place associated with World War II and the postwar years, and since 1980 there has been complete convergence (see table 3.6).

Expressed in terms of congressional districts, as Adam Sheingate says, "In 1960, the vast majority of Southern House members (61 percent) represented districts with at least 10 percent of their working population em-

TABLE 3.6. Decline of U.S. Agricultural Population, 1900–90 (percentage of population living on a farm)

| Percent | 1900 | 1920 | 1940 | 1950 | 1960 | 1980 | 1990 |
|---|---|---|---|---|---|---|---|
| Non-South | 32.1 | 22.2 | 17.1 | 11.4 | 6.3 | 2.7 | 1.7 |
| South | 60.8 | 55.3 | 42.0 | 27.2 | 11.2 | 2.8 | 1.3 |

Sources: Total state populations (the denominator): 1900–60 from *Historical Statistics of the United States, Colonial Times to 1970* (Washington, D.C.: Bureau of the Census, 1975), pp. 10, 24–37; 1980 and 1990, *1996 Statistical Abstract of the United States* (Washington, D.C.: Bureau of the Census, 1996), p. 28. Farm population (numerator): 1900–1950, *Historical Statistics of the United States: Colonial Times to 1970* (Washington, D.C.: Bureau of the Census, 1975), p. 458. 1960: *Census of Population 1960*, vol. 1, *Characteristics of the Population*, U.S. Summary, table 155; state totals, table 95. 1980: Bureau of the Census Report, *Estimates of the Number of Farm Residents*. Provided by Economic Research Service, U.S. Department of Agriculture. 1990: *Census of Population 1990: Social and Economic Characteristics Report* CP-2-1 (Washington, D.C.: Bureau of Census, U.S. Summary, table 15, state totals, table 4. South = 11 states of the Confederacy.

ployed in agriculture. In 1990, not a single southern representative met this criterion, and only 12 percent of congressional districts in the South contained an agricultural labor force greater than 5 percent."[10]

None of this considerable movement helps to explain why southern congressional districts outside their traditional mountain stronghold began to send Republicans to Congress. The movement of black rural southerners north gave them opportunities to vote that they had never had in the South, but the migration of rural southerners—white and black—into cities merely shuffled Democrats around the map, insofar as the newcomers voted at all.

Another trend is more promising in explaining the growth of the Republican Party in the South, namely the movement after World War II of northerners in significant numbers into southern states. This trend was facilitated by the growth in the South of residential air conditioning. Air conditioning made the South habitable all year around to northerners, many of whom had adopted the custom of visiting the South during the winter months, and who began to come down and establish all-year residences. This was a phenomenon of the 1950s and later. The leading historian of the rise of air conditioning in the South is Raymond Arsenault, who notes that in 1947,

> residential air conditioning . . . accounted for only 2 percent of the industry's business. By 1950 the figure had risen to 5 percent, but in most areas the air-conditioned home remained a novelty. In 1951, the inexpensive, efficient window unit finally hit the market, and sales skyrocketed, especially in the South. . . . By 1955 one out of every twenty-two American homes had some form of air conditioning. In the South the figures were closer to one in ten.[11]

Precise numbers on this phenomenon targeted to specific congressional districts are impossible to come by, but crude numbers for the states and the region as a whole support the general argument. We can demonstrate, for example, that residential air conditioning did arrive in the southern states after World War II and rapidly spread, especially to new homes as U.S. Census figures attest (see table 3.7).

The swift arrival of air conditioning can also be shown by watching trends in residential energy use, comparing winter and summer, South and non-South. The distinctive southern pattern shows rapid postwar growth in summertime energy use as compared to winter, tracking the introduction of southern air conditioning, which runs away from northern summer residential energy consumption over the same period (see figure 3.3).

TABLE 3.7. Residential Air Conditioning in the South, 1960–80 (percentage of households with air conditioning)

|  | 1960 | 1970 | 1980 |
|---|---|---|---|
| United States | 12.4 | 35.8 | 55.0 |
| South |  |  |  |
| Alabama | 16.7 | 49.0 | 70.7 |
| Arkansas | 14.0 | 46.5 | 71.3 |
| Florida | 18.3 | 60.5 | 84.0 |
| Georgia | 12.3 | 43.0 | 66.0 |
| Louisiana | 23.1 | 58.8 | 82.2 |
| Mississippi | 15.7 | 47.5 | 69.9 |
| North Carolina | 8.9 | 32.7 | 59.6 |
| South Carolina | 12.2 | 40.0 | 68.0 |
| Tennessee | 20.5 | 52.5 | 74.0 |
| Texas | 30.3 | 64.2 | 83.2 |
| Virginia | 12.2 | 43.3 | 64.8 |

Note: 1960 was the first year the Census asked if homes had air-conditioning units.

Source: U.S. Bureau of the Census, *U.S. Census of Housing, 1960*, vol. 1, *States and Small* Areas, part I, *United States Summary* (Washington, 1963), tables 7, 13, 26, and 29; "Detailed Housing Characteristics," in U.S. Bureau of the Census, *Census of Housing: 1970*, vol. 1, *Housing Characteristics for States, Cities, and Counties*, part I, *United States Summary* (Washington, 1972), tables 20, 21, 27, and 37; "Detailed Housing Characteristics," in U.S. Bureau of the Census, *Census of Housing: 1980*, vol. 1, Chapter B, *Characteristics of Housing Units*, part 1, *United States Summary* (Washington, 1982), tables 78, 79, 84, and 123; and ibid., parts 2, 5, 9–12, 19–20, 22, 26, 35, 38, 42, 44–45, 48, 50, table 64. Adapted from Raymond Arsenault, "The End of the Long Hot Summer: The Air Conditioner and Southern Culture," *Journal of Southern History* 50 (Nov. 1984), p. 611.

We can also note a shift in the postwar decades in which southern states, while continuing to receive new residents, presumably life-long Democrats from other southern states, in addition received greatly augmented streams of migration from other sections of the country. It is reasonable to presume that these non-southern states were where new Republicans were coming from.[12] Looking at the age distribution of the north-to-south migrants as compared with the south-to-south migrants, we find a pattern compatible with an influx of prosperous retirees from the North.[13]

The effects of air conditioning began to kick in during the mid-1950s, preceding the Voting Rights Act by about a decade. The first new postwar Republican safe seat in the South not held by a mountain Republican was

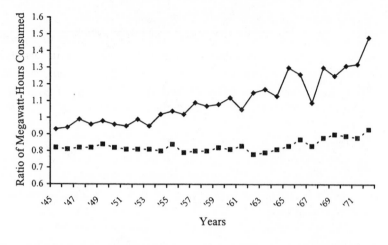

North = CT, IL, IN, ME, MA, MI, NH, NJ, NY, OH, PA, RI, VT, WI; South = AL, AR, DE, DC, FL, GA, KY, LA, MD, MS, NC, OK, SC, TN, TX, VA, WV.

Figure 3.3: Regional Summer–Winter Residential Power Consumption Ratios, September/January 1945–72. Sources: Federal Power Commission, *Sales of Electric Energy to Ultimate Consumers 1945–1949* (Washington, D.C.: Federal Power Commission, 1950); Federal Power Commission, *Monthly Sales of Electric Energy to Ultimate Consumers, January/July/September 1952/1954* (Washington, D.C.: Federal Power Commission, 1952, 1954); Federal Power Commission, *Sales of Electric Energy: By State and Geographic Divisions, January/July/September 1955/1957/1959/1960* (Washington, D.C.: Federal Power Commission, 1955, 1957, 1959, 1960); and Federal Power Commission, *Electric Power Statistics, January/July/September 1971/1972* (Washington, D.C.: U.S. Government Printing Office, 1971).

occupied by William Cramer, first elected in 1954, who represented St. Petersburg on the west coast of Florida, a big winter resort area.[14] This gives rise to the conjecture that many northerners who migrated South were reasonably well-off retirees. A fair number of them were used to voting Republican at home and would continue to do so after they relocated. Writing in 1960, Donald Strong of the University of Alabama thought so. He described the area as having "experienced a great influx of non-southern immigration. These immigrants have brought their Republicanism with them."[15]

From 1952 onward, the National Election Studies asked respondents where they were born as well as their party identifications, and so it is possible to track the incidence of northern-born Republicans in their samples of the southern voting population. These numbers show that starting in the mid-1950s, a very substantial share of the respondents identifying themselves as Republican voters were born outside the 11 southern states. Figure 3.4 indicates that migrants from outside the South made up as many as half of all Republican voters in 1964 and throughout most of the 1970s, and Figure 3.5 shows that a substantial number of migrants from the North were Republicans. These figures demonstrate a considerable augmentation of Republican strength in the electorate, obviously enough to begin to change the partisan landscape in the South, especially in those areas of the South where Republicans congregated in large numbers (see table 3.8).

By the 86th Congress, elected in 1960, seven southern seats were held by Republicans. Four were mountain Republican seats: Howard Baker and B. Carroll Reece from eastern Tennessee, Richard Poff from southwest Virginia, and Charles Raper Jonas from the Blue Ridge of North Carolina, a district that extended southeastward toward Charlotte (but was classified as 100 percent non-metropolitan as late as 1972).[16] The other three seats were Cramer's in Florida and two suburban seats: Bruce Alger's in Dallas and Joel Broyhill's in the northern Virginia suburbs of Washington, D.C.[17]

From the 1960s onward, north-to-south migration accelerated the transformation of the South into a region showing greater similarities to other parts of the country with its suburban Republicans and retirees voting according to habits they had picked up in their places of origin. Some-

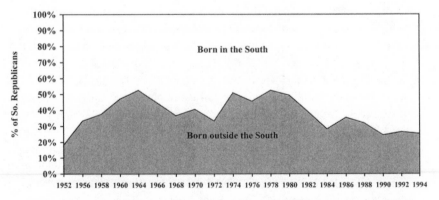

Figure 3.4: Southern Republicans, by Place of Birth, 1952–94. Source: Virginia Sapiro, Steven J. Rosenstone, and the National Election Studies. 1948–1994 Cumulative Data File [dataset]. Ann Arbor, MI: University of Michigan, Center for Political Studies [producer and distributor], 2001.

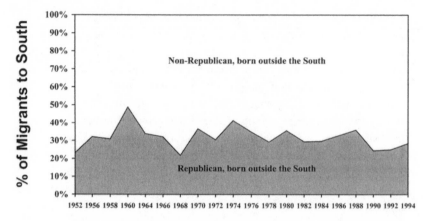

Figure 3.5: Partisan Affiliation of Southern Migrants, 1952–94. Source: See figure 3.4 for data source. Non-Republicans are respondents who identify themselves as Democrats or independents.

times these retirees were Democrats, as in the case of the Jews who moved to south Florida, and who sent the mainstream liberal Democrats Dante Fascell (1955–92) and Claude Pepper (1963–89) to Congress. Fascell and Pepper were both succeeded in Congress by Republicans of Cuban extraction. These Republican members appealed to fiercely anti-Castro Cuban immigrants who settled in the Miami metropolitan area as a result of the Cuban exodus that extended from 1960 to the early 1980s.[18]

Bruce Alger of Dallas and its suburbs was first elected in 1954, but it took a little time before his seat became safe, and his seat reflects the growing suburbanization of the South. In his precinct-by-precinct study of Alger's 1954 victory, Bernard Cosman identified a number of factors facilitating the Republican win: the lingering halo of Dwight Eisenhower's successful presidential run two years earlier, a split in the Democratic Party for the congressional nomination, and large numbers of non-Texans in the predominantly white-collar, upper middle-class electorate.[19] In the suburban precincts of Alger's district, which he describes one-by-one, Cosman records some of the heavier Republican votes in 1954 and 1956 as coming from "newly developed 'bedroom' subdivisions" indicating housing built in the early 1950s, presumably air conditioned.[20] Cosman says about one-third of Republican precinct chairmen were migrants from the North.[21] He also notes that Republican workers were in other respects different from the locals, tending to be Episcopalians, not Baptists, and businessmen, not

TABLE 3.8. Southern Partisanship, by Place of Birth, 1952–94

| Year | Born in South | | Not born in South | |
|------|------------|-------|------------|-------|
| | Republican | Other | Republican | Other |
| 1952 | 27 | 261 | 6 | 20 |
| 1956 | 36 | 262 | 18 | 38 |
| 1958 | 35 | 281 | 21 | 47 |
| 1960 | 46 | 294 | 41 | 43 |
| 1962 | 19 | 204 | 21 | 41 |
| 1966 | 21 | 168 | 17 | 36 |
| 1968 | 26 | 218 | 15 | 54 |
| 1970 | 38 | 232 | 26 | 45 |
| 1972 | 70 | 367 | 35 | 80 |
| 1974 | 50 | 408 | 52 | 74 |
| 1976 | 62 | 323 | 52 | 97 |
| 1978 | 49 | 287 | 54 | 131 |
| 1980 | 43 | 223 | 42 | 76 |
| 1982 | 47 | 203 | 30 | 72 |
| 1984 | 81 | 295 | 32 | 76 |
| 1986 | 80 | 289 | 44 | 90 |
| 1988 | 79 | 279 | 37 | 66 |
| 1990 | 65 | 282 | 21 | 65 |
| 1992 | 103 | 306 | 37 | 111 |
| 1994 | 118 | 195 | 40 | 101 |

Note: Values in columns represent number of respondents. Data for 1954 and 1964 were not available.

Source: See figure 3.4 for source.

lawyers. Many Republican districts like Alger's were prosperous; in the 93rd Congress (1973–74) the top five southern districts in median income were all represented by Republicans, as were seven of the top ten.[22]

By the 93rd Congress (1973–74) the six southern congressional seats with the largest percentage of residents over the age of 65 were all located in Florida, and half of them including the top two were held by Republicans.[23] At the same time nine of the top 16 southern seats with the largest contingent of residents born in different states were held by Republicans.[24] Four were in Florida. One was the northwest Arkansas seat held by John Paul Hammerschmidt, where Ozark Republicans combined with retirees coming down from the middle west and settling in newly developed planned communities and subdivisions.[25] Two were suburban Washington seats in northern Virginia, and one was the Norfolk seat with its Navy base held by William Whitehurst.[26]

Another way of looking at the phenomenon of migration: the census every year asks if residents had occupied the same house for the last five years. Eleven of the 15 southern districts scoring lowest on this measure in 1970 were represented by Republicans (mostly the same districts with out-of-state residents identified previously) (see table 3.9 and figures 3.6 and 3.7).[27]

Dixiecrats, conservative southerners having more in common with the national Republican Party than with the national Democratic mainstream, began to shift into the Republican Party where they felt more ideologically at home. This trend could be detected among voters in presidential elections for Dwight Eisenhower in 1952 and 1956 and also in 1964,[28] significantly, the year of the first of two Acts dealing with civil rights (the other was in 1965), which brought federal registrars to southern constituencies.

TABLE 3.9. Percentage of State Population Born Out of State, by Region, 1950–90

| State | 1950 | | 1960 | | 1970 | | 1980 | | 1990 | |
|---|---|---|---|---|---|---|---|---|---|---|
| | South[a] | Non-South[b] | South | Non-South | South | Non-South | South | Non-South | South | Non-South |
| Alabama | 8.7 | 3.0 | 9.3 | 4.2 | 10.1 | 5.7 | 11.9 | 8.0 | 13.2 | 9.5 |
| Arkansas | 12.3 | 10.5 | 11.3 | 10.8 | 10.4 | 13.5 | 11.0 | 18.9 | 11.8 | 20.1 |
| Florida | 27.2 | 27.1 | 24.2 | 35.7 | 20.4 | 39.8 | 16.6 | 48.0 | 14.1 | 50.1 |
| Georgia | 10.4 | 4.2 | 11.6 | 5.6 | 13.8 | 8.2 | 15.3 | 12.1 | 16.9 | 16.2 |
| Louisiana | 10.7 | 4.6 | 11.7 | 4.8 | 10.8 | 6.4 | 11.9 | 8.0 | 11.1 | 7.8 |
| Mississippi | 8.0 | 3.1 | 8.7 | 3.7 | 10.1 | 5.0 | 12.9 | 7.5 | 13.9 | 7.8 |
| North Carolina | 8.4 | 4.1 | 9.0 | 5.1 | 9.5 | 7.4 | 11.0 | 11.5 | 11.8 | 16.0 |
| South Carolina | 8.7 | 3.4 | 10.5 | 5.1 | 12.0 | 7.6 | 14.3 | 11.6 | 15.0 | 10.7 |
| Tennessee | 13.3 | 6.7 | 13.5 | 7.2 | 12.9 | 9.1 | 13.9 | 13.1 | 13.8 | 15.8 |
| Texas | 8.9 | 12.6 | 8.1 | 13.8 | 8.2 | 14.8 | 8.5 | 18.7 | 8.0 | 19.9 |
| Virginia | 10.4 | 15.1 | 11.1 | 17.8 | 10.9 | 22.6 | 11.0 | 26.4 | 11.2 | 30.8 |

[a]Refers to the percentage of a state's population that was born in any other southern state
[b]Refers to the percentage of a state's population that was born in any non-southern state or the District of Columbia

Note: The numbers include only those in the native-born population reporting a place of birth who were born inside one of the 50 U.S. states or the District of Columbia. Those born in outlying areas or abroad are excluded from these figures.

Sources: 1950: U.S. Bureau of the Census, *U.S. Census of Population: 1950*, vol. 4, *Special Reports*, part 4, Chapter A, State of Birth (Washington, D.C.: U.S. Government Printing Office, 1953), table 13, pp. 19–24; 1960: U.S. Bureau of the Census, *Census of Population: 1960, Subject Reports, State of Birth*, Final Report PC(2)-2A (Washington, D.C.: U.S. Government Printing Office, 1963), table 18, pp. 19–24; 1970: U.S. Bureau of the Census, *Census of Population: 1970, Subject Reports, Final Report PC(2)-2A, State of Birth* (Washington, D.C.: U.S. Government Printing Office, 1973), table 13, pp. 25–30; 1980: U.S. Bureau of the Census, *1980 Census of Population: Detailed Population Characteristics* (Washington, D.C.: U.S. Government Printing Office, 1983), vols. for southern states, table 194; 1990: U.S. Bureau of the Census, *1990 Census of Population: Social and Economic Characteristics* (Washington, D.C.: U.S. Government Printing Office, 1993), vols. for southern states, table 37.

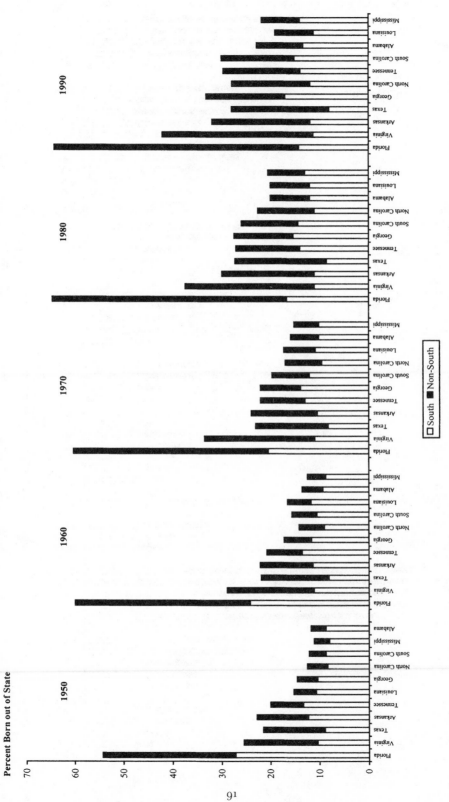

**Percent Born out of State**

Figure 3.6: State Population Born Out of State, by Region, 1950–90 (ranked by population born outside the South). Note: See table 3.8 for sources and definitions.

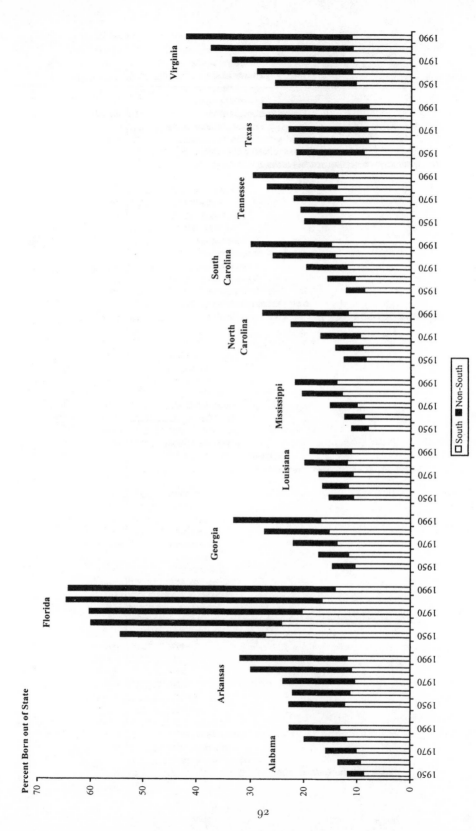

92

Figure 3.7: State Population Born Outside of South, by Region, 1950–90 (by state by year). Note: See table 3.8 for sources and definitions.

Not much later, ambitious young politicians could begin to contemplate running as Republicans for lesser offices and winning. For example, in 1972, when William Colmer, Democrat of Mississippi, retired, his legislative assistant went home to Pascagoula, switched parties, and was elected to the House as a Republican. His name is Trent Lott. He later became House Republican whip and Senate Republican leader.[29]

So in addition to significant movements of new voters into the South creating a Republican voting bloc, other Republicans were created through conversion or through the activation of new voters, especially of younger, white southerners, no doubt aided and abetted indirectly by results of the Voting Rights Act (1965). This Act enfranchised black voters who themselves did not vote Republican, but contributed to the liberal wing of the Democratic Party. It also stimulated the new registration of substantial numbers of white voters. This development undoubtedly helped not only to chase Dixiecrats out of the Democratic Party but also to attract Dixiecrats like Trent Lott into the Republican fold. Such converts were pushed by their diminishing prospects of leading a local Democratic Party liberalized by the influx of black voters, but also pulled by greatly improved prospects of Republican competitive success owing to the arrival on the scene of reinforcements from the North and new white registrants. And of course they were, many of them, genuinely and fiercely opposed to civil rights, increasingly high on the agenda of the national Democratic Party.

The perception that something like party realignment was taking place among southern politicians was reinforced by interviews conducted in the late spring of 1993 with southern Republican members of Congress, including future Speaker Newt Gingrich of Georgia, who was born in Pennsylvania and raised on army bases. Gingrich was the fourth Speaker in the twentieth century (out of 17) to represent a district outside the state of his birth. Two of the first three—Joe Cannon and Sam Rayburn—moved from the middle south to the then-western frontier as small boys.[30] Gingrich followed a more modern pattern. Whereas 30 years ago, almost all southern members represented districts in states where they were born, recently southern members have become more like those from the rest of the country—some native sons, but many outsiders. Indeed, among the Republicans, the new members of Congress elected in the bumper crop of 1994 were quite likely (12 out of 19) to be from out of state. The old style reflects a more settled rural pattern; the new transient style is more in keeping with lives lived in cities and suburbs.

Table 3.10 is another picture of convergence. In 1965 newly elected southern Republicans were somewhat more likely than Democrats to be

TABLE 3.10. State of Origin of New Members of Congress (number of newly elected members representing state in which they were born)

| Location | 1965 | 1995 | 1997 |
|---|---|---|---|
| Non-South | | | |
| Same | 47 | 39 | 29 |
| Different | 22 | 23 | 20 |
| Net | ca. 2–1 same | ca. 2–1 same | ca. 1.5–1 same |
| South | | | |
| Same | | | |
| Dem | 7 | 2 | 11 |
| Rep | 7 | 7 | 7 |
| Total | 14 | 9 | 18 |
| Different | | | |
| Dem | 2 | 1 | 5 |
| Rep | 0 | 12 | 3 |
| Total | 2 | 13 | 8 |
| Net | ca. 7–1 same | ca. 1–1.5 different | ca.2–1 same |

natives of the state they represented. By 1995, owing to the influx of southern Republicans, the South elected an enormous number of newcomers; and by 1997 the South and the non-South had pretty much converged at a 1.5–2 to 1 ratio of natives to newcomers.

These trends produced meaningful institutional consequences for the House of Representatives, resulting not only from the 1994 election, but from the series of events, starting in the 1970s, in which large numbers of Dixiecrat voters were subtracted from the ranks of the Democratic Party in the South. They now vote Republican and send Republicans to Congress. This plausibly explains why Dixiecrat members of Congress largely disappeared from the House Democratic caucus.

Two recent independent analyses of individual voting in House elections over time help to sustain this story. Both compare the effects of race with the effects of economic factors in producing votes for Republican candidates for the House in the South, and both conclude that the economic rather than the race factor was stronger.

Before the 1960s, in the South, rich and poor alike voted Democratic for the House. Afterward, the rate of decay in the Democratic vote among the well-to-do began to accelerate, with the results indicated in table 3.11.

African Americans, as they entered the southern voting population, voted overwhelmingly Democratic, regardless of their income level.[31] But whites, as indicated, voted their pocketbooks, and indeed from the 1960s

TABLE 3.11 House Vote by Income Level

| Income level | 1950s | 1960s | 1970s | 1980s | 1990s | Change 1950s–90s |
|---|---|---|---|---|---|---|
| *House vote for Democrats (whites only) in the South, by income level* | | | | | | |
| Lower third | 80% | 71% | 77% | 75% | 58% | −22% |
| Upper third | 81% | 69% | 66% | 52% | 27% | −54% |
| *House vote for Republicans (whites only) in the South, by income level* | | | | | | |
| Lower third | 18% | 25% | 24% | 27% | 40% | 22% |
| Upper third | 15% | 35% | 38% | 49% | 70% | 55% |

Sources: Democratic vote—National Election Studies, adapted from Mark D. Brewer and Jeffrey M. Stonecash, "Class, Race Issues, and Declining White Support for the Democratic Party in the South," *Political Behavior* 23 (June 2001), table 1, p. 139; Republican vote—National Election Studies, adapted from Byron E. Shafer and Richard G. C. Johnston, "The Transformation of Southern Politics Revisited: The House of Representatives as a Window," *British Journal of Political Science* 31 (Oct. 2001), table 1, p. 609.

to the 1980s in those districts with large black populations, they were less likely to vote Republican.[32] Shafer and Johnston report:

> For the 1960s and 1970s and 1980s, in every comparison—low-income whites in more and less black districts, middle-income whites in more and less black districts, or upper-income whites in more and less black districts—every category of white voter was less likely to vote Republican in the side of the comparison that included more black voters.[33]

This fortifies the view that those trends that were moving the South toward economic and social convergence with the rest of the country—urbanization, suburbanization, and migration from the North—were gaining strength as influences on the behavior of southern voters as compared with fallout from the peculiar institution of slavery.

Richard Fenno has depicted in microcosm and in rich detail many of the changes that appear in the aggregate statistics.[34] Over an eight-year period starting in 1970, he followed the fortunes of Jack Flynt, a senior conservative Democrat representing a dozen or so west Georgia counties. From the mid-1950s until the mid-1970s, Flynt's person-to-person representational style exploiting his deep roots in the communities of the district made a perfect fit with his constituents, who were overwhelmingly rural and small town whites and traditional southern Democrats. Redistricting in the 1970s reconfigured the district so as to embrace the outskirts of

Atlanta, bringing Flynt into contact with a large population of unfamiliar constituents, suburbanites and newcomers to Georgia. These included white-collar employees based in the industrial complex surrounding Atlanta's enormous, busy airport, for example, pilots working for Delta and Eastern airlines and other well-off Republicans. This led to a strenuous election contest in 1976 against a West Georgia College history professor, Newt Gingrich, who ran on the Republican ticket. Flynt, a committed opponent of civil rights, won this race, in part with the help of black Jimmy Carter voters, but the experience persuaded Flynt to make it his last term. He retired in 1978.

Fenno returned to the same territory in 1996. Jack Flynt's district by then had been reshaped by the Democratic Georgia legislature so as to elude the grasp of Newt Gingrich and later reconfigured again by a court order. Gingrich had long since jumped to more promising turf and entered Congress from a nearby district after the election of 1978. Since 1992, much of the territory and two-thirds of the population of Flynt's former Sixth District of Georgia, now the Third District, was represented by a Republican businessman, Mac Collins. Like Flynt, Collins was born and raised in a small town in Georgia and came from a family active in local politics. His early political career at the local level included both victories and defeats as a Democrat. In 1981, at the age of 37, he switched to the Republican Party; he became a county chairman of the Republican Party, was elected to the state Senate after two unsuccessful runs, and in 1993 was elected to Congress.

Fenno describes Collins as policy-oriented, issue-driven, and comfortable making connections with his increasingly suburban constituency through advertising, issue advocacy, and wholesale contact in sharp contrast with Flynt's one-on-one retail personal style.[35] Collins was a self-starter in his political career. He had to fight for the Republican Party label in his first run for Congress. He keeps a campaign office open all the time, raises modest but significant amounts of campaign money (which Flynt never did), and uses polls and television advertising.[36] He is well connected to congressional leaders of his party and he concerns himself with promoting Republican issues in a state where the congressional delegation switched over a 40-year period from entirely Democratic to predominantly Republican (see table 3.12). Whereas Flynt described the main industry in the district 25 years ago as textiles, Collins told Fenno "the dominant industry is people driving to Atlanta every day."[37] Fenno points out that the south end of the district in 1996 also included the suburbs of the city of Columbus.

TABLE 3.12. Georgia Congressional
Delegation, 1960–2000

| Year | Democrats | Republicans |
|------|-----------|-------------|
| 1960 | 10 | 0 |
| 1970 | 8 | 2 |
| 1980 | 9 | 1 |
| 1990 | 9 | 1 |
| 2000 | 3 | 8 |

## Southern Republicans in the 1990s: A Group Portrait

By 1993 (in the 103rd Congress) there were 48 Republican members of the House from the South, comprising 38.4 percent of all southern representatives and 27.3 percent of all Republicans in Congress. They came from every southern state except Mississippi (which had two Republican Senators) (see table 3.13).

In the spring of 1993 slightly more than half of them discussed in interviews the circumstances under which their districts became Republican and the course of their own political careers.[38] A synoptic look at these interviews bears out a number of the patterns disclosed by the aggregate numbers and reinforces Fenno's observations tracking the transition between Jack Flynt and Mac Collins. While maintaining their seats along the Appalachian ridge, Republicans tended to gather new strength in retirement communities, territory surrounding military installations, and the "new south" suburbs of transportation hubs and financial centers like Atlanta, Charlotte, and Dallas, as well as Washington, D.C.

Newt Gingrich, not unexpectedly, had the big picture:

> You have the Civil War Yankee vote in the mountains; that is still there. It hasn't changed a whole lot. It atrophied slightly, but not much.... You ... have a decisive shift of poor southern whites starting with Goldwater, which was essentially a racist reaction combined with the emergence of sort of the first wave of yuppies—we didn't call them that then ... entrepreneurial, wealth, business-oriented ... who see the Democratic Party as the party of labor, weak foreign policy, and confusion domestically ... [This] was really not a racist way, combined with the racist reaction

TABLE 3.13. House of Representatives Southern Republicans, by State and District, 1993 (103rd Congress)

| Member | Place of birth (date) | First elected | CC score | ADA score | ACU score |
|---|---|---|---|---|---|
| *Alabama* | | | | | |
| 1. Sonny Callahan[a] | Mobile, AL (1932) | 1984 | 96 | 5 | 96 |
| 2. Terry Everett[a] | Dothan, AL (1937) | 1992 | 86 | 10 | 96 |
| 6. Spencer Bachus[a] | Birmingham, AL (1947) | 1992 | 93 | 0 | 100 |
| *Arkansas* | | | | | |
| 3. Tim Hutchinson[a] | Bentonville, AR (1949) | 1992 | 91 | 5 | 100 |
| 4. Jay Dickey | Pine Bluff, AR (1939) | 1992 | 93 | 10 | 100 |
| *Florida* | | | | | |
| 4. Tillie Fowler[a] | Milledgeville, GA (1942) | 1992 | 93 | 15 | 83 |
| 6. Cliff Stearns | Washington, D.C. (1941) | 1988 | 94 | 5 | 92 |
| 7. John L. Mica[a] | Binghamton, NY (1943) | 1992 | 93 | 5 | 96 |
| 8. Bill McCollum[a] | Brooksville, FL (1944) | 1981 | 92 | 15 | 92 |
| 9. Michael Bilirakis[a] | Tarpon Springs, FL (1930) | 1982 | 85 | 20 | 80 |
| 10. C. W. Bill Young | Harmarville, PA (1930) | 1970 | 90 | 15 | 76 |
| 12. Charles Canady[a] | Lakeland, FL (1954) | 1992 | 93 | 10 | 100 |
| 13. Dan Miller | Highland Park, MI (1942) | 1992 | 80 | 10 | 88 |
| 14. Porter Goss | Waterbury, CT (1938) | 1988 | 85 | 5 | 88 |
| 16. Tom Lewis | Philadelphia, PA (1924) | 1982 | 94 | 10 | 96 |
| 18. Ileana Ros-Lehtinen[a] | Havana, Cuba (1952) | 1989 | 79 | 25 | 78 |
| 21. Lincoln Diaz-Balart | Havana, Cuba (1954) | 1992 | 75 | 35 | 75 |
| 22. E. Clay Shaw[a] | Miami, FL (1939) | 1980 | 92 | 15 | 84 |
| *Georgia* | | | | | |
| 1. Jack Kingston[a] | Bryan, TX (1955) | 1992 | 84 | 10 | 100 |
| 3. Mac Collins[a] | Butts County, GA (1944) | 1992 | 91 | 10 | 100 |
| 4. John Linder[a] | Deer River, MN (1942) | 1992 | 100 | 5 | 100 |
| 6. Newt Gingrich[a] | Harrisburg, PA (1943) | 1978 | 85 | 10 | 100 |
| *Louisiana* | | | | | |
| 1. Robert Livingston[a] | Colorado Springs, CO (1943) | 1977 | 73 | 10 | 95 |
| 5. Jim McCrery[a] | Shreveport, LA (1949) | 1988 | 83 | 5 | 91 |
| 6. Richard Baker | New Orleans, LA (1948) | 1986 | 94 | 0 | 100 |
| *North Carolina* | | | | | |
| 6. Howard Coble[a] | Greensboro, NC (1931) | 1984 | 75 | 10 | 92 |
| 9. Alex McMillan[a] | Charlotte, NC (1932) | 1984 | 94 | 15 | 84 |
| 10. Cass Ballenger | Hickory, NC (1926) | 1986 | 83 | 10 | 92 |
| 11. Charles Taylor | Brevard, NC (1941) | 1990 | 88 | 15 | 87 |
| *South Carolina* | | | | | |
| 1. Arthur Ravenel | St. Andrews Parish, SC (1927) | 1986 | 83 | 40 | 80 |
| 2. Floyd Spence[a] | Columbia, SC (1928) | 1970 | 98 | 15 | 92 |
| 4. Bob Inglis | Savannah, GA (1959) | 1992 | 89 | 10 | 100 |

TABLE 3.13. (*continued*)

| | | | | | |
|---|---|---|---|---|---|
| *Tennessee* | | | | | |
| 1. James Quillen | near Gate City, VA (1916) | 1962 | 77 | 5 | 92 |
| 2. John Duncan[a] | Lebanon, TN (1947) | 1988 | 71 | 25 | 84 |
| 7. Don Sundquist[a] | Moline, IL (1936) | 1982 | 92 | 5 | 96 |
| *Texas* | | | | | |
| 3. Sam Johnson[a] | San Antonio, TX (1930) | 1991 | 94 | 10 | 100 |
| 6. Joe Barton | Waco, TX (1949) | 1984 | 85 | 5 | 100 |
| 7. *Bill Archer* | Houston, TX (1928) | 1970 | 85 | 0 | 100 |
| 8. Jack Fields | Humble, TX (1952) | 1980 | 88 | 5 | 96 |
| 19. Larry Combest | Memphis, TN (1945) | 1984 | 94 | 10 | 100 |
| 21. Lamar Smith[a] | San Antonio, TX (1947) | 1986 | 96 | 20 | 88 |
| 22. Tom DeLay | Laredo, TX (1947) | 1984 | 92 | 5 | 100 |
| 23. Henry Bonilla | San Antonio, TX (1954) | 1984 | 98 | 5 | 96 |
| 26. Dick Armey | Cando, ND (1940) | 1984 | 96 | 0 | 100 |
| *Virginia* | | | | | |
| 1. Herbert Bateman | Elizabeth City, NC (1928) | 1982 | 83 | 10 | 84 |
| 6. Robert Goodlatte[a] | Holyoke, MA (1952) | 1992 | 84 | 5 | 96 |
| 7. *Thomas Bliley[a]* | Chesterfield Co., VA (1932) | 1980 | 94 | 15 | 96 |
| 10. Frank Wolf | Philadelphia, PA (1939) | 1976 | 96 | 20 | 84 |

[a]Interviewed in June 1993.

Notes: *Members in italics* were once Democrats. For members elected in 1992, voting scores are for the year 1993. For all others they are for 1992.

Source: *Politics in America* 1992, 1994, 1996.

against Lyndon Johnson and the Civil Rights Bill. The duality of those two could lead to . . . the emergence of a genuine network of Goldwaterites who permanently changed then to the Republican Party. So now these are the coalitions you've got. You've got a floating racist coalition which was Republican on the national ticket but very Democrat locally. . . . [T]his is the old world Democrat machine everywhere. . . . You have the rising suburbanites who are Republicans unless the Republican gets too racist. . . . [Y]ou have a whole wave of college-educated southerners merging with the influx of Yankees. . . . One of the interesting patterns you may have already picked up is that if you take a list of states and rank order them in terms of where the people are going . . . Georgia is radically more open to new people and almost all southern states are.

Q: Florida certainly.

A: Yes. Literally, when you go across the South, it is astonishing the immigration that is going on. Even in places in Mississippi: Biloxi and Pascagoula and those places . . .

Q: You date that from when?

A: The immigration began with the invention of air conditioning. . . . It is three big things. It is the impact of air conditioning. It is the extraordinary impact in the South of the best parts of the New Deal—REA, TVA, that sort of thing. And it is the intelligent use by [Rep. Carl] Vinson and [Sen. Richard] Russell [both Georgia Democrats] and other southerners of World War II government industrial build-up to insure that a lot of it happened in the South.

Some members represented territory combining the various components of southern Republicanism. Here is how Tim Hutchinson described his northwest Arkansas district:

The district, I think there are two sources of its Republican leanings. One is historic, in which the Ozark, mountain Republican . . . roots go back to the Civil War. The second big factor is the immigration and the people who moved into the . . . District . . . primarily from the upper midwest who are very much Republican in their voting patterns. We've seen since 1960 a huge influx of retirees and . . . companies that have moved into the district and brought in . . . management-level people with them with Republican leanings. But the retirees are a big factor. We have one of the largest retirement communities anywhere, Bella Vista, about 12,000, 13,000 retirees living there—almost all from the upper midwest: Illinois, Iowa, Ohio, Michigan. Eighty percent Republican.[39]

Unlike many of his older colleagues, Hutchinson began his political life as a Republican, and he grew up in the district. Although his parents were Democrats, they were conservatives. "I think the last Democrat daddy voted for was John Kennedy. But they both voted for Goldwater and [were] probably Republicans since then." This was well before Hutchinson went off to college, at Bob Jones University. "In 1964 I was in junior high school and took a liking to Barry Goldwater."

Lamar Smith of San Antonio has strong roots in his part of Texas. His great grandfather and grandfather, both Democrats, were active in politics. He became a Republican around 1975. The Democrats were too liberal for him and he wanted to be an accelerator in the Republican Party rather than a brake in the Democratic Party. He assumed at the time that becoming a Republican foreclosed elective politics.[40] His huge district, however, included at least three significant pockets of Republican strength in the 1990s. The affluent Anglo north side of San Antonio is the first. The second is the oil city of Midland, described in the *Almanac of American Politics* as "the headquarters of the people who run the Permian Basin . . . Midland remains one of the most Republican cities in America." The third consists of "the Texas hill country, much of it first settled by refugees from the failed German revolutions of 1848. They made good livings, even off barren soil, but they disliked slavery, instinctively favored the Union, and when Texas became one of the most heavily Democratic states in the Union after the Civil War, they insisted on voting Republican in every election. They still do."[41]

Smith was the second Republican to represent this territory, succeeding Tom Loeffler who held the seat from 1978 to 1986. Loeffler beat a Democrat who was too liberal for the district. Smith believes that the influx of new voters in the suburbs of San Antonio from about 520,000 to 720,000 people between 1980 and 1990 made it possible for a San Antonio resident to win the district.

Alex McMillan of Charlotte, North Carolina, described his district as:

> a doughnut with one little corridor running out to the north that circumscribed . . . the inner city of Charlotte, which is essentially minority, black. Structured that way. . . . Charlotte is a magnet city that is attracting people from all over the country. Many of them . . . tend to be Republican. . . . Charlotte is probably the center or epitome of the rural Piedmont south, which is distinctly different from the coastal plains which were formerly the large slave-owning sections. This is largely the center of the industrialized South or the new South. . . . Probably 20 percent of Charlotte's population is born there. They're either northern Republicans or they are southern Democrats who changed their location and feel free to break the tradition they've held in the Democratic Party.

In the years before the Supreme Court required equalization in the populations of congressional districts within each state, the state legislature of Texas protected Sam Rayburn's seat in the northeastern part of the state from change. Consequently, Rayburn's district throughout the 1950s was lightly populated—less populated than any seat in the country excepting the district covering the upper peninsula of Michigan. The city nearest Rayburn's territory was Dallas, one of the nation's most populous districts. Redistricting since then has moved the north Dallas district held by Sam Johnson northward toward fast-growing Plano (once in Rayburn's district), but it has its roots in the affluent, solidly Republican north Dallas territory—Highland Park, University Park—first captured by Bruce Alger and since held by two other Republican members.

Johnson said,

> When I first moved there in 1965, [Plano] was about 7,000 roughly in round numbers and it is now 150,000. . . . In the district before it was cut in the 1980 Census we had EDS . . . Texas Instruments, Rockwell International, Fujitsu . . . J.C. Penney's built a brand new headquarters. So they've moved nearly 10,000 people into the area . . . I think they came from Republican areas. I think Penney's up northeast in Connecticut or New York even. . . . Dallas is located pretty strategically from the standpoint of transportation, being in the center of the country. And in the South where the weather is good and the advent of DFW Airport between Dallas and Fort Worth.
>
> [I]n the '60s and '70s . . . the county organization was all Democrat. And as a matter of fact Collin County is probably a good example. That is the county immediately north of Dallas County, which about 28 percent of our constituents live in now. It was all Democrat until we elected a county judge—a Republican county judge—who was the first Republican elected in the county. And that was in . . . about 1978. . . . And now every elected position in the county is Republican, even the [justices of the peace] and the constables. Everyone.
>
> Q: What was it about that time that allowed people to start voting Republican?
>
> A: Texas was a one-party state at the time. It was conservative Democrat. And the conservative Democrats vote very much like Republicans do most of the time. So what happened, I think, is we started getting an influx of Mexican movement from the south and some liberals into Houston because of the ship channel down there and dock workers and that kind of thing. The party, nationwide as well, moved away from the conservative Democrats as you well know. They started jumping ship. [Texas Senator] Phil Gramm did that. He was a conservative and they kicked him out or refused to deal with him so he switched parties. And now he is a Republican. He was a conservative Democrat. [Texas Senator] Kay Hutchison's husband used to be a Democrat chairman in Dallas

County and then later became state Republican chairman. That's just the way the state was. You used to vote Democrat. I never did, but, you used to vote Democrat so you could vote for people because that was the only party they ran in.

I think it's the influx of population. See, Texas has gone from about 12 million [people] to 17 million today. And they are estimating 25 million by the year 2000. So you can see a great growth in the population and it is not all from the South. A lot of it is people moving down from the North.

An adjacent district to Johnson's was held in 1993 by Dick Armey, whom we did not interview. Armey's district was newly created in 1980 and centered in the largely new city of Arlington. Like Newt Gingrich, Armey is a former college professor with origins outside the South. He was born in North Dakota and has a Ph.D. in economics from the University of Oklahoma. His district was mostly empty land until the opening of the Dallas–Fort Worth Airport in 1972. Like Gingrich, whose district was near the Atlanta airport, Armey (first elected in 1984) drew his support from Republicans in the high-tech and defense-related industries attracted by the airport.[42]

Other members believe that migration had a strong impact on their districts. John Mica of Florida, who worked for William Cramer in 1970 and represents territory described in his literature as "the suburban area between Orlando and Daytona Beach," said:

I've always been a Republican. I campaigned for Nixon in 1959–60. I got interested in politics in high school and supported Nixon. I was [originally] from Binghamton, New York.

Q: You don't really consider yourself a southerner?

A: No . . . my district is all transplants. They are from New York or Ohio; they're from New Jersey, Pennsylvania.

Northern migrants had something to do with the conversion of Floyd Spence of South Carolina from a conservative Democrat to a Republican, but as Spence described it, his change of party was driven more by ideological conviction than rational calculation. He converted before there were any prominent Republicans in South Carolina, before, even, the conversion of Strom Thurmond.[43] It is not uncommon for this cohort of southern Republicans to have started in politics as Democrats, as we saw in the cases of Mac Collins and Alex McMillan. The somewhat older Spence (born 1928) said:

I served in the state legislature for six years as a Democrat....
[A]ll the while I was voting on the national level for Republicans
for president even though I was a local Democrat. We didn't have
any Republicans. Didn't know any Republicans. I hadn't seen any
Republicans. All I heard about them was bad.

Q: When did you change parties?

A: 1962.

Q: What was the impetus?

A: A group of young people calling themselves Republican had
moved in from the north. They wanted to know why I wouldn't
change parties and run as a Republican for Congress. And I
thought about it. I couldn't very well run as a Democrat, I didn't
think, given the way I felt philosophically. I'd get up here, you
know, and I would be blocked in—voting against my own beliefs
in a way. And feeling how I did about things I thought people just
voted for me regardless of party so I went and changed parties.
And the whole roof fell in. My kids were ostracized at school. My
minister called me up and said they were praying for me. I was
the first one in the state in public office to change parties.

Like Floyd Spence, a number of members identified political ideology as
a force in propelling them into the Republican Party. There can be no
serious doubt of the strong policy convictions of the southern Republicans
as a glance at their conservative coalition (median 91), liberalism (ADA,
median 10), and conservatism (ACU, median 95) scores reveals.

Jim McCrery of Louisiana tells a story much like Floyd Spence's:

When I was growing up I didn't even know that Republicans ran
for office in Louisiana.

Q: Were your parents Democratic?

A: Oh, sure. I was too.

Q: When did you switch over?

A: About six or seven years ago. When I went in to register to vote,
I think I was 19 or 20 at the time, the law changed . . . right when
I was 19 or 20. . . . So I went in to register to vote and told the
registrar that my father was a registered Democrat but had voted
for every Republican president in my lifetime. So I grew up hearing
my father talk about how good the Republican presidents were
and how bad the Democratic presidential nominees were. So I said
to the registrar of Garden Parish in Louisiana, I said, "I want to
register Republican." She said, "No, you don't." I said, "Yes, I really

do." She said, "No, you don't want to register Republican." I said,
"Why?" She said, "Well, you want to be able to vote for Sheriff
Turner don't you?" "Well, yes ma'am. Friend of the family." "You
want to be able to vote for clerk so and so?" And I said, "Yes,
ma'am." She said, "Well, if you register Republican you won't be
able to vote for them." I said, "I beg your pardon?" She said, "Well,
they run in the Democratic primary. And that is the election. There
is no general election because we don't ever have a Republican
primary. There is no Republican primary. So, if you register Republican you won't be able to vote in the local elections." I said,
"Oh gee, I don't want that." So I registered Democrat. And that is
how a lot of people my age came to be Democrats—because they
couldn't vote in local elections if they registered Republican.

Q: What changed?

A: It was a very gradual thing. It started at the presidential level and
now it is slowly but surely seeping down into the congressional
level. And then in some states it is even seeping down into the
local level. It hasn't in Louisiana and probably won't for some time.
Louisiana is different. But in South Carolina; you see a lot of local
Republican office holders. North Carolina. You are starting to see
that in Texas with the State Supreme Court. It is dominated now
by Republicans. . . . [W]hen Joe Waggonner [D-La.] retired in 1978
there was an open seat. And a lot more people ran for the seat
and a Republican . . . got in a run-off. I don't know how many
candidates. Probably 10 candidates or so running for an open seat.
So I knew it was possible for a Republican to win in that congressional district even though it would be very difficult. And so,
knowing that it was possible, it was easy for me to switch.

Q: That was what year?

A: Spring of 1988. But actually I made the switch in '87. As soon
as Buddy Roemer, my predecessor, was elected Governor, that
threw open his seat and that was in the fall of '87. And I was still
registered Democrat. So I had to make a decision then whether to
switch or not. It was easy for me to make the decision to switch
because I didn't want to be a Democratic congressman. I would
rather not serve than be a Democrat in Congress. . . . I had
watched Buddy Roemer . . . , for whom I worked about three and
a half years, a conservative Democrat fight his own party leadership day after day after day and get punished for voting his
positions. And I just didn't want to be a part of that. If I was to
serve in Congress, I wanted to serve as a member of a party that

agreed with me. And that is the Republican Party. So the decision was easy for me to switch and run as a Republican. I didn't care about winning as a Democrat. So it wasn't so much of a political calculation for me, although that was a part of it. If I didn't think I had a chance to win as a Republican I would not have run at all. So it was a part of the calculation but it was not the determining factor in terms of whether I ran as a Democrat or Republican. It was a philosophical determination.

In aggregate, southern Republicans in the 103rd Congress displayed the following characteristics:

1. Nearly half of the members born before 1945 were converts from the Democratic Party. Those born after World War II were much more likely always to have been Republican (see table 3.14).
2. About half of the native southerners were converts to the Republican Party. Almost all of the members born outside the South had always been Republican. Northern migrants have clearly been an important source of new blood for the Republican Party in southern states (see table 3.15).
3. Most of the younger members were home-grown southerners; over a third of the older members were migrants (see table 3.16).
4. They are virtually all quite conservative, with high ACU ratings, low ADA ratings.[44] Twenty-two of the 48 southern Republicans had a net score (ACU − ADA rating) of 90 or above in 1993.[45] Another eight scored 80 or above. Lincoln Diaz-Balart of south Florida and Arthur Ravenel of South Carolina scored a net of 40 points conservative above liberal. These were the most liberal of the 48 southern Republicans in the 103rd Congress.

TABLE 3.14. Party Affiliation by Age of Southern Republican House Members (103rd Congress)

| Date of birth | Once a Democrat | Always a Republican |
| --- | --- | --- |
| Born pre-1945 | 13 | 18 |
| Born after 1945 | 5 | 12 |

N = 48

Sources: Interviews and *Politics in America*, 1992, 1994; William Finnegan, "Letter from Miami: The Cuban Strategy," *The New Yorker*, March 18, 2004, p. 74.

TABLE 3.15. Party Affiliation by Region of Birth of
Southern Republican House Members (103rd Congress)

| Place of birth | Once a Democrat | Always a Republican |
| --- | --- | --- |
| Native South | 15 | 18 |
| Born outside South | 3 | 12 |

N = 48

Sources: Interviews and *Politics in America*, 1992, 1994; William Finnegan, "Letter from Miami: The Cuban Strategy," *The New Yorker*, March 18, 2004, p. 74.

I suppose there is a mild irony in the fact that it was the arrival in Congress in the 1970s of conservative Republicans that enabled the House of Representatives to move to the left and become a force for liberalism and for mainstream Democratic activism within the political system as a whole. This movement toward liberalism could not have happened until conservative Democrats, principally from the South, disappeared from the Democratic caucus. The disappearance could not have happened without the rise of the Republican Party in the southern states. The Republican Party could not have arisen without migration from the North: affluent retirees, people attracted to centers of white-collar employment, transportation, and finance, personnel surrounding military bases. All this demo-

TABLE 3.16. Age by Region of Birth of Southern Republican House Members (103rd Congress)

| Place of birth | Born before 1945 | Born after 1945 |
| --- | --- | --- |
| Native South | 19[a] | 14 |
| Born outside South | 12 | 3 |

N = 48

[a]Michael Bilirakis was born in Tarpon Springs, on Florida's west coast, in 1930; hence, we classify him as a native. However, he spent virtually all his early years in western Pennsylvania and worked his way through the University of Pittsburgh as a steel worker, returning only in 1960 to Florida to go to law school. He became a Republican in 1970, and in 1993 represented territory including his place of birth. There is a strong Greek American community there, descended from migrants who harvested sponges off the coast. The district also contains many retirees.

Source: Interviews and *Politics in America*, 1992, 1994, 1996.

graphic growth and change helped traditional white conservative south-erners resolve their disagreements with the national Democratic Party by moving into the ranks of the Republicans.

It makes sense to think that, sooner or later, political parties at the grass roots respond to demographic changes, and that demographic changes respond to changes in patterns of investment and technological capacity. Automobiles, arguably, created suburbs. Skyscrapers (steel skeletons, elevators) arguably, transformed cities. Barbed wire and the railroad changed the West. In the South, so it seems, a comparable technological innovation was air conditioning.

Could economic development have taken place without migration, and migration without air conditioning? I am inclined to doubt it mainly because Republican voting for Congress in the South did not take off immediately after the heavy investments of the late 1930s and World War II but waited a full decade for people to move down to produce its first safe seat. Were there other causes of southern economic development beside air conditioning? Undoubtedly, but one wonders whether in the absence of air conditioning they would have been sufficient to draw permanent settlers down from less tropical parts of the United States.[46]

# 4

## CONSEQUENCES: TOWARD
## A MORE RESPONSIBLE
## TWO-PARTY SYSTEM?

Roughly from the mid-1970s onward, party cohesion in the House of Representatives reached record high points owing to the decline in the population of Dixiecrats and a marked increase in the disposition of the House Democratic leadership to use the tools placed in their hands by the caucus to shape a partisan agenda. To a surprising extent, the House over the last quarter century has become the home of the sort of politics fondly anticipated in such utopian documents as the 50-year-old *Toward a More Responsible Two-Party System* issued by the long-gone Committee on Political Parties of the American Political Science Association.[1]

Party cohesion in roll-call voting is one indication of the modernization of congressional behavior (see table 4.1 and figure 4.1). The loss of independent power by committee chairmen, a second indicator, has also coincided with a sharp increase in the party loyalty of their voting (see table 4.2[2] The changes from the mid-1960s to 1980 and beyond are striking. In the earlier period 13 out of 20 chairmen were southerners, including leaders of all the most important committees. The average party unity score of this group was 45, well below the average of 56 for the group as a whole. By 1980 only five southerners led House committees, with a jumped-up party unity average of 56 (compared with 70 for the entire group of 1980 chairmen). In the 1990s the number of southern chairmen persisted at half a dozen with an average party unity score of 86, roughly the same as the average score (93) for the entire population of Democratic committee chairmen. These findings are consistent with the operation of two processes: both the shrinkage of southern influence overall in the

TABLE 4.1. Party Unity

| Congress | Southern Democrats | Non-southern Democrats |
|---|---|---|
| 80 (1947–48) | 79 | 88 |
| 81 (1949–50) | 67 | 89 |
| 82 (1951–52) | 61 | 92 |
| 83 (1953–54)[a] | 71 | 81 |
| 84 (1955–56) | 72 | 86 |
| 85 (1957–58) | 68 | 85 |
| 86 (1959–60) | 68 | 86 |
| 87 (1961–62) | 65 | 91 |
| 88 (1963–64) | 67 | 93 |
| 89 (1965–66) | 52 | 90 |
| 90 (1967–68) | 49 | 89 |
| 91 (1969–70) | 48 | 82 |
| 92 (1971–72) | 45 | 81 |
| 93 (1973–74) | 53 | 83 |
| 94 (1975–76) | 52 | 84 |
| 95 (1977–78) | 54 | 80 |
| 96 (1979–80) | 62 | 82 |
| 97 (1981–82) | 59 | 85 |
| 98 (1983–84) | 67 | 88 |
| 99 (1985–86) | 76 | 90 |
| 100 (1987–88) | 80 | 91 |
| 101 (1989–90) | 77 | 90 |
| 102 (1991–92) | 78 | 89 |
| 103 (1993–94) | 83 | 91 |
| 104 (1995–96) | 76 | 87 |
| 105 (1997–98) | 79 | 87 |

[a]Not adjusted

Note: All party unity scores, save for the 83rd Congress, have been adjusted to discount the effect of absences. The party unity score reported here is: Agree / (Agree + Disagree). *Congressional Quarterly* did not report the party unity scores for the 83rd Congress in a way that allowed for the adjustment.

Source: *Congressional Quarterly Almanac*, various years.

House Democratic Party and the liberalization of Democratic southerners who remained (see table 4.3).

These developments were rooted in trends operating to change the composition of Congress, especially technological and demographic trends leading to a two-party South. I have argued that in order to liberalize the House Democratic Party, and therefore to liberalize the policy outputs of the House of Representatives as long as Democrats controlled the House, it

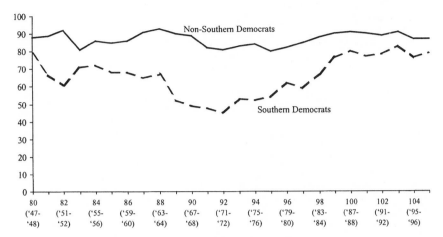

Figure 4.1: Southern and Non-Southern Democratic Party Unity Scores

was necessary for the Republican Party to prosper and grow in strength sufficient to create a two-party South. Without the rise of the Republican Party in the South, the consolidation of the House Democratic caucus into an instrument of mainstream Democratic liberalism could not have happened.

Almost none of this occurred in Sam Rayburn's time, and very little of it was visible while John McCormack was Speaker (1963–71). Most of the organizational changes happened on Carl Albert's watch (1971–77). Albert was more aware of them than some of his colleagues, but he was a Speaker little inclined to use in an aggressive way the new levers of power the caucus pressed upon him.[3] And this was also true, but to a lesser extent, of Albert's successor Tip O'Neill (1977–87). O'Neill's Speakership coincided with the presidencies of Jimmy Carter and Ronald Reagan. Carter presented O'Neill a problem because he and his aides had run against Washington and had a disdain for Congress[4] and because he ran a highly ineffective legislative liaison operation that dovetailed badly with whatever help he might receive from a newly empowered Speaker.[5] Even so, O'Neill was notably forthcoming. For example, he put Carter's early energy program on a fast track, using new organizational powers to set up a special committee that quickly reported a bill much to Carter's liking.[6] That this bill then languished for months in the Senate is another story. O'Neill's was the era of task forces and the submissions of bills to multiple committees, both innovations in House leadership tending to constrain the

TABLE 4.2. Party Loyalty of Chairmen, Committee Chair Party Unity Scores, 1965, 1980, and 1993

| Committee | 1965 Chair | Unity | 1980 Chair | Unity | 1993 Chair | Unity |
|---|---|---|---|---|---|---|
| Agriculture | Cooley-NC | 47 | Foley-WA | 85 | de la Garza-TX | 80 |
| Appropriations | Mahon-TX | 64 | Whitten-MS | 46 | Natcher-KY | 92 |
| Armed Services | Rivers-SC | 30 | Price-IL | 92 | Dellums-CA | 99 |
| Banking | Patman-TX | 81 | Reuss-WI | 78 | Gonzalez-TX | 95 |
| Budget | | | Giaimo-CT | 53 | Sabo-MN | 98 |
| District of Columbia | McMillan-SC | 21 | Dellums-CA | 79 | Stark-CA | 96 |
| Education and Labor | Powell-NY | 71 | Perkins-KY | 70 | Ford-MI | 97 |
| Foreign Affairs | Morgan-PA | 94 | Zablocki-WI | 92 | Hamilton-IN | 83 |
| Government Operations | Dawson-IL | 87 | Brooks-TX | 74 | Conyers-MI | 97 |
| House Administration | Burleson-TX | 42 | Thompson-NJ | 60 | Rose-NC | 93 |
| Interior and Insular Affairs/Natural Resources | Aspinall-CO | 70 | Udall-AZ | 72 | Miller-CA | 98 |
| Interstate and Foreign Commerce/Energy and Commerce | Harris-AR | 68 | Staggers-WV | 70 | Dingell-MI | 92 |
| Judiciary | Celler-NY | 61 | Rodino-NJ | 59 | Brooks-TX | 89 |
| Merchant Marine and Fisheries | Bonner-NC | 15 | Murphy-NY | 53 | Studds-MA | 99 |
| Post Office and Civil Service | Murray-TN | 47 | Hanley-NY | 81 | Clay-MO | 89 |
| Public Works | Fallon-MD | 80 | Johnson-CA | 93 | Mineta-CA | 95 |
| Rules | Smith-VA | 19 | Bolling-MO | 86 | Moakley-MA | 98 |
| Science and Astronautics/ Technology | Miller-CA | 81 | Fuqua-FL | 64 | Brown-CA | 98 |
| Small Business | | | Smith-IA | 81 | LaFalce-NY | 89 |
| Standards of Official Conduct | | | Bennett-FL | 56 | McDermott-WA | 98 |
| UnAmerican Activities | Willis-LA | 56 | | | | |
| Veterans Affairs | Teague-TX | 42 | Roberts-TX | 41 | Montgomery-MS | 72 |
| Ways and Means | Mills-AR | 56 | Ullman-OR | 65 | Rostenkowski-IL | 94 |
| Average | | 56.6 | | 70.5 | | 92.7 |

Source: *Congressional Quarterly Almanac*, 1965, 1980, 1993. Party unity scores are for the years 1965, 1980, and 1993 for each committee chair. The scores for 1993 are adjusted for absences.

influence of committees and subordinate them to the Speaker as the agent of the caucus.[7]

But O'Neill did not himself put forward an integrated Democratic program, not even after the election of 1980, when Ronald Reagan became president and a Republican majority took over the Senate, leaving O'Neill

TABLE 4.3. Party Unity Scores of Southern Chairmen

| 1965 | | 1980 | | 1993 | |
|---|---|---|---|---|---|
| Chairman | Score | Chairman | Score | Chairman | Score |
| Cooley | 47 | Whitten | 46 | De La Garza | 80 |
| Mahon | 64 | Brooks | 74 | Natcher | 92 |
| Rivers | 30 | Fuqua | 64 | Gonzalez | 95 |
| Patman | 81 | Bennett | 56 | Rose | 93 |
| McMillan | 21 | Roberts | 41 | Brooks | 89 |
| Burleson | 42 | | | Montgomery | 72 |
| Harris | 68 | | | | |
| Bonner | 15 | | | | |
| Murray | 47 | | | | |
| Smith | 19 | | | | |
| Willis | 56 | | | | |
| Teague | 42 | | | | |
| Mills | 56 | | | | |
| Average: 45 (57) | | Average: 56 (70) | | Average: 86 (93) | |
| Share of chairmanships: 13/20 or .65 | | Share of chairmanships: 5/22 or .23 | | Share of chairmanships: 6/22 or .27 | |

Note: Figures in parentheses are party unity averages for all committee chairmen.

Source: *Congressional Quarterly Almanacs* 1965, 1980, 1993.

as the senior Democratic officeholder in the nation's capital. Very near the end of his life O'Neill (ghosted by the talented Gary Hymel) wrote: "When I was Speaker, I would sometimes be criticized for not establishing a lot of leadership policy positions. On the things that were important to me and the party, we had positions. But a Speaker who issues too many pronouncements and insists on his positions all the time cannot be successful in bringing people together."[8]

O'Neill upheld traditional Democratic values with sufficient tenacity to attract strong personal criticism from Republicans in the House, and even an expensive televised advertising attack campaign paid for by Republican funds.[9] More expressive of O'Neill's old-shoe style was the fact that throughout his Speakership, O'Neill maintained an occasional golf date with Bob Michel, his Republican counterpart in the House, and stories—probably exaggerated—were put about that O'Neill and President Reagan cultivated good personal relations after hours.[10]

Nonetheless, important changes were brewing in the congressional environment.

## The Retreat from Bipartisanship
## in Committee

The packing of the Rules Committee in 1961 is an example of confrontation between a bipartisan coalition on a committee and the majority of the majority party. It was the first and most dramatic such confrontation in modern times, but not the only one. Many of the committees, especially the stronger ones, were run through bipartisan coalitions. These coalitions were not always or necessarily manifestations of the alliance between Dixiecrats and Republicans that was the source of liberal Democratic frustration, in part because not all committees dealt with civil rights or with other subject matter central to the major conflicts that agitated American sectional politics in the post–New Deal era. But this exemption from the battleground can scarcely be granted to the Ways and Means Committee, a body whose legislative writ includes tax legislation, social security and social welfare, Medicare, and the regulation of foreign trade.

Under the stewardship (1957–74) of Wilbur Mills, the Ways and Means Committee operated consensually, across party lines. Carl Albert's account reflects the received wisdom:

> One of the first bills that [Mills] . . . presented as chairman had come out of a divided committee and was beaten on the floor. Wilbur Mills never forgot his humiliation. From that day onward, he never produced a bill until he was certain it would pass. He was absolutely obsessed with having the overwhelming support of his committee, including the support of its ten Republican members, before producing a bill.[11]

This operational style produced a strong alliance between Mills and John Byrnes of Wisconsin, who for many years (1963–72) was the ranking member on the Republican side.[12] Byrnes recalled:

> Of course, the person I got the closest to was Wilbur Mills. Part of the reason that the period I had in Congress was so enjoyable was that our relationship was an enjoyable one. Wilbur was a very fair chairman. . . . The system encouraged it, and Mills was sympathetic with . . . the idea that what you tried to do is develop a consensus . . . [Y]ou've got to have some Republicans to have a consensus . . . [D]uring that period, you had ten Republicans and fifteen Democrats. I could get those Republicans pretty much to be together. . . . On the Democratic side, though, there were always two or three Democrats who were more philosophically attuned with the Republican position. . . . If they were going to really make

it an issue, rather then try to find a consensus, you could end up thirteen to twelve with the Republicans winning . . .

There was another factor that I think dictated this idea for the consensus of a committee. . . . [W]e had what they called the 'closed rule'— no amendments—which meant that you had to come in with something that was going to be fairly satisfactory to the membership, otherwise they were going to be raising hell about that closed rule, which they were doing anyway, more and more. So that more and more you had to look to make sure you had developed something that was consistent with what the House would accept and which was fairly a consensus bill.

All during that period the effort in the committee was to have at least twenty-two members in support of a proposition; try to get something that would produce at least that kind of result. Nobody on the committee really, in the early stages, had the idea that your objective should be to develop issues. It was more that if you had a problem, let's try to find a solution, rather than to develop partisan issues—the Democrats favoring this, and the Republicans favoring something else. The attitude was: let's try to develop a consensus. As a result of that, it was a pleasant operation. You weren't constantly fighting on philosophical or other grounds and issues. You were trying to look for ways where we could compromise differences and move along. So it was exciting. It wasn't a press release type of committee operation—with the chairman issuing a release and the ranking member of the committee issuing a release . . .

If it had been otherwise, I probably would have retired from Congress earlier. But it was part of the thing that made life worthwhile and interesting. You knew that you did leave some kind of an imprint because any idea that finally developed into a consensus, you knew that you were part of that process.[13]

By the mid-1970s, these conditions changed. Julian Zelizer makes it a point to say that when Al Ullman of Oregon took over as temporary chairman in 1974 while Mills recovered from surgery, he "earned the respect of liberal Democrats by designing legislation without consulting Republicans."[14] Allen Schick says, "Ullman abandoned Mills's practice of involving Republicans in the development of legislation. With no stake in the committee's work, the Republicans defected in droves."[15] Randall Strahan comments:

After the 1970's reforms—especially the new procedures requiring election of committee chairmen by the Democratic caucus—created strong incentives for a more partisan orientation and greater attentiveness to majority party members . . . Ways and Means Republican Barber B. Conable, Jr., (N.Y.) [said,] "There can't be a [bipartisan] consensus . . . because his position as chairman depends on his party, not on us." As another committee Republican described Ullman's situation as chairman, "He always had to be looking over his shoulder at the Democratic caucus."[16]

In 1974, Wilbur Mills had refused to permit a floor vote on the famous tax bugaboo of liberals, the oil depletion allowance. In 1975, Catherine Rudder reports Ullman

> supported this position with the suggestion that the matter be taken up in a subsequent bill, but [William] Green (D-PA) and Sam Gibbons (D-FL), along with five new members of the Ways and Means Committee, gathered the required 50 signatures and petitioned for a caucus vote. That amendment and another . . . were permitted. Green and his allies won the removal of the allowance on the floor of the House. . . . Having lost that battle, Ullman began to realize his subservient position vis-à-vis the caucus. In short, the Ways and Means Committee had been and would probably continue to be overruled on certain matters, given the current predilections of the Democratic caucus.[17]
>
> One member of the committee . . . commented, "The changes in the Ways and Means Committee and the House changes are tied together. The chairman must react differently from the way he reacted in the past. He's not protected by seniority. This causes a tremendous change in the way the committee operates."
>
> To the extent that the changes have undercut Ullman's ability to lead the committee, Ullman has tried to overcome this difficulty by making use of the Democratic caucus on the committee. He tries to forge agreement in closed meetings among the Democrats. He employed this method with the energy bill by setting up task forces composed of Democrats and with the tax revision bill in which the final compromise was hammered out in a secret caucus meeting. Inevitably, this method of operation arouses the ire of Republicans whose response is to vote en masse against Ullman in committee. This method also breaks up the conservative coalition of Republicans and southern Democrats on the committee. A senior Republican complained, "The Republicans feel cut out and therefore resist supporting the chairman. . . . The committee is polarized. It's partisan. The Republicans are responding to being cut out of the process." Said another, "The Republicans have to act together. . . . It's the only way we have to make our position felt." Ullman, in turn, has publicly mentioned that he resents the consistent and staunch Republican opposition that he has confronted in the committee.[18]

Ullman was not reelected in 1980. His successor, Dan Rostenkowski, was by instinct and by practice a believer in bipartisan accommodation. His biographer, Richard Cohen, reports:

"Rostenkowski always talked about how we are the Cadillac of committees," said Tom Downey of New York. "He overstated the point a bit. He
remembered the committee in its best, collegial days under Mills." As
the years passed, the changes in the House eventually forced Rostenkowski to abandon some of his bipartisan instincts. "When Dan assumed
the captaincy, he made a strong point that he wanted a majority in each
party," said Republican [Bill] Frenzel [Minn.]. "But he failed to do that
... the House was becoming more polarized. And the Democrats were
driving that."[19]

The Ways and Means Committee in the Mills–Byrnes years was famous
for the bipartisanship of its atmosphere, for the collegiality of its internal
operations, and for the effectiveness of its collective work on the floor of
the House and in conference. It was not the only committee that ran in
this fashion. Richard Fenno's great ethnographic portrait of the Appropriations Committee tells much the same story, of a committee in which
internal norms are not those of partisanship but rather of devotion to a
mutually shared mission of guardianship over the U.S. Treasury. These
norms were well established by the middle of the twentieth Century, sustained by mechanisms of recruitment and internal socialization on both
sides of the aisle, and universally reckoned to be bulwarks of the committee's extraordinary influence in the political system at large, where its con-
clusions about the shape of the U.S. budget, year after year, provided by
far the most important imprint on the entire process.[20]

I quote at length Fenno's painstaking description of the Appropriations
Committee's practices as of the mid-1960s leading to "minimization of
partisanship."

The norms which define the committee's various decision-making
roles emphasize that committee decisions should not be majority party
decisions. They should be majority and minority party decisions, worked
out cooperatively at every stage and whenever possible. Committee members believe that interparty agreement is a prerequisite for their influence
in the chamber. Normally each subcommittee would rather produce a
bill which satisfied the minority than a bill which maximizes the advantages for a majority. They want to be able to go to the House floor and
say—as they normally do—"This is one [sub]committee where you will
find no partisan politics. We carry on the hearings and we mark up the
bill and we compromise our differences. We bring a bill to the floor of
the House each year with the unanimous approval of the [sub]committee
members." "The subcommittee's approach has never been partisan and
the subcommittee was unanimous in its findings. The recommendations

were unaltered by the full Committee and the bill was reported to the House by a unanimous vote."

Subcommittee integration holds the key to Committee integration. And, for the subcommittee, the condition of integration is that the key votes of chairman and ranking minority member mesh rather than conflict. The attempt to achieve such role reciprocity is reflected in the expectation that the two cooperate and consult in Committee decision-making. When they do, partisanship will automatically decline. Thus, one ranking minority member described the relationship with his chairman:

"I have worked closely with him and can say that we have never had a minute's disagreement during the time we served together. As ranking minority member, I received every consideration which could possibly be expected from [the] chairman. In fact it can be safely said that under [his] chairmanship there were no parties in the subcommittee—we were all working for the same goal and working shoulder to shoulder."

[A]n important exchange of rewards occurs. The chairman gains support for this leadership and the ranking minority member gains intra-committee influence. The Committee as a whole ensures against drastic change in its internal structure by giving to its key minority member a stake in its operation. Chairmen and ranking minority members will, in the course of time, exchange official positions. To the degree that the roles associated with the positions mesh, a switch in occupants will not heighten conflict in the subcommittee.[21] . . .

The close working relationship of Clarence Cannon and John Taber, whose service on the Committee (at the close of the 87th Congress) totaled 70 years, and who exchanged the position of Committee Chairman and ranking minority member for 20 years, highlighted and strengthened the reciprocity of roles existing in the group. Despite their radically different personalities and voting records, the two men concurred that "We have a lot in common," "We stand shoulder to shoulder," "We usually agree," and "We are both on the conservative side" when it comes to the business of the committee. "Many times," said Cannon, "the two of us could sit right here at this table and go over the whole schedule—authorizations and all. If we saw something that ought to come out, we'd take it out; if we saw something that ought to go in, we'd put it in."

It was Cannon and Taber who inaugurated and sustained the powerfully integrative arrangement whereby the ranking minority member as well as the Chairman served as ex officio member of every subcommittee. Committee members who watched them in action reiterated that, "They work very closely together," "They fight for the same things," or "They've been here so long they understand each other." "Mr. Cannon confides in Mr. Taber and he confides in absolutely nobody else," said a veteran subcommittee chairman. A senior staff member described the mutual understanding that had been built up over the years and that checked the force of partisanship:

They understood each other. They knew they were members of opposite parties and that party loyalties would pull. But they knew where they each stood. They differed widely on such things as public power. But they would vote against each other on that and then join the next day and take up the fight together. They knew where to find each other on the issues. They knew each other's idiosyncrasies. But they forgot past battles and didn't dwell on old issues. In this way they were both big men. They had been together for a long time. They went through many eras together. They were old men and they grew old together.

In a system where the teaching of committee norms and role behavior is accomplished primarily by example, the impact of the Cannon–Taber comity multiplied itself as a model for others. Their counterparts on the subcommittees—long-time chairman/ranking minority twosomes such as Representatives Gary (D., Va) and Canfield (R., NJ) (1949–1961); Whitten (D., Miss.) and Andersen (R., Minn.) (1949–1963); Kirwan (D., Ohio) and Jensen (R., Iowa) (1949–1963); Fogarty (D., R.I.) and Laird (R., Wisc.) (1959 to present [1966]); Mahon (D., Texas) and Ford (R., Mich) (1959–1965); Thomas (D., Texas) and Ostertag (R, N.Y.) (1959–1965); Rooney (D., N.Y.) and Bow (R., Ohio) (1959–present [1966]), have had an example to follow as well as time to work out such idiosyncratic techniques of accommodation as might be necessary.[22]

This is not a picture of committee democracy, but rather of sharply restrained partisanship that had evolved into a subculture grounded in a bipartisan consensus. It is difficult to overestimate the power of this subculture to shape the attitudes of participants toward the political process. A decade after Fenno wrote his elaborate account, the novelist John Hersey spent a week following Appropriations Committee alumnus Gerald Ford, by then the occupant of the White House, on his daily routine. Listening to President Ford evaluate the prospects for a portion of his legislative program, Hersey says:

The President, thoroughly at home with Congressional give-and-take, talks zestfully, predicting how this man and that man will finally come down. He names some who are dead set against him; he speaks their first names with fondness.

The President stirs with pleasure—it almost seems as if he has suddenly walked through a door into his real self. Familiar names: the old horse-trading routines. Even his hands seem independently to enjoy themselves now as they settle into the little enactments of bargaining they know so well—counting, weighing, arresting; a finger encircles a thumb (We have that man), knuckles rap the desk (Try again), the whole hand flaps (He's hopeless), reminiscences about motions to recommit like memories of great football games. The names like candies in his mouth: Frank, Gale, Hugh, John, Al, Herman, Gaylord, Barber, Mike.[23]

As in the case of the Rules Committee, not every committee of the House of Representatives, even when a bipartisan coalition existed, was restrained in its partisanship. The Education and Labor committee was noted for its partisan divisions, in which pro-education and pro-labor Democrats clashed regularly with anti-federal aid to education and anti-union Republicans.[24] Both parties assigned members to the committee upholding the party's point of view. But even on the Education and Labor Committee, at least on education matters, John Brademas of Indiana has testified that during his last decade in Congress (in the 1970s):

> As a subcommittee chairman, . . . planning hearings on a bill I had introduced, I would invite the senior Republican on the committee to call some of his own witnesses to testify. Then in markup session, I would ask him what amendments he, to support the measure, felt essential and, in both committee and floor debate would praise his efforts as we joined forces to produce a majority for the bill.[25]

Partisan differences threatened the peace and civility of the Foreign Affairs Committee, the main business of which was the annual foreign aid authorization, after the Eisenhower presidency and the departure from the committee (1963) of Walter Judd (Minn.) when the Republican Committee on Committees appointed foreign aid skeptics.[26] But hot spots of partisan contentiousness within the committee system were, on the whole, exceptional. The consensual Appropriations Committee was very large, occupying the efforts of 50-plus members; the conflictual Rules Committee was small, 15 members, all selected in part because they could "take the heat" of partisan combat on the Hill without having to worry overmuch about electoral retribution at home.

Many committees, even when despotically or hierarchically run, such as Agriculture or Armed Services, frequently treated senior members on both sides of the aisle well. Here is what a Republican member told Richard Fenno about the Interior Committee under Wayne Aspinall: "[John] Saylor [R-Pa., ranking member] and Aspinall work so completely together it wouldn't make any difference who was chairman. They don't let politics in. When someone brings up something political, they put the lid on it right away. It couldn't be less partisan."[27] Fenno continues:

The two men had some strong policy disagreements—over conservation and public power; and in that sense, the preceding comment overstates its case. What Aspinall and Saylor shared was a desire to maintain the Committee's reputation for careful, expert, and independent handling of its legislation and, consequently, the confidence of the House. To this end, they worked in conspicuous harmony on all internal procedural matters and compromised on substantive matters whenever possible.[28]

In an interview, Aspinall described his relationship with Saylor:

We did our arguing back and forth in the committee. John Saylor . . . and I used to go to it in the committee meeting, but when we went out of the committee, the consensus was determined. And although there were some arguments on the floor to show the different viewpoints, we never tried to get the Congress to believe in something that the committee wouldn't accept. I'll say this for Congressman Saylor—he's been gone now for almost seven years—he was a valiant fighter in the committee for the purpose of carrying the position of the minority—or as some would say—the opposition. He did his work as an oppositionist on the floor, but never, never tried to upset the action of the committee. And, consequently, our result was, I guess, 100 percent—about as good as you can get, as far as that's concerned.[29]

A remarkable example of bipartisan comity occurred on the uncontroversial Science and Technology Committee. This committee was formed (as the Science and Astronautics Committee) in 1959 as a response to the 1958 Russian success in space with Sputnik. Its jurisdiction other than a few odds and ends consisted of the authorization of the NASA budget, mostly a bipartisan occasion for patriotic cheerleading. Over the years, the committee used its jurisdiction over the National Science Foundation to acquire a portfolio in expertise about science policy generally. Under the leadership of an active subcommittee chairman, Emilio Daddario (D-Conn.), (until he left the House in 1970), it was instrumental in establishing the Office of Technology Assessment (1972)[30] as a freestanding congressional agency and in 1976 the committee reestablished the science advisory office in the Ford White House after President Nixon had closed it down three years earlier.[31]

These were examples of bipartisan efforts enacted while Democrats controlled Congress. When the ranking Republican, Charles Mosher of Ohio, retired in 1977, the Democratic chairman of the committee, Olin Teague of Texas, prevailed upon Mosher to become the committee's staff director, heading up what was already a nonpartisan, professionally accomplished staff. Mosher served 14 months.[32] This was, to put it mildly, an unusual career move for a, by then, veteran member of Congress. It illustrates the high level of bipartisan trust achieved by the committee, perhaps higher than many, but not unique.[33]

On such committees, subcommittees were workshops where those members so inclined could develop a mastery of subject matter satisfying diverse goals: influence within a Washington policy sub-system, sometimes the economic interests of constituents, sometimes both. Increased partisanship threatened the insulation of these workshops and introduced important changes into the working conditions affecting members.

This process of change was illustrated by the House Armed Services Committee. Bruce Keith meticulously documents a decline in the Armed Services Committee's influence on the House floor—its ability to pass bills unamended—from the 91st Congress (1969–70), when Carl Vinson's successor Mendel Rivers (D-S.C.) was chairman, to the 94th Congress (1975–76), under the leadership of Melvin Price of Illinois. Keith comments:

> [O]perating as it had as a nonpartisan committee, the 91st HASC's Republican membership, as a group, was even more loyal to, and in harmony with, the committee majority's goals than the committee's total Democratic membership had been in the past. . . . [T]he higher ranking Republicans participated in the deliberations of HASC's "policy committee" and the Republican member choices for subcommittee billets were regularly satisfied.[34]

The dumping of the four committee chairmen in 1975 (including Hebert of Armed Services) was a powerful indicator that the seniority system had been destabilized. Even so, it was a full decade before the caucus voted (121–118) to replace another chairman, and it happened to Price, by this time age 80, who had succeeded Edward Hebert as the Armed Services Committee chairman in 1975. The move was strongly opposed by Speaker O'Neill,[35] and by the Steering and Policy Committee, which voted 24–0 to endorse Price; but it was strongly supported by the junior members of the Armed Services Committee. One of them, 34-year-old Dave McCurdy of Oklahoma was quoted as saying, "They've got to stop counting the generals and start counting the troops."[36]

The issue was allegedly Price's age and lack of vigor, not policy. "We just want somebody who is going to work and be dynamic," McCurdy said. The next ranking member was the 74-year-old Charles Bennett of Jacksonville, Florida, who was passed over, as were the next four Democratic members who did not run in deference to Bennett. By a vote of 125–103 the caucus chose as chairman (over Bennett) Les Aspin of Wisconsin, age 43, the committee's seventh-ranking member. A defense intellectual with a Ph.D. from MIT, Aspin had earlier been a Pentagon whiz kid in the McNamara era, and despite his gadfly show-horse style, no doubt learned from his former boss Senator William Proxmire,[37] he was universally regarded as knowledgeable on defense issues.

Margaret Shapiro in the *Washington Post* wrote: "In the past few years, Price has become frail, and it often appeared that the committee was being run by its ranking Republican, Rep. William L. Dickinson (R. Ala.). In addition, the committee is dominated by conservative Democrats who have supported [President] Reagan's defense build-up when most House Democrats have not."[38]

Within two years, Aspin was in hot water with the Democratic caucus, which at the next opportunity, at the start of the 100th Congress, voted 130 to 124 to reject the Steering and Policy Committee's recommendation (by a vote of 22 to 8) that he be retained as chairman. Three committee members ran to replace him. After an intensive two-week long campaign, and three successive secret ballots, Aspin was restored to his chairmanship by a caucus vote of 133 to 116 over Marvin Leath of Texas.

Among the supporters of the conservative Mr. Leath was Ron Dellums of California, possibly the most liberal member of the Armed Services Committee and of the Democratic caucus. He later wrote:

> The Democratic caucus—a rambunctious and liberal-leaning group whose leadership was now emerging from the "Watergate class" of 1974—pressed the leadership of the party harder on the MX, on Central America, and on other military and foreign policy issues. Aspin's use of the Armed Services chairmanship to thwart the caucus's effort to terminate the missile system, and his support for the Reagan backed Nicaraguan "contras", distressed many in that group . . . [W]hile Aspin did not abuse members on the committee in the way that Hebert had done, neither did he run its deliberations with open solicitation of the views of all. He was a loner in many respects, and those with whom he did consult were often not members of the committee.[39]

Once the original recommendation of the Steering and Policy Committee to reappoint Aspin was rejected, the committee then voted (16–11) to endorse the most senior member of Armed Services, Charles Bennett of Florida.[40] Bennett survived the first secret ballot of the caucus (Aspin 91, Leath 69, Bennett 44, Nicholas Mavroules of Massachusetts 35), but lost in the second (Aspin 108, Leath 91, Bennett 47) and so under the rules had to drop out.[41]

Amid copious protestations that he had learned his lesson, Aspin re-
sumed his chairmanship.[42] The freedom of a chairman to make cross-party
alliances had become vulnerable to second-guessing by the caucus. Junior
members of the committee on the Democratic side of the aisle might monitor the behavior of chairmen and organize against them in the caucus as
Marvin Leath did (following Aspin's tactics against Price two years earlier)
and in open opposition to the wishes of the Speaker and the Steering and
Policy Committee. Had Marvin Leath's own voting record in the support
of Democratic Party positions not been so weak, he might well have succeeded in overturning Aspin.[43]

The attack on Les Aspin's chairmanship was an important sign of a
change that had already taken place in which the management options
available to committee leaders were sharply curtailed. The powers of the
caucus to replace chairmen, relatively newly acquired powers, meant that
something like a party line on policy could be enforced. No wonder the
party unity scores of chairmen soared in the 1980s and 1990s. This re-
striction on the behavior of chairmen was bound also to have a significant
impact on the Republicans and their style of opposition.

## Two Strategies of Opposition

John Byrnes of Wisconsin repeatedly referred to his collaborative working
relationship on the Ways and Means Committee with Wilbur Mills as "enjoyable." It should come as no surprise that in an institution where the
work is organized primarily around committees that the manner in which
committees are run has a deep impact on whether or not members of
Congress enjoy their working lives.

In 1973 Albert Hunt did a feature story in the *Wall Street Journal* about
Byrnes's probable successor, Barber Conable of Genesee County, New York,
referring to Conable's "legislative acumen and diligence" making him "an
important Republican force in the committee's key jurisdictional areas."
Conable is quoted as saying, "I went on Ways and Means to be astride the
great issues."[44] By the 1980s, working conditions were less enjoyable for
senior Republicans, Conable included. William Connelly and John Pitney
interviewed him in the late 1980s as part of a study of House Republicans.
They report: "Conable attributed his own retirement [in 1984] in part to
his waning influence on Ways and Means: 'In the later years, anything I
got was by the grace of Danny [Rostenkowski, the committee chairman].' "

"Some House Republicans," Conable said, "don't even get crumbs. All you get from Jack Brooks (D-Texas, Chairman of the Judiciary Committee) are fang marks."

Connelly and Pitney quote from another former member:

> [At one time] you were looked upon by your colleagues on the other side of the aisle as first, a member of the House, second, as the member from [your state], and third, as a Republican. That order has been reversed. Now the defining characteristic that labels everybody initially is party. If a member is a Republican, they don't much care about him.[45]

It was certainly not true that committee work in the earlier period was universally regarded as a respite from the rigors of partisan combat. But for some committees this was the case. These committees frequently took great pride in delivering to the floor proposals that had bipartisan approval and reflected bipartisan cooperation in the framing of legislation. And in those committees, members of the minority party who took a substantive interest in legislation, and who were prepared to do homework, could expect to be taken seriously.

These conditions sustained a strategy of half-a-loaf opposition that focused on opportunities for Republicans to make a meaningful impact on the course of legislative work. Members of the minority party who espoused this strategy argued from the premise that it was the legislation that mattered, and that they could maximize their influence over legislative substance by restraining their opposition and accommodating to the formation of bipartisan majorities.

Bob Michel of Illinois, Republican leader from 1981 to 1994, was a forceful advocate of this point of view. When he announced his retirement he said, "I didn't come to Congress on a campaign of trashing Congress. . . . Are you going to be a player, or are you just going to be a constant, harping critic?"

Michel, who represented a district surrounding Peoria, Illinois for 38 years, was an active practitioner of politics as a branch of human relations, deploying an impressive array of social skills. For many years he pitched for the Republican side in the annual congressional baseball game and sang with a sturdy baritone on numerous festive occasions. In the early days, before congressional benefits included reimbursement for frequent trips back home, he said, "Those of us who were raising families saved money by piling in the doggone station wagon" with a group of colleagues including Dan Rostenkowski (D) of Chicago and Harold Collier (R) who drove erratically. Michel said, " 'Gosh darn, Harold,' the others would say,

'Can't you keep that thing from jerking around? We're trying to sleep.' "
He made friends readily on the floor of the House: "Oh shucks," he said,
"some of the debate was dull as can be [but] you use the time visiting
with members . . . gassing with the members on the other side of the
aisle."[46]

> When Newt [Gingrich] succeeded me, [Michel said,] I said congratula-
> tions and said here you are with a majority, something I've never been
> able to have, but take it in good grace. Talk to the minority and because,
> you know, I reminded him about [Sam] Rayburn's [D-Tex.] Speakership,
> when he and Joe Martin [R-Mass.] changed places a couple times, going
> way back. So you may not always be in the majority, you may be in the
> minority again. You like to be treated the same way. So do unto others
> as you'd have them do unto you.
>
> Well, Newt, let's face it, his personality wasn't exactly that type. Part
> of it at that time was they weren't political adversaries, they were real
> enemies. . . . I [am] reminded of how [it was] when Tom Foley [D-Wash.]
> was Speaker. Tom was so good, from the standpoint of Speaker, and me
> in the minority, that we alternated our weekly meetings between our
> offices. That was a great gesture on the part of Tom. There were those
> on my side who would say, well, we were too cozy or we talked too much
> or I wasn't vigorous enough in my trashing the Speaker.
>
> My whole methodology in making things go and that I had to do it
> was, when you're in the minority, you ain't gonna win nuthin' with a
> solid vote on your side and none on the other side. The pragmatism, the
> practical situation is that you've gotta get votes from the other side to
> make anything go.[47]

Until the early 1980s, this was more or less the prevailing wisdom
among Republicans, but it was by no means the only strategy on offer to
Republican members. Notable for his development of the main alternative
to the get-along, go-along style espoused by the Republican leadership was
Newt Gingrich of Georgia, a self-identified bomb thrower, leader of a group
that believed that his colleagues had been too acquiescent in their minority
status and needed to pursue a strategy of overt obstreperousness with the
ends in view of discrediting Democratic stewardship of the House and
overturning the Democratic majority.

Gingrich's closest ally, Robert Walker of Pennsylvania, told Connelly and
Pitney:

> We've had an attitude among many of our more senior members that
> because they didn't see any way out of minority status, that they found

it easier to cooperate with Democrats to get a percentage of the action in the House rather than presenting alternatives, and so . . . much of what came to the floor ended up being bipartisan in nature as it came out of the committee. The only people fighting the committees tended to be people from off the committees, and so . . . we had no real case to take to the country.[48]

Gingrich said that his tactics were not anti-Congress:

No, only if they define the institution as corrupt and Democratic. I mean, if by the institution they mean the current model of Democratic control of the House, the current one-sided control of the Rules Committee, the current rigging of the rules, the current liberal domination of scheduling and the current one-sided stamping on behalf of the Democrats, then yes, I'm interested in breaking up the Democratic monopoly of power.[49]

There was in fact little in the way of empirical evidence to sustain the view that bringing the House into disrepute would elect Republicans. But even if convincing national electorates that the House was in disarray operated indiscriminately against all incumbents, there were still more Democratic incumbents than Republicans.

The effort began modestly, in the O'Neill era. Gingrich and his allies (who around 1983 took to referring to themselves as the Conservative Opportunity Society) adopted the tactic of using the time set aside each day in the House calendar for individual speeches unconnected with pending business on the floor to launch a concerted attack on Democratic management of the House. They had noticed that the C-SPAN television network accepting the daily feed from House-owned cameras covered this part of the House day with the same automated impartiality with which it covered actual floor debate. To an untutored television spectator, wild allegations delivered to an empty House were indistinguishable from the real business of Congress. From the point of view of Gingrich and his colleagues, this offered a free gift of publicity; the somewhat spurious stamp of officiality was an added benefit.

The tactic so enraged Speaker O'Neill that he directed the House cameras to violate the agreement governing their presence in the chamber and pan around to show the sea of empty chairs to which Gingrich and his allies were playing. Soon thereafter Gingrich goaded O'Neill into characterizing an attack on absent members as "the lowest thing I have ever seen in 32 years service," words that were taken down and ruled unparliamentary.[50]

This event—a big tactical victory for Gingrich—took place in May 1984, more or less pursuant to a strategy that Gingrich had laid out publicly in January. As Steven Roberts reported in the *New York Times*:

> Junior members made a decision to "systematically challenge the way the Democrats run the House," according to Representative Gingrich, the Georgian who heads the loose-knit hit squad that includes about a dozen members.
>
> Since Monday, for instance, these Republicans have repeatedly interrupted the House and asked for unanimous consent to bring up bills that would legalize school prayer, mandate a balanced budget and give the President power to veto part of any legislation that reaches his desk. Now, he must veto the whole bill or sign it.
>
> "It's going to be like a Chinese water torture," boasted Mr. Gingrich. "For the next 10 months, the country will see the Democratic leadership consistently block issues that have majority support in this country."
>
> Then, he adds, Republican challengers will try to use these issues against Democratic incumbents in the fall.[51]

This stage of the Conservative Opportunity Society's campaign was mostly a matter of being annoying and unaccommodating, and creating unfavorable publicity. In spite of the risks of such a strategy for the prospects of President Reagan's legislative program in the Democratic-controlled House, COS thinking began to dominate Republican Party strategy.[52] David Rogers wrote in the *Wall Street Journal*:

> No one has seemed more isolated than Minority Leader Robert Michel, a Taft Republican who was Mr. Reagan's faithful general in the last Congress but has since been ignored too often by the White House and his friend the Speaker. "There's no question that the leadership in terms of the floor has moved away from Michel," said a Democratic leadership aide.[53]

Observers point to a marked shift toward the right in the Republican Party in the House from the 1960s to the 1990s and the virtual elimination of northeastern moderate Republicans. John Gilmour comments:

> I did the following tabulation using the Poole and Rosenthal DW-NOMINATE scores.[54] These scores are designed to retain meaning over time. Higher numbers means more conservative. The table [table 4.4] shows the number of moderate-to-liberal (.2 or lower) and conservative

TABLE 4.4.  Growth of Republican Conservatism, 1960–94

| DW-NOMINATE Score | 87th Congress (elected 1960) | 104th Congress (elected 1994) |
|---|---|---|
| .2 or lower (liberal) | 63 | 7 |
| .5 or higher (conservative) | 16 | 94 |

Source: Keith T. Poole and Howard Rosenthal, *Congress: A Political-Economic History of Roll Call Voting* (New York: Oxford University Press, 1997); calculated by John B. Gilmour, personal communication, May 23, 2002.

(.5 and higher) Republicans in the 87th (1960) and 104th (1994) Congresses.

These numbers would sustain an argument that the GOP was moving toward intransigence anyway. The burden of my argument, however, is that in their basic sympathies the center of gravity in the Republican Party as measured by voting was always well to the right, as a comparison of the quite similar voting records of Bob Michel and Newt Gingrich shows (see Appendix table A.1).[55]

David Cohen, an influential liberal lobbyist from the 1960s onward, points out,

> Party responsibility was influenced by . . . Republican discipline . . . Republicans were disciplined about who got on the power committees. . . . Their policy committee got behind recommittal motions and expected the Republicans to vote for them, often changing the thrust of legislation. Lots of that happened in the 1961–71 period—before the record teller vote took command and Democrats were influenced by Republican practices.[56]

It is recognized that Sam Rayburn was induced to pack the Democratic side of the Rules Committee in 1961 largely because his non-aggression pact with Joe Martin broke down when the Republicans replaced Martin as their leader. It is also pertinent to emphasize that Martin's successor, Charles Halleck, proceeded to pack the Republican side of the Rules Committee by replacing the relatively tractable Henry Latham and Hugh Scott with the more consistently partisan Hamer Budge, Carroll Reece, and then when they left Congress, Katharine St. George, Allen Smith, Elmer Hoffman, and William Avery. These last observations argue that notwithstanding the disappearance of liberal Republicans, the Republicans who ran the

party in the House from the 1960s onward for the most part were conservative in their sympathies and what was at issue in the split between
Michel and Gingrich in the 1990s (as, to a lesser extent, was also true of
the earlier differences between Joe Martin and Charlie Halleck) was not
ideology but strategy of opposition.

## An Era of Ill-Feeling

By the mid-1980s Democrats had controlled the House for over 30 consecutive years—an unprecedentedly long time. There began to appear
stories in the newspapers regularly describing the partisan atmosphere on
Capitol Hill as unprecedentedly toxic.[57] The alert Congress-watcher Norman Ornstein gave a thorough rundown of Republican grievances as of
May 1985: "short counts of Republican votes [on the floor], abuse of proxy
voting [in committees] . . . unfair committee and subcommittee assignments."[58] In an especially inflammatory incident, the House determined,
more or less on a party-line vote (10 Democrats joining 180 Republicans
versus 236 Democrats) that Frank McCloskey, Democrat of Indiana, had
won a disputed election in 1984 for Representative from the Eighth Congressional District.[59]

When McCloskey was sworn in Republicans let fly on the floor of the
House with what Ornstein described as "rank vitriol." "You know how to
win votes the old-fashioned way, Mr. Speaker," one member said, "you steal
them." Members used words like "corrupt," "rotten," "thugs," and "rape."
"After the debate," Ornstein wrote, "Republicans stormed out of the chamber en bloc." He quoted moderate upstate New York Republican Sherwood
Boehlert: "There is a cloud hanging over this chamber. The tolerance level
is going down, down and down. Motives are being questioned. Integrity is
being challenged. Name-calling is rampant. Emotionalism is at a fever
pitch, with all-too-frequently nasty results."[60]

There was a precedent for much of this, but it was just over the time
horizons of most contemporary Washington journalists and national politicians: the McCarthy era of the early 1950s, 30 years earlier. The political
atmosphere in those years was also extraordinarily ugly: blacklisting, witch
hunts, loyalty oaths, legislative committees on Un-American activities at
national and state levels, a national "loyalty-security" program, careers
blighted, firings, denunciations, suicides. In retrospect, this seems a peculiar way for the strongest nation on earth to celebrate victory in World
War II. To be sure, there was a core of reality around which the vastly
exaggerated anxieties swirled: the American political system was learning

by trial and error how to wage a Cold War and how to cope with the threat to U.S. interests posed by the Soviet Union.

Amid the uproar, Senator Joseph McCarthy of Wisconsin stood out as a remarkably successful political entrepreneur, with his flamboyant charges of subversive activity, spies, and foreign agents in the government: in the State Department, the U.S. Information Agency, and even the U.S. Army. A very great deal has been written about this period, and so it is something of a puzzle that students seeking to explain the rancorous partisanship of the 1980s and 1990s in Washington did not ponder the parallels with the last such sustained episode in American national politics.

One parallel deserves special consideration: both the 1950s and the later period were notable for the incorporation of anti-system rhetoric into the behavior of ostensibly conservative, mainstream actors. It is not unexpected in a political system as large and as varied as the United States that at all times somewhere in public life crackpots, extremists, sociopaths, and malcontents of many different sorts—left and right—would exist. What needs explaining is why at certain times and places extremist rhetoric is accorded credence and given amplification by more respectable, moderate, and centrist actors. On this reading of the situation, what needs explaining is not why a Joe McCarthy, or a Newt Gingrich, made wild charges but rather why, in McCarthy's case, his far more mainstream colleague Robert A. Taft would encourage him to "keep talking and if one case doesn't work out, he should proceed with another one."[61]

Consider the situation of the national Republican Party in February 1950, when McCarthy rather suddenly emerged into the spotlight. The last big event in national politics had been the presidential election in the autumn of 1948. This was a disaster for the Republican Party, in which Harry Truman, a relatively unpopular, unelected Democratic incumbent, who had succeeded to the office on the death in 1945 of the larger-than-life Franklin Roosevelt, trounced the combined forces of Henry Wallace and Strom Thurmond, both leading significant renegade factions of the Democratic Party, as well as the mainstream Republican nominee, Thomas E. Dewey of New York. After this debacle, Republicans might well have wondered if there were any circumstances at all in which they could contemplate winning the presidency in a regular election. This was the climate in which the uproar created by McCarthy's charges of communist infiltration into the Democratic-led government was welcomed rather than resisted—or toned down—by establishment Republicans. Of Taft, by far the most important Republican in the Senate, William S. White, who covered the Senate in those years for the *New York Times*, wrote, "The debacle of 1948 and the Eastern challenge to [his chairmanship of the Senate Republican Policy Committee] in early 1949—stirred [Taft] in most unfortunate ways. It seemed even to some of his friends and admirers that he began . . . to adopt the notion that almost *any* way to defeat or discredit Truman's plans was acceptable."[62]

Not all Republicans felt that way, of course. Margaret Chase Smith of Maine and Ralph Flanders of Vermont were early and notable senatorial critics of McCarthy. But far more notable were Republican defenders of McCarthy in the Senate, leading figures like Taft of Ohio, Styles Bridges of New Hampshire, William Knowland of California, and Everett Dirksen of Illinois.[63] The Republican national party apparatus sent McCarthy around the country to speak at dinners and gatherings of the faithful, and public opinion polls showed that his grass-roots popularity—contrary to the beliefs of many Washington politicians—was heavily concentrated among Republicans.[64]

Richard Rovere commented that after the election of 1952, Dwight D. Eisenhower's first landslide, it was believed in Washington that McCarthy's campaigning had defeated eight sitting U.S. Senators or candidates for the Senate.[65] Once Eisenhower took office, a Republican administration at last, McCarthy's status should have changed. But McCarthy, now chairman of a committee, continued to make ugly charges, and he was still defended by Republicans—especially Senators and others from the isolationist wing of the party who had favored Robert Taft for president. Eisenhower adopted a policy of calculated passivity toward McCarthy's attacks on the foreign policy and defense establishments—much to the detriment of both.[66] What might have ended more quickly took two years' time and required the unpleasant turmoil of embarrassing televised hearings, the famed Army-McCarthy hearings, before McCarthy's influence finally blew itself out in a motion on the floor of the Senate—supported by only half the Republicans—to censure McCarthy.[67]

Compare the saliency of Republican despondency over losing their best shot at the presidency since 1928 as a key factor in encouraging McCarthy with the equally obtrusive saliency in the 1980s of the Republican failure over what seemed like an endless period to control the House of Representatives. Fewer and fewer Republican members could claim that they had much of a stake in a system that perpetuated their minority status and—owing to changes in the management of the Democratic Party in the House—increasingly deprived them of influence over legislative outcomes. In these circumstances the strategy of no-holds-barred opposition advocated by Newt Gingrich and his allies was bound to gain ground.[68]

Despite—or perhaps because of—similarities with the McCarthy era, it is not an exaggeration to refer to the period from sometime in the middle of the O'Neill Speakership onward as an era of ill-feeling in the House of Representatives, an era that has not yet run its course. This ill-feeling was expressed in many ways and had a profound effect on the functioning of the House. By the time Jim Wright became Speaker, in 1987, relations between the parties had already become strained.

Unlike his predecessors in the Speakership, Wright pursued a strategy of leadership that explicitly mobilized the Democratic caucus to pursue a broad-gauged Democratic program. In the single-minded pursuit of this goal, Wright accentuated tendencies already present to do without the participation of Republicans in the conduct of legislative business. An important byproduct was further to weaken the credibility of go-along, get-along Republicans among their Republican colleagues. By drawing sharp partisan lines, Wright gave Republican moderates—moderates in style, not necessarily in policy preferences—no place to go but into the camp of Republican militants.

There was some irony in this: in 1976 Wright had become majority leader by a single vote in an election in which the two leading candidates, Richard Bolling and Phillip Burton, were expected to be liberal steamrollers. Wright was widely perceived to be of the three the candidate with the soft touch, and certainly the candidate with the fewest passionate enemies.[69] When he succeeded O'Neill, however, Wright pressed forward with an unprecedentedly proactive agenda. John Barry, the journalist who covered Wright's Speakership most intensively says, "He had waited patiently for power, submerging his own agenda through the forty years of politics it took him to become Speaker; now that he had it he intended to use it."[70]

In some ways Wright's initial approach was harder on his fellow Democrats than on Republicans. As he took the reins of leadership, he expanded the whip system and appointed a Chief Deputy Whip (David Bonior, D-Mich.) without consulting or even informing the whip the Democratic caucus elected, Tony Coelho (D-Calif.).[71] He appointed a non-freshman Texan (Jim Chapman) to the Steering and Policy Committee to represent the freshman class, without consulting the freshman class.[72] He attempted (but failed) to annex sole authority to appoint the House Administration Committee, Wayne Hays's former stronghold, with its jurisdiction over petty details of routine life like parking and travel vouchers, threatened the Chairman of the Ways and Means Committee (Dan Rostenkowski, D-Ill.) with reprisals in the caucus if he persisted in bipartisan policy-making on trade issues, and he delayed reappointments to the Rules Committee saying, "I just wanted them to remember they were the Speaker's appointees."[73] He dominated the committee assignment process and grabbed extra office space. The hallmark of all these acts was a driving desire to consolidate power and to neglect concessions to collegiality.[74]

Susan Rasky gave a mixed report in the *New York Times* on Wright's first year as Speaker:

> In the year since Mr. Wright assumed control of the House, he has led that sometimes fractious body through a legislative blitzkrieg of budget, appropriations, tax, trade, environmental, housing, health, and highway and welfare-revision bills. He has also staked out for himself and the Democratic party a highly visible position, squarely at odds with the White House, on policy in Central America . . . [T]he Speaker's determination to set a legislative agenda and his unabashed use of personal and institutional powers to propel it have embittered a Republican minority already frustrated by its lack of influence in a House where Democrats hold sway, 257 to 177.
>
> "The degree of partisanship, the strength of feeling, is more than it has ever been," said [third-ranking House Republican] Rep. Dick Cheney (R-WY). . . . "We had our problems with Tip O'Neill, too, but with Wright it is somehow more bitter."[75]

Republicans were annoyed by Wright's pursuit of an independent foreign policy in Central America and by all manner of managerial issues involving, in particular, the prerogatives of the minority on the floor.[76] One ugly eruption occurred on October 29, 1987. The House Rules Committee reported out a modified closed rule on a budget reconciliation bill that prohibited all points of order against the legislation (including objections that the bill violated provisions of the Budget Act), prevented the minority from offering instructions on a motion to recommit, and included a $6 billion welfare reform initiative without separate debate or vote. A coalition of Republicans and disaffected Democrats defeated this rule on the floor by a vote of 217 to 203. A standing House regulation prevented Wright from bringing up a different rule on the same day—so Wright promptly adjourned the House and reconvened it a few minutes later, technically on a different legislative "day." A new rule for the bill, lacking the welfare provision, was approved, but the bill itself fell short of passage, 207 to 206, as the customary 15 minutes allowed for electronic voting elapsed. Wright, putting his thumb back on the scale, held the vote open for 10 additional minutes while he rounded up Jim Chapman, his obliging colleague from Texas, to switch his vote, allowing the legislation to pass by a single vote. This abuse of the clock although certainly not unprecedented enraged Re-

publicans already irritated at Wright's management style. Rep. Dick Armey
(R-Tex.) sarcastically referred to the incident as "black Thursday-
Thursday," referring to the separate legislative "days." In an interview with
*National Journal* the usually cool and collected Dick Cheney called Wright
a "heavy-handed son of a bitch," and Republicans also responded by tying
the House in procedural knots the following day, even demanding a roll-
call vote on approval of the previous day's journal.[77]

Republican staffers compiled statistics showing a downward trend in
the number of open rules allowing unrestricted amendment of bills reaching the floor, therefore an upward trend in tight control by the majority
of legislative action (see table 4.5).[78]

Four months later, interparty relations appeared to have slipped a notch.
A prominent young Republican member, Vin Weber of Minnesota, said:
"The dislike of Speaker O'Neill was ideological. . . . He was really the sym-
bol of Northeastern liberalism. The dislike of Speaker Wright is different.
Republicans think he is basically and fundamentally unfair; that he does
not have the respect for the institution like Tip; that deep down he is a
mean-spirited person, ruthless in the truest sense of the word."[79]

It was therefore, understandably, not at all unwelcome among Republicans when Gingrich, encouraged by his personal coup against Tip O'Neill,
went after Jim Wright personally. Proclaiming Wright "the least ethical
Speaker in the 20th Century" he filed charges against the Speaker with
the House Committee on Standards of Official Conduct and enlisted the
support of the nonpartisan progressive watchdog group, Common Cause,
in calling for a thorough investigation of Wright's personal finances. This
was the culmination of a systematic campaign of vilification. Eleanor Clift
and Tom Brazaitis report:

TABLE 4.5. Open and Restrictive Rules, 1977–88

| Congress | Speaker | Open rules | | Restrictive | | Total rules |
|---|---|---|---|---|---|---|
| | | Number | % | Number | % | |
| 95 (1977–78) | Tip O'Neill | 213 | (88) | 28 | (12) | 241 |
| 96 (1979–80) | | 161 | (81) | 37 | (19) | 198 |
| 97 (1981–82) | | 90 | (80) | 22 | (20) | 112 |
| 98 (1983–84) | | 105 | (72) | 40 | (28) | 145 |
| 99 (1985–86) | | 65 | (64) | 36 | (36) | 101 |
| 100 (1987–88) | Jim Wright | 26 | (57) | 20 | (43) | 46 |

Source: *Congressional Quarterly Weekly Report* 45 (Oct. 10, 1987), p. 2450.

Gingrich began making public charges against Wright in 1987. He would travel around the country saying that Wright was a "crook" and when his remarks were reported in the media the mounting file of clippings helped persuade the House ethics committee to investigate. Though Gingrich later confessed that some of the charges he raised were "a fishing expedition," the committee appointed an independent counsel who spent six and one half months and $8 million uncovering enough ethical improprieties that Wright resigned after a debilitating battle.[80]

The independent counsel produced a large number of separate complaints—69 different counts—requiring some sort of answer by the Speaker. But in fact the committee was pursuing only two points of substance. One was a sweetheart deal with a publisher that permitted Wright to receive an unusually high royalty for a book of his speeches. This constituted, at most, an unseemly exploitation of a loophole in regulations forbidding members of Congress most outside sources of income, but not book royalties. The second was a claim that Wright and Mrs. Wright had regular business of long standing with and received "gifts" from a Fort Worth entrepreneur who had or might have had an interest in federal legislation. Whereas the association between the Wrights and the entrepreneur, George Mallick, was real, the allegation that Mallick was somehow exploiting the relationship to affect legislation was to some observers far-fetched.[81] But the committee—evenly divided between Democrats and Republicans—found against Wright on both issues. Ground down by the embarrassing persistence of the Ethics Committee investigation, and its very bad publicity, Wright resigned his Speakership on May 31, 1989, and from Congress on June 30. His Speakership had lasted five months longer than one Congress (the 100th).

Toward the end of Wright's travail, Tony Coelho, the House Democratic whip, resigned so as to avoid having to explain his personal business to the Ethics Committee.[82] The confrontational strategy seemed to be working extremely well. The Democrats moved Tom Foley, a soothing figure, up from majority leader to Speaker.

Meanwhile in the Senate, the newly elected President Bush lost John Tower, his nominee for Secretary of Defense in a bruising confirmation battle. Bush reached into the House of Representatives for his next choice, and asked Republican whip Dick Cheney to head the Defense Department.[83] This created an unexpected vacancy in the second spot in the House Republican leadership. At that moment (March 10, 1989), Jim Wright was on the run, only two months from resigning his Speakership. Newt Gingrich stepped forward from the backbenches and offered himself as candidate for whip. Bob Michel had other ideas and supported his colleague from Illinois, Ed Madigan, a nine-termer and stalwart member of the Agriculture Committee. He was Cheney's chief deputy whip and had served as deputy to Trent Lott, Cheney's predecessor. "Moderate Mr. Madigan," wrote Jeffrey H. Birnbaum in the *Wall Street Journal*, "is a legislative craftsman who, without fanfare, has won bipartisan support to pass some bills the Republicans care about."[84] In a close-run contest (vote 87 to 85 with two members not voting), Gingrich and his aggressive strategy prevailed.[85]

When Jim Wright became a victim of hardball politics, a wave of misgivings did not sweep the House. To the contrary, Wright's departure was like catnip to Republicans who themselves had felt ill used by developments in the legislative process over what had seemed like a very long time.[86] Newt Gingrich said on national television (referring to Democrats): "I think the country is going to be further shocked when the news media digs deeper to discover that it doesn't stop with Coelho and Wright, that it goes on to more and more people . . . at least I think another 9 or 10, maybe more than that."[87]

## Tyranny Tempered by Assassination

The central management problem confronted by Democrats in their 50-year run as the dominant party in the House was finding ways to express party majority sentiment through the legislative agenda. Eventually, this was accomplished through increased reliance on the Democratic caucus. It was done, however, not by binding the votes of Democrats on the floor, the traditional use of the caucus, but by retrieving decisions that had been put on automatic pilot (principally committee assignments) and exercising political discretion over them. The Speaker had been given a great deal of power as the agent of the caucus, power which it made no sense for the Speaker to use so long as the caucus was split into large opposed factions.

By the time of Tip O'Neill and Jim Wright, however, Democratic factional difficulties had greatly abated, and the formal powers of the Speaker were quite substantial. These powers O'Neill used gingerly, Wright more vigorously, indeed possibly with more vigor than the broad church of the Democratic Party even without its large congregation of Dixiecrats could comfortably accommodate. Tom Foley's gentler style was less divisive.[88] Had he not been caught up in a comic-opera fiasco that the news media, skillfully abetted by a group of enthusiastic Republican members, pumped up into a Wagnerian Götterdämmerung, it is conceivable that over the medium run some of the resentments of House Republicans over such serious matters as the allocation of committee staff and of time for debate on the floor could have been addressed and ameliorated.

The fiasco was a faux scandal over the mismanagement of the House Bank. The House Bank story deserves—but will not here receive—its own lengthy melodramatic recapitulation.[89] Briefly, the General Accounting Office in the exercise of its post-audit supervision of the routine administration of the legislative branch reported in September 1991 that 8,331 bad checks had been written against members' accounts at the House Bank during the year ending June 1990. It had found comparable overdraft activity in earlier years. The Bank (hastily closed by a vote of the House in October 1991) was a peculiar institution, 150 years old, more or less a cooperative enterprise that had been set up solely for the convenience of members of the House. Its funds consisted entirely of automatic monthly deposits of members' salaries for those members wishing to participate. It made no investments and paid no interest on members' accounts. It was nominally supervised by the Sergeant-at-Arms. Overdrafts were covered by subsequent deposits.

Since only money already earned and belonging to individual members was involved, it required a stretch to turn the GAO report into a public scandal. But in the atmosphere of the Era of Ill Feeling, the stretch was easily accomplished. The Ethics Committee was asked to report and in March 1992 proposed to identify the two-dozen worst overdrafters and declare that they had "abused their banking privileges." Because the names would be those of elected officials, vulnerable to bad publicity, this was rather more punitive than a private club posting on a bulletin board the names of members in arrears in their dues.[90]

But it was not enough for purposes of partisan combat. Republicans seized what looked like a golden opportunity to discredit the management of the House as an institution and demanded more disclosure. With the news media in full cry against secrecy, perks, and privileges, Speaker Foley capitulated in short order. The names of 325 sitting and former members who overdrew their accounts between 1988 and 1991 (one overdraft in 40 cases, over 500 overdrafts in 14 cases) were publicly released. The Bush administration's Attorney General empaneled a special prosecutor—a retired Republican judge—to determine if crimes had been committed. The answer, ultimately, after months of uncertainty, was no. But in the mean time leaders of the House had to determine how much raw information about members' finances the special prosecutor was entitled to inspect. The special prosecutor demanded all the Bank's records. "The records," Speaker Foley wrote, "include all banking transactions over a 39 month period—

every single check (whether it covered an overdraft or not) deposit slips and monthly payments—of each member or former member whether he or she had overdrafts or not."

As in so many matters, Bob Michel found himself at odds with red hot members of his own party and ready to stand with Speaker Foley in defense of the House. *CQ* reports: "In an impromptu talk with reporters . . . he agreed with the Democrats' main concerns, suggesting that [Special Prosecutor Malcolm] Wilkey was on 'a broad fishing expedition. . . . Before you get all carried away here, there are certain institutional prerogatives that we have as a co-equal branch of government.' "[91] Shortly, Michel and Foley were themselves swept aside. Democrats were split, Republicans united, in votes to comply fully with Wilkey's subpoena to turn over all House Bank records without a court test.

The political havoc caused by this "scandal" (no public money, no crimes) at the next election was spectacular. *CQ* reported:

> Only six of 17 current members accused of having "abused their banking privileges" by the House ethics committee were reelected. Of the 46 members with 100 or more overdrafts, 25 (54 percent) retired or were defeated. Of the 389 with fewer than 100 overdrafts or none at all, 80 (21 percent) retired or were defeated. Most of the damage came in the primary season. On November 3, [1992,] challengers beat 24 incumbents. . . . All but five of the defeated had overdrawn their House bank accounts at least once during the 3 1/4 years studied by the ethics committee. Five had at least 140 overdrafts.[92]

The House was becoming less and less Bob Michel's sort of place. In an August 1993 interview with his hometown paper, the *Peoria Journal Star* (Ill.) he unburdened himself a little, calling the Republican conference "the most conservative and antagonistic to the other side" he had seen since he came to Congress in 1957, and describing the 47 Republican freshmen elected in 1992 as follows: "Seven are thoughtful moderates and the other 40 are pretty darn hard-liners, some of them real hard-line."[93] This was taken as a signal that he would be announcing his retirement from Congress soon as, by October, he did.[94] Newt Gingrich had in the mean time communicated that whether Michel left or not he would be a candidate for Republican leader in the next Congress.[95]

There was worse news for Democrats in the election of 1994. Not only did Foley himself lose his seat after 30 years of service to his predominately Republican constituency, but the Democratic Party nationwide suffered a loss of 52 seats while no Republican incumbent lost. This was the sort of landslide that within living memory had usually buried Republicans, not Democrats. After 40 years, the Republican Party finally won a majority in the House of Representatives. There were 73 freshman members, 65 from formerly Democratic districts. Many of them had been recruited by GOPAC, Newt Gingrich's political action committee devoted to recruiting Republican activists to run for public office.[96]

Thus began the short, turbulent speakership of Newt Gingrich. In a mere four years (January 1995–December 1998), Gingrich presided over quite a lot of excitement, notably two episodes of deadlock on budgetary questions, which caused the shutdown of the government—and which were blamed largely on his intransigence—as well as the beginnings of an extremely unpopular presidential impeachment.[97]

As a prelude to his takeover of the machinery of House leadership, Gingrich had persuaded a large number of House Republicans to run for office in the 1994 election on a consolidated manifesto, a "Contract with America" he called it. This was primarily an advertising gimmick, and the fact that American voters had largely ignored it, indeed never heard of it, did not intrude on the credit-claiming that went on after the new, Republican-controlled Congress met in January 1995 in an atmosphere of unbridled Republican euphoria.[98]

Gingrich, as Speaker, promptly drove through the Republican conference numerous proposals to change House rules.[99] These moved an enormous amount of the organizational furniture around in the House, everything from abolishing some committees and reshuffling their responsibilities, and renaming most of the rest, to terminating the age-old practice of permitting a bucket of ice-chips to be delivered each morning free of charge to each member's office.[100] Some of the changes tended to weaken the influence of the House in the political system overall. These measures included arbitrarily shrinking the size of committee staffs by one-third and defunding legislative service organizations like the Office of Technology Assessment, which had helped the House capitalize on its strong division of labor by supporting the substantive expertise of individual members who had been assigned to specialized subcommittees and committees. The subcommittee bill of rights had originally been an enactment of the House Democratic caucus and not incorporated into the rules. The Republicans treated subcommittees quite differently, forbidding them to hire staff. This was permitted only to committee chairmen, who were themselves hand picked by the Speaker. Done under the rubric of party responsibility, many of the conference's moves gave the Speaker more discretion, which he promptly used.[101]

The House inspector general was ordered to conduct an audit of House financial records while it had been under Democratic control. He in turn commissioned a $3.2 million study by Price Waterhouse which uncovered "handwritten ledgers filled with scratched-out numbers," "outdated and poorly designed computer systems," inadvertent overpayments on travel vouchers, poor documentation of expenses and other indications of laxity and managerial disarray, but nothing that could be used for partisan purposes.[102] A few time bombs were set in place to go off down the road: term limits were placed on committee and subcommittee chairmen (six years) and on the Speaker (eight years). Many rules were enacted affecting committee business: no joint referrals, no closed committee meetings, no proxy voting, limits on the number of subcommittees.

Among the forces at work in the "revolution" (as it was widely described) were what looked like a retrospective orientation reflecting simple inexperience in managing the machinery, difficulty in adjusting to the fact that the Republicans were now a majority and consequently had to attend to maintaining a governing consensus, and hunger for the redress of Republican grievances that had built up over the years.[103] In the engine room of House politics for half a century had been the fundamental tensions that divided the Democratic Party. Meanwhile, all but ignored by observers, Republicans were running a far more ideologically compact and hierarchical operation.[104] Committee assignments, for example, had been more successfully monitored by ranking members of key committees than the divided Democrats had done and filtered through a process dominated by a coalition of senior members from the large state delegations.[105]

Gingrich and his leadership team took centralized control a step or two farther. His relationship with the Appropriations Committee did not resemble relations between Sam Rayburn and Clarence Cannon, as David Maraniss and Michael Weisskopf report:

> Gingrich visited the Appropriations Committee for a closed-door meeting with Chairman Bob Livingston of Louisiana and his thirteen subcommittee chairmen, collectively known as "the cardinals" . . . Livingston had been handpicked for the assignment by Gingrich and [majority leader Dick] Armey, who passed over three committee members with more seniority in their search for someone they considered tough enough for the job. Ralph Regula of Ohio seemed a shade too soft and moderate. C. W. Bill Young of Florida had other missions more important to him. And John Myers of Indiana had failed the Gingrich test set up before the 1994 elections: He did not raise enough money or help the Republican team with sufficient time and energy. . . .
>
> The Speaker reminded the chairman and his cardinals that they would be making deep cuts in programs they had funded for years.

"You're going to have to be in the forefront of the revolution," he said. "You have the toughest jobs in the House. If you don't want to do it, tell me." He said that he would meet individually with each cardinal to discuss the leadership agenda for each of the thirteen bills they would be shepherding through the committee and onto the House floor. There would be no confusion about the philosophy of every bill and Gingrich's priorities. He instructed the cardinals to write him letters reaffirming their commitment.[106]

Richard Fenno writes:

[T]he new Speaker abolished some committees and subcommittees, appointed the Committee Chairmen, extracted loyalty pledges from committee leaders, controlled committee staff, selected committee members, created and staffed ad hoc task forces to circumvent committees, established committee priorities and time lines, and monitored committee compliance.[107]

As Gingrich steamed ahead, relations between the parties continued unpleasant. In March 1997, a bipartisan group of members, alarmed at the ugly spirit pervading House business, put together a weekend retreat in Hershey, Pennsylvania, for the whole House aimed at recapturing a spirit of civility. About half the members showed up, many with their families, heard some inspirational speeches, took field trips, mingled a little. Two years later they did it again, "sharing their feelings in discussion groups, singing 'Kumbaya' and line dancing."[108] Polite noises were made about benefits to overall morale, but a bucolic weekend every other year could scarcely outweigh partisan sentiments generated over the long run, never mind feelings that surfaced during the sharply partisan impeachment and trial of President Clinton that took place between the two retreats, from August 1998 to February 1999.[109]

As time went on, Gingrich's hold on the Republican conference slipped.[110] Even well before the impeachment failed to produce a conviction in the Senate, there were mutinous rumblings among the House Republican rank and file, especially among hard-right members who thought Gingrich was making too many compromises with Bill Clinton.[111] And to what avail? Republicans lost a net of three seats in the 1996 election and five seats in the 1998 election. Their majority was so thin as almost to be vulnerable to the actuarial hazards of by-election turnover. Confrontation with Bill Clinton on budgetary matters had earned Gingrich enormous unpopularity out in the country and as he maneuvered to deal with that problem he fell afoul of strong ideologues in his own caucus. As Gingrich later wrote:

> By mid-June 1997. . . . Most of the Republican members were angry with the leadership for not leading more effectively and . . . angry at a number of the sophomores who from the time of their first coming into the House in 1994 had made life harder by being so aggressive and confrontational. For their part, the militant sophomores were . . . angry at the leadership for not putting up a tougher fight . . . against Clinton and . . . for conservative values.[112]

As militants became restive they seriously explored the possibility of replacing the Speaker. At one point it looked like they would back Bill Paxon of New York, whom Gingrich had appointed "leadership chairman," but this caused the defection of majority leader Dick Armey, who disliked being bypassed. The plot blew up, causing Paxon to resign his Gingrich-appointed position and permanent embarrassment to Armey, who denied complicity in the attempted coup, a denial that was not widely believed.[113]

While the 1997 plot fizzled, dissatisfactions with Gingrich among Republicans least happy with compromise persisted. After the disappointing 1998 election Rep. Matt Salmon (Ariz.) "confirmed to *Roll Call* that he and several other Republicans had spread the word to Gingrich that they would risk a Congress with no Speaker if Gingrich refused to resign his post."[114] This could have been accomplished with the House narrowly divided by simply withholding their votes for Speaker.

Less than a week after the election, Gingrich withdrew as a candidate for Speaker of the 106th Congress. *Roll Call* reported:

> Minority Leader Dick Gephardt (D-MO) who spoke face-to-face with Gingrich less than a dozen times during his four-year reign, had few kind words . . .
> [He said:]
> "I hope that whoever succeeds Newt Gingrich as Speaker will immediately begin the process of repairing the damage that was wrought on this institution over the last four years."[115]

There was precedent for some of this. Republican rank-and-file dissatisfactions had erupted from time to time over the years, especially after elections when Republicans did less well than expected.[116] These eruptions not infrequently targeted their own party leadership. Of the five Republican leaders preceding Newt Gingrich, two, Joe Martin and Charlie Halleck, had been dumped by vote of the Republican conference at the instigation of aggrieved younger members who thought they could manage things better. Gerald Ford ascended unscathed to the vice presidency by appointment when Spiro T. Agnew resigned, in an apparent plea bargain, one step ahead of federal prosecutors. John Rhodes burned out in 1980 in much the same circumstances as his successor, Bob Michel, who was hustled toward the exit by impatient junior members of the Republican conference (as the GOP caucus in the House is called).[117] So was Newt Gingrich himself a mere four years after his coronation.[118]

This pattern is as close as a democratically governed institution gets to the sort of arrangement described by the famed founder of the BBC, Lord Reith, as his notion of the ideal form of government: "Tyranny tempered by assassination."[119] It is a pattern—strong, centralized leadership, abrupt departures—that Gingrich, upon taking over, accentuated rather than invented. Republicans in the House in the time of the Gingrich Speakership never learned how to manage their narrow majority in the bipartisan environment created by a Democratic president. By the turn of the millennium the Republicans had a new Speaker, Dennis Hastert, of Illinois, by many accounts deeply under the influence of party whip Tom DeLay of Texas whose deputy he had been. Their majority, one of the smallest in congressional history, was precarious and relationships with the Democratic leadership remained extremely hostile.

It might be argued that day-to-day rancor between the parties and a lack of informal communication between their leaders are natural byproducts of strong partisanship itself when partisanship is permitted unconstrained expression. In any event, by the beginning of a new millennium both strong party regularity and pervasive partisan hostility were, so it seemed, well entrenched in the politics of the House of Representatives.[120] And these can plausibly be described as consequences of the party realignment of the immediately preceding era.

# 5

## OVERVIEW: HOW CONGRESS
## EVOLVES

---

In a turbulent world, Americans have been able to rely upon great stability in their political institutions.[1] They rarely have felt a need to reflect or to regret that they have been unfairly deprived of the keen stimulus of occupying armies, or the refreshment of an internal revolution, or the shock of some other constitutional upheaval leading to a wholly new and different domestic political order. These have frequently erupted in various places in the modern world over the last half century, transforming the governments under which large chunks of the world's population exist, but not in the United States. Nevertheless meaningful change has come to the American political system within living memory, and even to that seemingly rock-solid fortress of continuity and stasis, the United States Congress. And this is true even from the standpoint of liberals who have been impatient with the workings of the system.

### Innovation and Stalemate

Looking at the last half century of Congress as a historical whole from this point of view, as we have been doing, it is possible to discern an alternating and somewhat overlapping pattern of activity and retrenchment, of focus and stalemate in congressional affairs. Three times during the 50-year period Congress has gone through episodes of high productivity and strong coordination; and through three somewhat longer episodes Congress has more or less ridden at anchor in the political system at large. Neither one mode nor the other is exclusively "natural" to Congress. Al-

though the legitimacy of congressional behavior in either mode is frequently the subject of hot dispute, both roles are historically characteristic
of Congress, and both fully express the powers of Congress as contemplated
in the overall constitutional design. This design confides to Congress two
complementary assignments: to represent the American people in at least
some approximation of their variety and diversity, and to provide a forum
for the processing of significant policy initiatives. When there is great variation and disparity in the opinions of Americans about public policy, this
fact is bound to be recognized in pulling and hauling on Capitol Hill; when
there is unanimity and resolution, Congress moves its business with dis-
patch.

It is possible to be brief and schematic in identifying episodes of concentrated congressional activity over the last two generations. In these
historical moments, Congress initiates or ratifies sizable expansions of federal activity, focuses its energies effectively, and undertakes policy innovation. These moments include: the enactment of the New Deal (ca. 1933–
36) in which the political innovations of Franklin Roosevelt's first 100 days
occurred: the revision of banking laws, the formation of the Securities and
Exchange Commission, the establishment of a social security system, and
the passage of the Wagner Act, among other events.[2] Second, the creation
of wartime agencies in Washington (ca. 1939–46) greatly increased the
administrative capacities of central government and broke through prewar
congressional resistance to governmental economic forecasting and planning and to an administratively augmented presidency. This episode includes, inter alia, the enactment of the 1939 Reorganization Plan to
Amend the Budget and Accounting Act of 1921, the establishment of the
Office of War Mobilization and (later) Reconversion, the Employment Act
of 1946, which created, among other things, a Council of Economic Ad-
visors, the consolidation of civilian control of the armed services into a
Defense Department, the establishment of the Central Intelligence Agency,
the Atomic Energy Commission, and the National Science Foundation.[3]
The third episode was the New Frontier–Great Society, (1963–69). This
period saw the completion of the New Deal: medicare, the enactment of
civil rights laws, and the creation or enhancement of federal bureaucracies
dedicated to less advantaged clientele, such as the Departments of Health
and Human Services and of Housing and Urban Development.[4]

Interspersed with these episodes of innovation have been episodes of
stalemate and retrenchment. We remember, for example, the thwarting of
the later New Deal (1937–41) in which President Roosevelt attempted, and
failed, to pack the Supreme Court after the Court found many early New
Deal measures unconstitutional. Roosevelt then attempted, and failed, to

defeat conservative Democratic members of Congress in the 1938 election (with the single exception of John O'Connor of New York) and Congress no longer produced a cornucopia of new legislation. In time, "Doctor New Deal" gave way to "Doctor Win-the-War."[5] Then from roughly 1950, when the Truman administration began to be bogged down in loyalty-security issues, and all through the Eisenhower administration, when the threat of a presidential veto prevented all but the most consensual of congressional initiatives, on into most of the Kennedy presidency, in which the dominance of conservative committee chairmen in Congress narrowed the president's agenda (ca. 1950–62), Congress and the presidency existed in a sort of equilibrium described as a "deadlock of democracy."[6] Since 1968, there has been a period of consolidation in reaction to the most recent set of policy innovations, and during much of this time the presidency has been in Republican hands and Congress has been split between the parties or has oscillated between them. During most of these three periods, political innovation as Democrats defined it has been resisted or stalemated, and little or no consensus has existed favoring new departures in governmental policy (see table 5.1).[7] Private activity has been preferred to the leadership of central government.

That periods of stalemate should last, on average, about twice as long as periods of innovation ought not greatly to surprise even the most casual student of human nature. In important respects the U.S. population resembles the population that attempted to build the Tower of Babel. The point of that biblical fable is perfectly straightforward: to undertake great public works it helps if everyone speaks the same language.[8] Finding that language in the expression of common goals and organizing concerted strategies to accomplish those goals are not trivial tasks when formal power and autonomy are dispersed as they are in the United States and it is necessary legislatively to mobilize the consent of majorities over and over—successively first in subcommittees, then in committees, then on the floors of two legislative chambers, and finally behind the occupant of the White House. Obviously, alternative forms of coordination are available (though not under the U.S. Constitution): parliamentary government on the party-responsible first-past-the-post Westminster model, for example, makes leg-

TABLE 5.1. Periods of Congressional Innovation and Stalemate, 1933–98

| *Innovation* | New Deal 1933–37 | | War time 1939–46 | | Great Society 1964–68 | |
|---|---|---|---|---|---|---|
| *Stalemate* | | 1937–41 | | 1947–63 | | 1969–98 |

islative coordination relatively simple, but frequently leads to policy zig-zags and sometimes to insufficiencies over the long run in the consent of the governed. Parliaments that are constituted of party coalitions arising from variants of proportional representation sometimes fail to coordinate at all. Still another form of coordination that is fairly prevalent world-wide—dictatorship—is scarcely relevant to the politics of a free and self-governing people. Far more relevant is the simple fact, illustrated in table 5.1, that it takes time to gather up the consensus necessary to move a bicameral representative body that exists independently within a consti-tutional separation of powers.

Crises of various sorts, notably a depression, a war, and a presidential assassination, respectively, have done a great deal to press Congress toward bouts of innovative activity.[9] In contrast, explicit reforms of congressional procedures have played little or no immediate role in galvanizing forward motion on the policy front. The entire era's most comprehensive overhaul of procedures, the reform of the committee system in 1946, came at the start of a long period of stalemate.[10] Other important institutional changes included Lyndon Johnson's redesign of the seniority rules for assigning Democratic senators to committees, which occurred during the Eisenhower lull, the 1961 packing of the House Rules Committee, and various reor-ganizations and reforms of the House in the mid-1970s.[11] All these changes were significant, but not right away. Some of them created institutionalized settings for the more successful and more coordinated deployment of the resources of the majority party in Congress, but none was sufficient in and of itself to create an avalanche of new and innovative public policies. These sorts of avalanches require the cooperation of the president. Even so, the most important facts about the capacity of Congress to respond—to presidential leadership or to leadership within Congress itself—are en-coded in Congress's own organizational structure, and in the ways in which over time the changing composition of Congress makes an impact upon congressional organization.

## Overview of the House

As late as 30 years ago, an observer might have said that of all of the institutions of American government, the House of Representatives had been least touched by change since the creation of so many of the insti-tutions of modern America—professions, universities, corporations, and the modern House of Representatives—in the early years of the twentieth century. Not since 1919 had an ongoing committee assignment in the

House violated the criterion of seniority.[12] New committee assignments were doled out by committees on committees of each party much influenced by the leaders of key state delegations.[13] Committee chairmen—always those most senior in committee service in the House majority party—dominated the policy-making process within their respective domains, frequently collaborating with ranking minority members, but sometimes not. The Republican conference—the assembly of all Republican members—was considerably more successful than its counterpart body, the House Democratic caucus, in expressing and maintaining a party mainstream ideological position. This was understandable in light of the fact that Republicans in the House were, on the whole (as is true of Republicans in general), far more ideologically united.[14] The Democratic caucus, active in Woodrow Wilson's day, by the late 1940s was for the most part moribund, meeting to do serious business only once in every two years, and then only to nominate and elect party leaders and to ratify the work of its Committee on Committees. The so-called leadership—Speaker, majority leader, whip—in the interim had custody of all the routines and schedules that are at the heart of the management of a complex legislative body, but they were constrained to exercise their power incrementally and in deference to the factional divisions of the majority party.

Change, however, finally came to the House of Representatives. Its main outlines, so long as the Democrats controlled Congress, were these: committee chairmen, once beyond reach, were deposed and threatened with removal on several occasions after 1970, mainly for being out of step with mainstream sentiment among the members of the Democratic caucus; the Democratic Committee on Committees was reconstituted to give party leaders much more influence, including the power unilaterally to appoint members to the key scheduling committee, the Rules Committee; and uniform rules of committee conduct were required to be written so as to spread power downward and outward to subcommittees and their chairmen. As subcommittees gained autonomy and party leaders gained responsibilities, power slipped away from the chairmen of full committees, who were the major losers in the transformations that took place.[15]

The main engine of change was the House Democratic caucus. Because the House has been predominantly in the hands of a Democratic majority over the last 60 years, what happened to the Democrats is of paramount concern in following developments in the House. From 1937 until quite recently, the divisions within the caucus were sufficient to neutralize any attempts to use the caucus to coordinate the majority party. Southern Democrats—about 100 strong during most of the period, and virtually all of them from safe seats—made up almost half of the Democratic members of the House, sometimes a little less depending on Democratic electoral fortunes in the rest of the country. About two-thirds of the southern Democrats were Dixiecrats, which meant that they were opposed to Democrats from the rest of the country on many issues of public policy and perfectly willing to make coalitions with House Republicans to stop liberal legislation. They had little trouble enlisting the active collaboration of the Republicans. So the actual ideological division in the House as a whole was frequently closely balanced when conservatives were not slightly in the lead. This made of the House the graveyard of many liberal proposals during the late Roosevelt, Truman, and Kennedy presidencies.[16]

From time to time House members closer to the mainstream of the national Democratic Party would become restive. A small uprising took place after the 1958 election, for example, when a flood of newly elected liberal Democrats washed over the House. As Speaker Rayburn saw all too clearly, this was bound to have no legislative consequences over the short run, since liberal initiatives could not survive an Eisenhower veto. A few young leaders of the party in the House in their impatience organized what later became a programmatically oriented shadow of the caucus, the Democratic Study Group.[17] This group in time embraced most ideologically mainstream Democratic members. It took more than a few years for the House Democratic leadership to become comfortable with the Study Group, which at its most effective acted as the sort of communications system and rallying point that the official Democratic whip system could not be, because of the obligation of the whips to serve all Democratic members, whatever their ideological stripe.

By the 1970s, the caucus had been persuaded to absorb many of the functions of the Study Group, and had revived as an instrument of House leadership after a long period of quiescence. This could happen because numerous Dixiecrats had disappeared from the House and they had been replaced by Republicans. It is not intuitively obvious that a substantial gain of seats in the House by the Republican Party would be a proximate cause of the liberalization of the House, but that, more or less, is what happened. It was, to be sure, not the new Republican members themselves, most of whom were ferociously conservative, who were the instruments of change but rather the drastic revision in the makeup of the Democratic caucus that did the job, enabling the caucus to take initiatives that only a few years earlier would have torn it apart.

Indirectly these changes were the product of the nationalization of the South, of demographic changes that had made the South more like the rest of the country, and of the party realignments that made it possible for southern Republicans to run for House seats and win. Promiscuous and ill-founded claims of party realignment at the national level have given the whole idea of realignment a bad name among careful analysts. But if there has been a party realignment anywhere in America these past 50 years, it has occurred in the South, and it led to liberalization in the House of Representatives.

When, after the election of 1994, the Republicans got their chance to manage the House, the tools for centralized leadership by the Speaker had already been put in place by the Democrats. House Republicans tend to follow relatively centralized and hierarchical management practices, dominated by the large state delegations and ranking committee members as befits a more ideologically homogeneous party. They deal with internal dissatisfactions by overthrowing their elected leaders on a fairly regular basis.[18] Thus, the rearrangements, sometimes quite drastic, in House procedures instigated by the Republican "revolution," when the Republicans at long last elected a majority of members, were consistent with the ways in which the Republican congressional party had done business in the past. Whether these rearrangements would survive a party turnover, or persist over a long period of time, was anyone's guess.

## Stories about Change

All this movement ought to inspire a reconsideration of the proposition, frequently asserted, that as a piece of eighteenth century political machinery Congress is ill-equipped to deal with modern challenges by virtue of its resistance to and incapacity for change.[19] Fair-minded observers must concede that there may be many reasons to find fault with Congress and with many aspects of public policy as they emerge from Congress. It seems doubtful, however, that a lack of change can be pinpointed as the source of difficulty. Students of Congress will be familiar with analogous complaints in the 1960s and 1970s about the incompetence and senility of conservative congressional committee chairmen who were, in the mysterious exercise of their diminished and enfeebled powers, completely thwarting the forward march of liberalism as orchestrated by competent and non-senile presidents, journalists, public interest advocates, and professors. The proper diagnosis should have been: if only these committee chairmen had actually been senile, how much easier it would have been for liberals to get what they wanted.

As an institution that is venerable in years, certainly as governmental institutions go, well-bounded, highly legitimate, and resourceful, it cannot be expected that the Congress of the United States would transform itself into something unrecognizable with the touch of every passing breeze. If a serious, functioning institution exists, then it is to be expected that institutional inertia would exact a toll on any effort to make changes. Yet changes have come to Congress, and many of these changes have proved to be meaningful for the life of the institution and, ultimately, consequential for public policy. A short list of some of the means by which these have come about in the history of Congress would include:

1. *Institutionalization.* At an early point in the life of the Constitution, Congress had not developed a large number of the organizational characteristics that are familiar to present-day observers. The development of some of these characteristics has been studied in the case of the House of Representatives under the rubric of "institutionalization."[20] This is the name of a process that refers to the growth of organizational features tending to define and harden the external boundaries of the institution, manage and promote internal complexity, and establish universalistic, impersonal criteria for internal decision-making. Many of these features were observed to have developed over the course of the nineteenth century, to have slowed down during the Civil War, and to have achieved very near to their contemporary form soon after the turn of the twentieth century. These included the modern committee system, and modern criteria for the selection of party leaders, as well as the diverse duties adhering to the positions of party leadership themselves, seniority in committee assignments, and quasi-judicialized methods for disposing of contested elections. All of these contemporary and persistent organizational features are, even today, contingent and subject to modification.

2. *Technology.* Change in the modern Congress has also come in part as a response to changes in various underlying conditions of modern life. A technological innovation such as television, with its power to focus the attention of millions, could be counted on to impinge upon the lives of politicians who depend on millions of people for their votes, though no one could predict precisely how it would do so. The nationalization of the South, with its eventual impact on the rise of southern Republicans and, paradoxically, on the liberalization of the House, rests at least in some respects on a technological footing, for example, on the mechanization of agriculture that depleted the nation, and especially the most rural part of the nation, the South, of its rural population. Or consider the effects of air conditioning, that made intolerably hot places in the summer habitable and made of some of these places targets for year-round settlement by retirees, new white-collar industries, and other migrants from places with political traditions that differed from local habits and customs.

3. *Socio-political movements.* Changes in Congress can equally be seen as the product of social and political movements. The demographic movements that brought rural southerners to the cities and northern Republicans south have already been mentioned. World War II attracted southerners, both black and white, to the North to work in factories supporting the war effort. This greatly accelerated the movement of black Americans into the voting population and helped to create more northern safe urban Democratic congressional seats.[21]

4. *Political innovations, frequently deliberate.* Finally, political changes elsewhere in the system have had an impact on Congress. Some, like the changes creating myriads of safe congressional seats, may retard as well as accelerate the prospects for other changes. As seats become safe, David Brady has argued, landslides creating critical elections become harder to produce.[22] Other political events may have facilitated change more straightforwardly. As the presidency expanded, for example, Congress found that it too had to expand its capabilities in order successfully to exercise its responsibilities to check and balance and to keep track of what was going on. It is possible to trace the recent growth of congressional staff and its professionalization to the stimulus of institutional innovation in the modern presidency.[23] Changes in the rules and procedures of presidential nominations, not trivially abetted by television, have given Washington politicians added visibility and influence in what has come to be a process dominated by primary elections and hence by publicity. At the same time, the influence of state party leaders has been diminished in the selection process.[24] This combination of technological innovation and political reform may be the best explanation available to account for changes in the career possibilities confronting U.S. Senators and therefore may explain changes in the role of the Senate in the political system. The Voting Rights Act, by providing for the registration of African American voters in the South, undoubtedly stimulated the redistribution of white voters between the parties, facilitated the rise of the Republican Party in the South, and liberalized southern Democratic parties.

Change happens frequently enough, and in sufficiently unexpected ways, even in the life of an organization as stable as the U.S. Congress, to require the attention of observers as they monitor the performance of contemporary political institutions. It has not been my purpose in this essay to give an exhaustive census of changes that may have affected Congress, but only to call attention to some of the more important ways in which Congress has adapted in recent years to some of the complex and surprising challenges of life in our times.

Over the period of time covered by this study, the House has been led at various times by different combinations of strong and weak Speakers, united and divided parties, independent and well-coordinated committees and subcommittees. At one point or another the House has faced demanding, cooperative, distant, and hostile presidents. From the effective end of the New Deal, in the late 1930s, to John Kennedy's assassination in the early 1960s, the House was mostly a bottleneck in the policy-making process mainly because of the demands of presidents more liberal than the majority of the House. But there was no liberal Democratic majority in Congress despite the predominance of liberals in the national Democratic Party. The history of Congress since then has consisted, among other significant events, of an uneven, but discernible, movement away from a long-running conflict between the two majorities, congressional and Democratic, and toward a situation in which the main competing coalitions have been effectively mobilized by each of the two dominant political parties. What occurred was less a massive change in sentiment among the American people producing a reliably liberal Congress and more a realignment toward the national norm of party competition in the southern stronghold both of conservatism and of the Democratic Party.

The stand-off in Congress between the two majorities that existed for a very long time was broken only after local demographic changes worked their way through the political system and had an effect on the composition of the House of Representatives. These changes might well have occurred earlier but for institutional barriers—such as the malapportionment of congressional districts. The overthrow of these barriers required a series of decisions by the Supreme Court before the underlying demographic factors could assert themselves.[25] Arguably, political factors continue to exercise an important influence. Minority–majority districts, packed with minority voters under requirements from the Bush (the elder) Justice Department, cause the under-representation of minority voters in adjacent districts, thus creating or protecting Republican seats that might otherwise fall to Democrats.[26] Procedural changes in the House organization had to be put in place so that the Democratic caucus could be used to influence the conduct of committee business. Liberal Democrats in the North and West had to win their share of elections to the House. And the Republican Party, after a century, had to make inroads in the South.

So to make the claim that institutional evolution is founded upon social and demographic changes is not to claim that there is anything simple or automatic about the influence of these changes on political institutions. If the evolutionary process were automatic, there would be nothing like the complicated story that unfolded in the preceding pages. Indeed, if the evolution of political institutions could rely on the straightforward orchestration of an invisible hand, it seems unlikely that the movement toward the liberalization of the House would have been accomplished through the addition of Republicans, as actually occurred.

According to a radio program of my youth, people who pass every day through New York City's Grand Central Station bring with them a thousand different stories. Much the same can be said of the U.S. House of Representatives and the American political system more generally. The story I have chosen to extract from this very large set of alternatives and tell has a beginning but no real ending—at least not yet. As modern technology came to the southern United States, its population began to change. With changes in population came changes, at long last, in the parties of the region. These in due course had their impact on the composition of the national body that directly represents the people and finally, with co-operation from the president, on the work product of that institution. But the story only pauses at that point, as the next phase of the institution's history unfolded and continues to unfold in reaction to the phase immediately preceding it, and in response to new electoral results.

The many citizens and many observers all over the world who have good reasons to concern themselves with the policy outcomes that Congress produces will not need to be advised to continue to stay tuned.

# APPENDIX: METHODS AND SOURCES

Among the many pleasures a reader may experience in reading the book by Ivor Crewe and Anthony King on the rise and fall of the British Social Democratic Party is the authoritative evocation of the lives and times of a substantial fraction of the British political class during the years (1981–87) when the SDP flourished.[1] Britain, being a tight little island, creates within it well-bounded communities. Some of the very best writing on British politics is quasi-anthropological in character and attends to the ways in which the values and status systems of these communities shape the fortunes of their members as well as the policies and strategies they pursue. I think of work by Hugh Heclo and Aaron Wildavsky on the private government, as they call it, of public money; or by Peter Hennessy on the hidden wiring of the unwritten British constitution or on Whitehall; or of anything by the late, much-missed Noel Annan.[2]

Crewe and King's *SDP* is very much in this tradition. In this book one can read sentences like these: referring to a major public figure, Roy Jenkins, they write: "He was a very grand person. Everyone said so."[3] How can such utterances occur in a work (especially a very good work) of social science? Obviously Crewe and King have not sent a questionnaire around to "everybody" and gotten back unanimous agreement on the item: "Is Roy Jenkins a (check one) very grand person, grand person, not-so-grand person, non-person?" What they are doing is taking advantage of their intimate acquaintance with common opinion, which implies, indeed proclaims, the prior existence of networks of communication and evaluation, and of a subculture filled with social facts, widely shared within a population, that can be described and consulted.

The House of Representatives in the United States is another such subculture, embedded in the much larger American society whose political life is in general by no means as well-bounded or easily studied as British political parties. But as students have frequently noted, from its early years Congress has created its own inner political world with its own social facts.[4] The study of the internal structure of this world repays the close observer with understanding about how public policy of great significance to life in the United States is made. And that is the business of this book.

A short description of the making of this book would simply say that it is the product of 40 years, more or less, of study, reflection, and data collection, some of it aimless, some of it focused, and of a year or so of writing. As is true of anyone my age, I have actually lived through the half century of congressional history reported on here. For most of that period I have been paying attention to Congress, teaching and writing, watching and listening.[5] I have done my share of time on Capitol Hill, trudging around to congressional offices and committee rooms, reading and clipping the newspapers, and observing, meeting, interviewing, and getting acquainted with a fair number of the people whose names turn up in the text and footnotes of this account.

I have derived both pleasure and benefit from the complementary and parallel activities of several generations of congressional scholars, journalists, and students. I hope in the appropriate places I have noted my particular obligations to these colleagues, and to the members of Congress and congressional staff as well as the unelected practitioners of politics working on or near Capitol Hill who helped me understand what was happening while it was happening, but in addition I want to add a general word of gratitude. It takes a village, as the saying goes, to do empirical research in the social sciences, and especially research requiring extensive observation and fieldwork. The untidy village of congressional scholars has produced quite a lot of good journalism, history, and political science over the last half century, and has sustained and inspired me as I have gone about my own work.

In writing this book, I drew upon several streams of material, each imposing somewhat different ground rules for their wise and responsible use.

1. *Personal observation.* Early in the spring term of 1961, my Ph.D. not yet actually awarded, I was asked by Leon Epstein, the chairman of the University of Wisconsin Political Science Department, where I was then teaching, to cover the great congressional scholar Ralph Huitt's course on Congress, while Ralph was on leave.[6] I had never taken a course on Congress, graduate or undergraduate. My doctoral dissertation was on community power, a totally different topic. I did know a fair bit about the

Senate, from general reading and from following the newspapers as a teen-aged politics junkie, not so many years earlier, but the House was a mystery to me. Where was the literature? There was a little bit but not much. David Truman's formidable *The Congressional Party*; Steven K. Bailey's prize-winning *Congress Makes a Law*; some hard-to-find, very stimulating work by an eccentric sociologist named Lewis Anthony Dexter that my friends in the Congressional Fellowship Program were passing around hand-to-hand in mimeographed form.[7] From the same semi-underground sources came artful newsletters by a young California congressman, Clem Miller—later published as a supplementary textbook.[8] That was about it.

I did the best that I could with the course. The experience piqued my interest in the subject. Here was this lively little organization on Capitol Hill, pulsing with vitality, centrally important in the political life of our nation, and on the whole quite neglected by scholars. In June of 1961—after the course was over—the *APSR* ran two extremely good articles on the House by Charles O. Jones and Nicholas Masters, both Wisconsin Ph.D.s, one a doctoral student of Ralph Huitt's, plus a bravura performance on the Senate by Ralph himself.[9] By then I was thoroughly intrigued and wanted to learn more. That summer I moved to Washington, D.C., en route to my next teaching post at Wesleyan University, and undertook a program of self-education. My friend Aaron Wildavsky, then teaching at Oberlin College, had made the acquaintance of Oberlin's freshman member of Congress, Charles A. Mosher. Mosher, a moderate Republican in his mid-fifties, had been editor and publisher of the weekly *Oberlin News Tribune*, and a former Ohio state legislator. As time permitted, he liked to take courses in the Oberlin Government Department toward a master's degree from his alma mater. Aaron sounded Mosher out: would Mosher let me hang around for a week, just learning the routines of a congressman's life? He agreed.

In the early 1960s, members of Congress occupied two-room suites in two office buildings a block from the Capitol, since named for Speakers Joseph Cannon and Nicholas Longworth but then known as "old" (built at the turn of the century) and "new" (built in the 1920s). There were tour-ists in the Capitol building but security was informal, and the hallways—especially in the office buildings—were not crowded. Not many scholars could be spotted doing what I was doing, which was just watching and listening, and occasionally asking Mosher to explain what was going on, getting a sense of his time horizons, his points of reference, the rules of thumb he used to evaluate situations and policies. I learned, for example, that he paid a good deal of attention to what the other Ohio Republicans thought about things, that though a loyal party man he was in general open-minded about most public policy, and that he worried a great deal about what new proposals would cost.[11]

It was a worthwhile week, and I was hooked on the method.[12] There was no C-SPAN in those years, no way to learn about the routines of the institution other than do what I was doing, and so my learning curve was steep.

My next stop was Bob Kastenmeier, Madison, Wisconsin's congressman, a liberal Democrat, who had visited my classroom. His administrative assistant was possessive and protective, and so my access wasn't as good as with Mosher, but it was still very helpful to see a different style of being a congressman, from a different ideological and party perspective. By the end of the summer I had spent a week with a few other members, including two Wesleyan alumni, Abner Sibal and Emilio Daddario, both from Connecticut, one a Republican, the other a Democrat.

At some point during the summer of 1961 I decided to make the acquaintance of participants in the most significant House political battle of the era, the packing of the Rules Committee that had taken place just six months before I arrived on Capitol Hill, and so I scheduled interviews with some of the main actors and began to show up fairly regularly at hearings held by the expanded Rules Committee. These were held in the committee's old meeting room in the Capitol, where the committee sat around a long table under an enormous rococo chandelier with spectators, the press, and witnesses in chairs crowded together at the edges of the room. By the time I got around to seeking out members for individual interviews, I was a familiar face to some of them.

One member, in particular, proved especially forthcoming: Carl Elliott of Alabama, a lanky country lawyer whose love of higher education knew no bounds. He had been one of the new additions to the committee in January. His office was in the very farthest reaches of the 5th floor of the old House office building, as far from the House floor (and from the tourists) as a member could get. After breaking a couple of appointments, he finally agreed to see me on a Saturday afternoon and we hit it off. So I stayed a week with him at the end of which he offered me a job as his legislative assistant. I couldn't do it, but I was able to introduce Elliott to my close friend Micah Naftalin, a young government lawyer, who was bored out of his mind at the Housing and Home Finance Agency. Micah took the job. After that, I had a reliable place to hang my hat whenever I was able to spend time on Capitol Hill.[13]

Over the next few years I visited Capitol Hill often: summers, Christmas and spring breaks, intersessions in the Wesleyan calendar. Clement E. Vose, my Wesleyan chairman, accommodated my teaching schedule to make it possible for me to spend an unusual amount of time doing field work in Washington. This was rare flexibility in support of research at a liberal arts college and was absolutely essential in the building of intellectual capital. I spent time with members as targets of opportunity presented themselves, including a week with John Brademas of Indiana, another with Robert Giaimo of New Haven, Connecticut, and an especially valuable stretch of time with Richard Bolling of Missouri during the period in late 1961 when he ran for majority leader and granted me total access to his activities during that extremely challenging episode in his life. I combined this period of close-up observation with access to Bolling's correspondence, perhaps two dozen follow-up interviews, and conscientious clipping of the newspapers to produce my article, "Two Strategies of Influence in the House of Representatives."[14]

As the years have gone on, I have gotten to know a fair number of members of Congress. Not as many, to be sure, as scholars who have spent most of their careers in or near Washington, D.C., but over four decades the numbers have mounted up. From time to time I have done formal interviewing, on one focused project or another, but there have also been many informal occasions: meetings, conferences, briefings, retreats, lunches, dinners, and so on.[15]

Occasionally, I have quoted from my transcribed notes of interviews that originally were not for attribution. With the passage of time, a sort of statute of limitations kicks in. In most cases, the member quoted is deceased and some of these interviews are 40 years old. In other cases, only non-sensitive material is involved. Not a great deal of the information I have gathered through personal observation is directly visible in the body of this work, but it is this information that told me where to look for more systematic sorts of evidence and provided my basic orientation to the institution of the House and the way it has developed over the years.

2. *The written record: news articles, published memoirs, contemporary narrative accounts.* A lot of contemporary written material is not indexed or preserved, and tends to disappear, such as, for example, memoranda put out by the Democratic Study Group or newsletters to constituents written in members' offices. Some of it has sat undisturbed in my personal files for many years. Good historians who follow along in due course will unearth even more of this sort of thing than I have been able to do. In addition, there is the written record that has been preserved, notably, for Congress, in the weekly reports and annual almanacs of *Congressional Quarterly*, in official records of Congress and its committees, in places like the *New York Times*, and the main news weeklies, in *Roll Call* and *The Hill*, the semi-weekly parish pump publications of the congressional community,

and other journals. These records are invaluable for, among other things, reliably reconstructing the sequences of events and identifying the main public players. And, like interviews I may have done myself at the time, they record the on-the-record responses of actors to events as they unfolded.

Published memoirs are in a special category. On the whole, American politicians do not write their own memoirs, and so these have to be treated at best as on-the-record interviews—as told to the ghost-writer—rather than as unguarded diaries. At worst they may be purposely misleading. Or they may merely show signs of careless cosmetic work. How, for example, ought we to evaluate this anecdote, which appears in the memoirs of former Speaker Tip O'Neill (written with William Novak):

> Bill Bates, a close friend of mine and a Republican from Massachusetts, was serving on the Armed Services Committee. Old Carl Vincent [*sic*] was the chairman and Bill used to complain to me about how Vincent would monopolize two or three hours of the Committee's time before he finally turned things over to the ranking Republican.
>
> One day, when Bill finally got to ask a question, Vincent said to him, "Are you a new man on this Committee?" Bill had been there for twelve years, but the old man conducted hearings as he pleased. He wasn't aware of the other members.[16]

This is a great story, and I believe it, but it would have improved O'Neill's credibility at least a little if he had accurately rendered the spelling of Carl Vinson's name. It raises the interesting question: while I suppose that Tip O'Neill gave a series of interviews that eventuated in his memoirs (he nowhere discloses how the memoirs were actually produced),[17] did he ever actually read the book once it was written?

Memoirs are usually retrospective, which means they are not quite the same as contemporary news coverage. Once in a while, as in the case of Rep. Clem Miller's remarkable newsletters, they are written on top of events, and so can be treated as one would treat eyewitness accounts.

Miller had an unusual literary style and the assumption has always been that he wrote his newsletters himself. The "editor" of the collected newsletters was a professor of Political Science at Ohio University named John W. Baker whose main contribution to the book seems to have been to scramble the chronological order of the letters and to remove names of members mentioned in the text. One infers this simply by comparing the book with the original newsletters, of which I own precious mimeographed copies. There is nothing explicit mentioned in the book about John W. Baker's role in its production.

A lack of candor about who actually wrote what prevails in the Washington ghost-writing industry. The most famous example, I suppose, is *Profiles in Courage* (New York: Harper, 1956) a book of inspirational vignettes that won John F. Kennedy a Pulitzer Prize for biographical writing that he may or may not have done all by himself. The consensus at the moment seems to be that he wrote the book but with a great deal of help. My opinion of the book is that it is a lightweight production no matter who wrote it. The politics of the Pulitzer selection committee that year must have been quite something to have produced a winner so unrepresentative of first-class modern historical scholarship.[18]

Kennedy's book is in any event about U.S. Senators. Closer to home are books with the names of members of Congress on the cover and not infrequently written in the first person but pretty clearly not actually written by the member in question. The quotation above from the literary oeuvre of Tip O'Neill is one example. O'Neill's other book, *All Politics is Local* (New York: Times Books, 1994) was copyrighted in the names of O'Neill and Gary Hymel (listed on the cover as junior author). No explanation is given about how that collaboration worked.[19]

The academic text *The Speaker* (Washington, D.C.: Congressional Quarterly, 1995) contains four chapters "by" former Speakers of the House. Of these editor Ronald M. Peters, Jr., says: "I want to thank Danney Gobel and Gary Hymel for their assistance to Speakers Albert and O'Neill respectively, and to Drema Johnson for her assistance to Speaker Foley."[20] It is impossible to tell what "assistance" covers. In the case of Tip O'Neill, probably quite a lot.[21] Peters says: "Speaker O'Neill passed away just after completing his chapter." O'Neill's "assistant," Gary Hymel, was a reporter in New Orleans before coming to Washington in 1965 to work for Hale Boggs in the Democratic whip's office. He stayed on when O'Neill succeeded Boggs as majority leader after Boggs was killed in 1972 in an Alaska plane crash and in 1981 became a Washington lobbyist. There is no serious doubt that he knew O'Neill's mind thoroughly. Their collaborations were written in O'Neill's voice but Hymel is in his own right a perceptive observer of Congress. He spent no trivial amount of his time as a staff member helping political scientists and is well known and highly respected in the congressional research community.[22]

Part of the ghost-writing skill is finding and reproducing the voice of the ostensible memoirist. I give especially high marks to Michael D'Orso for bringing to life the rhetorical style of my friend the late Carl Elliott.[23] I am sure others are equally skilled. A novel collaboration was worked out by Jeffrey Biggs and Speaker Thomas S. Foley. Biggs, who had been Foley's press assistant, wrote the bulk of their joint book, *Honor in the House*

(Pullman: Washington State University Press, 1999) in his own voice; Foley, unmistakably in *his* own voice, interpolates long passages of elaboration and tells some wonderful stories. This is a successful and candid way of disclosing who is responsible for what.[24]

Ghost-writing, whether adequately acknowledged or not, pervades the Washington political culture. There is no practical way of avoiding it and I have not done so. Too many telling anecdotes have found their way into Washington memoirs. These anecdotes constitute the lore of the Washington community, and embody too many of the social and cultural realities that members of the House, staff, and observers live with to be excluded from any realistic account of the contemporary Congress. The time I have spent on the Hill interviewing members and observing politics there has helped me in sorting out which among the cleaned up versions of history memoirists have seen fit to publish I am willing to pass along as reliable or reasonable.

3. *Scholarly studies by others, mainly grounded in interviews and observations like my own.* I rely, in particular, on devoted ethnographic work on Congress by Richard Fenno, who has done more than any other single individual to bring to the printed page an intimate understanding of the professional lives of members of Congress. About 40 years ago, before he was universally acknowledged to be the leading field worker in contemporary political science, I had an opportunity to do a little field work on Congress in tandem with Dick Fenno and came to admire his extraordinary gifts in doing that demanding work. Three gifts in particular impressed me: his patience, a willingness to wait and wait while seemingly nothing was going on until he could grasp the underlying pattern of an interaction; his unobtrusiveness, an ability to melt into the background while events, untouched by his presence, flowed around him; and his sensitivity to what he was hearing, an ability to pick up the exact rhetoric of the people he was listening to, and to render it utterly scrupulously and accurately in his notes and in his reports. These reports have been copious—something like fifteen books so far—and have been a gold mine for students of Congress.

Fenno is a strenuous advocate of the view that professional students of politics should make an extraordinary effort to get to know politicians and to study them in their native habitat, i.e., interacting with constituents and with one another.[25] This is more difficult than it may at first appear to be, requiring long hours, sometimes considerable expense, and not infrequently complicated logistics. Not many people have the stamina to do a lot of fieldwork, as Fenno has, but a fair number have done some of it, and whenever possible I have made use of their findings and reports.

4. *Documents and statistics.* I recall more than one person in and around Congress in the 1960s saying to me that Tom O'Brien, Democrat of Illinois, the elderly former Sheriff of Cook County and Mayor Daley's man on the Ways and Means Committee, always got priority placement for his appointees to committees.[26] This was back in the days when the Democratic Committee on Committees was made up of the Democrats on Ways and Means. Rep. Henry Reuss of Milwaukee, Wisconsin recalls:

> I had not asked for assignment to the Banking Committee when I arrived in 1955. Instead, I had requested Public Works, because it had jurisdiction over the St. Lawrence Seaway and I wanted to work on this prize for Milwaukee. But the reigning regional Democrat on the all-powerful Ways and Means Committee, which governed committee assignments, was old Tom O'Brien of Chicago. Old Tom feared that I, a Milwaukean, would start complaining about the "Chicago Water Steal", a perennial Milwaukee gripe that Chicago was taking too much water from Lake Michigan to flush its sewage down the Chicago River. So he put me on the Banking Committee instead.[27]

O'Brien's influence was alleged to go beyond shunting inconvenient freshmen from his region onto a track where they would cause Chicago no trouble. The claim was that when more than one freshman was placed on a committee, O'Brien's man would rank first, and hence, in due course, according to the workings of the seniority system, would get first crack at a subcommittee chair. This is the sort of assertion that can be checked with hard evidence. I checked it. Although Mr. O'Brien in fact did not have this power when he first came on the Ways and Means Committee in the 81st Congress (1949–51), by the 86th and 87th Congresses (1959–62) he was able to secure first place for all Illinois freshmen on committees to which they were appointed.

With respect to committee seniority, the Rules of the House say only that members are to be seated in the order in which they are presented in the resolution prepared by the party committees on committees. The success of Illinois in gaining committee precedence thus broke no rules, but did fly in the face of two customs. One, cited to me repeatedly in congressional interviews, provides that members of equal seniority shall be placed on committees in alphabetical order if they are from the same state, and if they are from different states, in the order in which their respective states entered the Union. The second custom is described by Nicholas Masters. The Democratic members of the Ways and Means Committee represented different geographic areas in negotiating committee assignments, e.g., in the 86th Congress Aime Forand represented the New England Democrats, Tom O'Brien the Democrats from Illinois and Wisconsin. "Each zone representative, *speaking in order of seniority*, nominates candidates from his zone for the various committee vacancies, usually with supporting arguments. Thereupon the committee votes on each of the vacancies [each member having one vote] and the nominee having the highest number of votes is designated to fill it."[28]

Now consider this process in the 86th Congress, (1959), when Mr. O'Brien was fourth in seniority on Ways and Means, behind representatives of zones representing Arkansas, Delaware, Kansas, Oklahoma, the New England states, California, Alaska, Arizona, Nevada, and Utah—a group that included some 19 freshmen Democrats, nine of them from states entering the Union before Illinois. Aside from Harris McDowell of Delaware, who had previously served a term in Congress, *none* of these nine freshmen preceded freshmen from Illinois on the committees to which they were appointed, and four, all from New England, found themselves from one to five places behind freshmen from Illinois. The cases of these four New Englanders are especially in point, because Majority Leader McCormack, both as the most senior member of the New England delegation and as majority leader, was intimately engaged in the process of making committee assignments. However in this domain, clearly Mr. O'Brien enjoyed something of a privileged position, a matter of some consequence, since the line of succession to subcommittee and committee chairmanships was determined by the outcomes of decisions such as these.[29]

Thus, the folklore could be verified as true after the election of 1958, when lots of freshmen had to be placed on committees. But opportunities to test O'Brien's influence in that fashion didn't come up often, since a substantial influx of new members was required, and this was not often supplied by electoral results. The source of O'Brien's influence was identified by informants as dating back to the 1937 election of Sam Rayburn as majority leader when O'Brien swung 16 Illinois Democrats behind Rayburn's candidacy.[30]

On reading voting records. There are minor discrepancies between voting records of some members and their reputations. Wright Patman of Texas was regarded as a liberal because he was a prairie populist on banking issues, central business in his committee, although his overall voting record was sometimes more conservative than that. Similarly, Albert Thomas of Texas voted liberal but was regarded as tight-fisted on the Appropriations Committee by liberal members.

Nonetheless, I rely heavily on voting statistics in determining the bloc

structure of the House—as members generally did as well. Interest group
ratings—statistics about voting published by interest groups as a way of
identifying friends and foes—frequently involve a restricted selection of
issues and do not always give a full picture of members' commitments.
However, within their domain they are helpful in describing the main lines
of alliance and adversarial relations among members. Here, for example,
is a table from William Connelly and John Pitney's book on House Republicans, illustrating, quite effectively, that the very important differences in
the leadership of Bob Michel of Illinois and Newt Gingrich of Georgia had
nothing to do with where they stood on the issues coming before the House
for a vote (see table A.1). Virtually everyone who writes about Congress
uses these sorts of numbers, and I am no exception.

In the text I use three different, but related, measures placing individual
members on an ideological spectrum. Agreement with the conservative
coalition involves the fewest number of issues; party unity adds more issues. A third set of measures notes agreement and disagreement with
liberal (Americans for Democratic Action, ADA) and conservative (American Conservative Union, ACU) interest groups. These groups pick roll-call
issues that are meaningful to them—not always the same issues on both
sides of the spectrum, by the way—and rate members accordingly. In general it is a matter of convenience which score is used. On the whole, they
are much in agreement with one another. Because the conservative coalition score involves fewer issues than party unity scores, some individual
members' scores are liable to jump around from Congress to Congress if
they are irregular voters. Here, for example, is Wright Patman's record
over an 18-year period. During one two-year sequence he bounces from a
conservative coalition net support score of 46 to a net opposition score of

TABLE A.1. Michel and Gingrich Voting Scores in 1992

| Vote score type | Michel | Gingrich |
|---|---|---|
| Party unity | 87 | 94 |
| Conservative coalition | 95 | 98 |
| Presidential support | 93 | 88 |
| ADA | 10 | 10 |
| AFL-CIO | 25 | 22 |
| Chamber of Commerce | 88 | 88 |
| American Conservative Union | 87 | 100 |

Source: William F. Connelly, Jr., and John J. Pitney, Jr., *Congress'*
*Permanent Minority? Republicans in the U.S. House* (Lanham, Md.:
Rowman & Littlefield, 1994), p. 59.

minus 48, a distance of 94 points (see table A.2). The amplitude of his swing from year to year was never again that great, but it is easy to see with this voting record why Patman was never regarded as much of an ally by the Dixiecrats even though he represented a predominantly rural district surrounding Texarkana, bordering Arkansas.

More matters of definition: a great deal of the discussion in the text requires a uniform definition of the term "the South." I use the 11 states of the old confederacy as my benchmark: Virginia, North and South Carolina, Georgia, Florida, Tennessee, Alabama, Mississippi, Louisiana, Arkansas, and Texas. Mason and Dixon's line ran between Maryland and Pennsylvania, and several states—Maryland, Delaware, Oklahoma, Kentucky, and Missouri—which for my purposes would be considered border states, maintained Jim Crow institutions in some cases well into the 1950s. Notoriously, for example, African and Asian diplomats driving between the U.N. in New York City and their embassies in Washington, D.C., down Route 40 were routinely refused service in restaurants south of Philadelphia—well north of the territory I define as the South. West Virginia, which seceded from Virginia in 1861 in order to remain in the Union, is also definitely not south for my purposes. The Census Bureau includes all

TABLE A.2. How Wright Patman Voted, 1959–76

| Year | CC support | CC opposition | Net | Swing |
|------|-----------|--------------|-----|-------|
| 1959 | 73 | 27 | 46 | — |
| 1960 | 26 | 74 | −48 | 94 |
| 1961 | 17 | 78 | −61 | 13 |
| 1962 | 19 | 50 | −31 | 30 |
| 1963 | 27 | 67 | −40 | 9 |
| 1964 | 33 | 67 | −34 | 6 |
| 1965 | 24 | 65 | −41 | 7 |
| 1966 | 19 | 81 | −62 | 21 |
| 1967 | 24 | 57 | −33 | 29 |
| 1968 | 27 | 47 | −20 | 13 |
| 1969 | 33 | 44 | −11 | 9 |
| 1970 | 45 | 25 | 20 | 31 |
| 1971 | 38 | 21 | 17 | 3 |
| 1972 | 39 | 26 | 13 | 4 |
| 1973 | 30 | 29 | 1 | 12 |
| 1974 | 35 | 38 | −3 | 4 |
| 1975 | 33 | 42 | −9 | 6 |
| 1976[a] | 36 | 5 | | |

[a]Wright Patman died in June of 1976.

Source: *Congressional Quarterly Almanacs*, 1959–76.

of these additional states—Maryland, Delaware, Oklahoma, Kentucky, Missouri, and West Virginia—as southern states for many purposes, and some scholars follow suit.[31] *Congressional Quarterly* includes Oklahoma and Kentucky in its definition of southern states when calculating its conservative coalition scores. I follow V. O. Key[32] and others who have adopted a more restricted definition. Readers should be aware that minor discrepancies between my findings and those of other scholars may be accounted for by differences in the way we define "the South".

I use the word "Dixiecrat" in a non-pejorative sense to describe members of the Democratic Party from the South (voters and members of Congress), who vote contrary to most of their counterparts in the national Democratic Party. Southern Democrats who vote with the national party I refer to as "mainstream" or "national" Democrats. A more restricted view would argue that the term "Dixiecrat" should be reserved for southern Democratic opponents of civil rights legislation, since many southern Democrats favored the economic development measures of the early New Deal. While this is true, it is also true that by the late 1930s, there was a solid phalanx of southern Democrats who opposed President Roosevelt and voted with Republicans on issues not directly related to civil rights.

I refer at several points to a substantial part of my investigative procedures as "quasi-anthropological" in character. This requires drawing a distinction between "quasi" and conventional anthropology. Both sorts of anthropology entail personal presence on the research site, sometimes called "participant-observation," but authentic, traditional anthropology means total immersion for a protracted period of time in the social setting that is being studied. As T. M. Luhrmann says, "If you study Malagasy villagers who plant rice and perform cattle sacrifice, you work in the rice paddies and offer up a cow."[33] Typically, professors in pursuit of knowledge about Congress do not themselves get elected to Congress (though some—not necessarily students of Congress—have done so) and so there is a constraint on the extent to which they participate. They can, however, observe, making themselves present in the Capitol and by permission in many of the places members of Congress congregate and can see first hand what is going on. Presence usually entails some sort of interaction with others but in the prevailing etiquette of congressional fieldwork this is usually kept to an unobtrusive minimum.

An example of this approach was my week-long encampment in members' offices in order to get a feel for the everyday routines of their lives. This method blends seamlessly into what we might call informal interviewing, taking advantage of events as they come along to elicit reactions and commentary from members. The best data of this sort is frequently not the product of interviewer-to-subject communication but rather results from being present while local inhabitants communicate with one another.

One miserably hot summer day in the 1960s, for example, a member took me off to the steam room in the House gym, where we sat around for an hour or two. Clad mostly in a clipboard, I watched elderly gentlemen—all members of Congress—loom up out of the fog and engage in informal chat. I observed that they identified themselves to one another by the geography and chief products of their home districts. Members, I learned, didn't necessarily know one another all that well. They are trapped in their routines, and in their offices, and interact mostly with their staffs, with other members of their committees, and in one or two other settings where they may be thrown together, such as at prayer breakfasts, or in state delegation meetings, or interest group caucuses. But members span several generations, and there are a lot of them, and there is constant turnover—averaging between 10 and 20 percent every two years—and it turns out to be quite difficult to get to know members on an informal basis from the other party or who work in other buildings or on other committees. This underscores the costs of the vastly improved transportation from Washington that draws members to their home districts more regularly and more frequently today than in earlier years, and the benefits of travel on business by committees, the so-called junkets, that give members informal opportunities to get to know one another. Committee travel under favorable circumstances introduces cross-pressures of human sympathy capable of attenuating the bitterness of partisan combat. Many of these reflections occurred to me as I sat there in the steam. It also occurred to me to recommend that students thereafter work equipped with the sort of writing instruments that function under water.

A second feature of the quasi-anthropological approach (shared with other ethnographers) is the use of multiple sources and types of data, including eyewitness accounts of others, newspaper clippings, and official statistics. Third, there is the commitment to what anthropologists are now calling "thick description," which requires the rendering of some account of these various streams of data in a coherent narrative form that attempts to capture the world-views of the natives, as explained in the local language.

Two other features of research activity such as I am describing make me want to call it "quasi" anthropology rather than simple garden-variety anthropology. One is the copiousness of the written record on the research site. It is, of course, not unheard of for traditional anthropologists to study modern settings, but it is not typical of them to do so, and frequently the only written material about the locality they study is what they themselves produce. This raises issues of veracity that the alternative sources of documentation available in a modern setting may help to dispel.

A final feature of an enterprise like this one that distinguishes it from traditional forms of anthropology is that one's research site is continuously available to other investigators as well as casual observers. I was never the only observer around, as evidently was the case for Margaret Mead or Malinowski off on their South Sea islands.[34] There is a scientific trade-off between finding a pristine research site and working where there is the possibility that observers can check their impressions with one another. On the whole, I think the chance to corroborate and correct impressions is valuable and increases an investigator's—and a reader's—confidence that we are making an approximation to the truth in our reports.[35]

This raises the issue of the relationship between my report and the accounts of others who have taken an interest in congressional institutions and their history. In general, my book is not about the congressional literature.[36] Though it relies in part on what other scholars have learned about Congress, it is first and foremost about Congress. The events that have marked the evolution of Congress are not my exclusive property, however; they belong to all of us who study Congress, jointly and severally. So, unavoidably, there will be overlap between the story I tell and other treatments of the contemporary Congress, sometimes in agreement, sometimes in disagreement.[37]

Emphases are bound to vary in the way different scholars see a complex landscape. These should in principle be no more troubling than the similarities that are bound to crop up as independent scholars traverse the same, publicly available, terrain. But, of course, there are always practical problems associated with keeping scrupulous score of the influence of others on one's own work. I had occasion, for example, to think of the possibility that I might tread on the toes of (or become too reliant on) a study of congressional change being written in my department by an outstanding young colleague of mine, Eric Schickler, roughly at the same time I was drafting a large part of this book. And so I deprived myself of the pleasure of reading his book until after I had found my own voice and finished my own draft.[38] To my relief, I see we intersect at some points but each have our own story to tell. I am glad now to commend his very accomplished work to students of congressional history. While it had no impact on my thinking, I'm certain it will in the future as it takes what is sure to be a highly valued place in the literature.

# NOTES

*Preface*

1. Nelson W. Polsby, "The Institutionalization of the U.S. House of Repre-sentatives," *American Political Science Review* 62 (March 1968), pp. 144–168; Nelson W. Polsby, Miriam Gallaher, and Barry S. Rundquist, "The Growth of the Seniority System in the U.S. House of Representatives," *American Political Science Review* 63 (September 1969), pp. 787–807.

2. Nelson W. Polsby, *Consequences of Party Reform* (New York: Oxford University Press, 1983).

3. As a very able historian, the late Lawrence Stone, put it: "There is a clear risk of Whiggish teleological distortion if the main question uppermost in the mind of the historian is how we got from there to here. On the other hand, it is just this explanation of the present which is the prime justification for an interest in history." (Lawrence Stone, "The Charles Homer Hoskins Lecture: A Life in Learning," *ACLS Newsletter* 36 [Winter–Spring 1985], p. 21).


*Introduction*

1. For example, one important alternative would be to study changes in congressional rules over time, a focus that has produced a number of first-rate studies, e.g.: Sarah Binder, *Minority Rights, Majority Rule: Partisanship and the Development of Congress* (New York: Cambridge University Press, 1997); Eric Schickler, "Collective Interests, Institutional Innovation, and the Development of the United States Congress," (Ph.D. diss. Yale University, 1997); and Steven S. Smith, *Call to Order: Floor Politics in the House and Senate* (Washington, D.C.: Brookings Institution, 1989).

Another way to write the history of the modern House would be syste-matically to track formal attempts at reform, from the Legislative Reorganiza-tion Act of 1946 through the varied projects of the 1970s, including the Bolling

Committee and the Obey Commission. George Galloway of the Library of Congress, who was instrumental in guiding the work of the Joint Committee on the congressional reorganization of 1946, has written about the results of that effort in *Congress at the Crossroads* (New York: Thomas Y. Crowell, 1946). See also Leroy N. Rieselbach, *Congressional Reform: The Changing Modern Congress* (Washington, D.C.: CQ Press, 1994); Roger Davidson and Walter Oleszek, *Congress against Itself* (Bloomington: Indiana University Press, 1977); Burton D. Sheppard, *Rethinking Congressional Reform* (Cambridge, Mass.: Schenkman, 1985); and David W. Rohde, *Parties and Leaders in the Post-Reform House* (Chicago: University of Chicago Press, 1991).

### 1. The House in Sam Rayburn's Time

1. See D. B. Hardeman and Donald C. Bacon, *Rayburn: A Biography* (Austin: Texas Monthly Press, 1987).

2. For illustrations of this consensus, see, e.g., James T. Patterson, "A Conservative Coalition Forms in Congress," *Journal of American History* 52 (March 1966), pp. 757–72; Richard Bolling, *House Out of Order* (New York: Dutton, 1965), p. 200; George B. Galloway, *History of the House of Representatives* (New York: Crowell, 1961), p. 147; William E. Leuchtenburg, *Franklin D. Roosevelt and the New Deal 1932–1940* (New York: Harper and Row, 1963), p. 252; Neil MacNeil, *Forge of Democracy* (New York: David McKay, 1963), p. 283.

3. Leuchtenburg, *Franklin D. Roosevelt and the New Deal, 1932–1940*, p. 61.

4. James T. Patterson, *Congressional Conservatism and the New Deal: The Growth of the Conservative Coalition in Congress, 1933–1939* (Lexington: University of Kentucky Press, 1967), p. 31.

5. Indeed, William Leuchtenburg argues, to me persuasively, that the heroic image of Franklin Roosevelt in those days made a distinctive mark on all subsequent presidents. See *In the Shadow of FDR: From Harry Truman to Bill Clinton*, 2d ed. (Ithaca, N.Y.: Cornell University Press, 1993). Presidents are routinely evaluated after 100 days in office and regularly found wanting. For example, see Tom Wicker, *JFK and LBJ: The Influence of Personality upon Politics* (New York: Morrow, 1968), who laments John Kennedy's "Hundred Days that never came" (p. 147); and Richard E. Neustadt's argument deploring the 100-day yardstick, "The Presidential 'Hundred Days': An Overview," *Presidential Studies Quarterly* 31 (March 2001), pp. 121–125.

Martin Shapiro refers to a "New Deal myth" and gives a Court-oriented version of these expectations, which he describes as "A selective version of reality made larger than life and employed as a guide to the interpretation of all subsequent reality." He says:

> The myth is simply stated. President Roosevelt took office in 1933 with overwhelming public support and immediately initiated a set of ingeniously pragmatic government programs to save the nation from the De-

pression. In the grip of a sterile and outmoded laissez-faire economic philosophy, the Court declared these programs unconstitutional. In his righteous wrath, the President then rose up to threaten the Court with his "court packing" bill, and in 1937 the Court surrendered. ("The Supreme Court from Warren to Burger," in Anthony King, ed., *The New American Political System* [Washington, D.C.: American Enterprise Institute for Public Policy Research, 1978], pp. 189–90.)

Herbert Stein describes a comparable myth in the field of presidential economics and disputes the claim that Roosevelt invented governmental intervention in the economy:

> Tourists in Leningrad are shown the cruiser "Aurora" moored in the Neva at the spot from which it fired the shell into the Winter Palace in October, 1917, opening the Revolution. But the guide neglects to say that the Winter Palace was occupied at the time not by the Czar but by Alexander Kerensky. . . . Just so the story of the "Keynesian" revolution in fiscal policy. (*The Fiscal Revolution in America*, 2d rev. ed. [Washington, D.C.: AEI Press, 1996], p. 6.)

A recent, vivid retelling of the accepted story is David Kennedy, *Freedom from Fear: The American People in Depression and War, 1929–1945* (New York: Oxford University Press, 1999), pp. 135–53.

6. Jerry Voorhis, *Confessions of a Congressman* (Garden City, N.Y.: Doubleday, 1947), p. 55.

7. Quoted in Paul H. Douglas and Joseph Hackman, "The Fair Labor Standards Act of 1938 I," *Political Science Quarterly* 53 (December 1938), p. 507.

8. Ibid., pp. 507–8.

9. A careful journalistic reconstruction of the politics of the court-packing fight concludes: "Sumners' decision, so quickly arrived at, so stubbornly held to, bulked largest in the final White House determination to let the Senate deal with the plan before the House" (Joseph Alsop and Turner Catledge, *The 168 Days* [New York: Doubleday, Doran, 1938], pp. 66–68). Joseph P. Lash quotes the contemporary comment by FDR's astute assistant Tom Corcoran: "The significance of the Court fight, wrote Corcoran in one of his autobiographical fragments, was precisely in Roosevelt's loss of the fundamental support of the South" (*Dealers and Dreamers: A New Look at the New Deal* [New York: Doubleday, 1988], p. 315).

10. In 1937, the membership of the Rules Committee was as shown in the accompanying table. Four Republicans plus five southern Democrats plus Chairman O'Connor could easily outvote the four remaining New Deal Democrats. In the 1938 election, O'Connor—the brother of Roosevelt's erstwhile law partner Basil O'Connor—was defeated. He was the only anti–New Deal Democrat to be beaten in Roosevelt's otherwise unsuccessful effort to conduct

TABLE TO NOTE 10. Rules Committee Membership, 1937

| Democrats | Republicans |
|---|---|
| John J. O'Connor, Chairman (NY) | Joseph W. Martin, Jr. (MA) |
| Adolph J. Sabath (IL) | Carl E. Mapes (MI) |
| Arthur H. Greenwood (IN) | J. Will Taylor (TN) |
| Edward Eugene Cox (GA) | Donald H. McLean (NJ) |
| William J. Driver (AR) | |
| Howard W. Smith (VA) | |
| J. Bayard Clark (NC) | |
| Martin Dies, Jr. (TX) | |
| Byron B. Harlan (OH) | |
| Lawrence Lewis (CO) | |

Source: Committee on Rules, *A History of the Committee on Rules* (Washington, D.C.: U.S. Government Printing Office, 1983), p. 256.

a purge of unfriendly Democrats in that year. See Sidney M. Milkis, "Presidents and Party Purges: With Special Emphasis on the Lessons of 1938," in Robert Harmel, ed., *Presidents and Their Parties* (New York: Praeger, 1984), pp. 151–175; J. B. Shannon, "Presidential Politics in the South, 1938, I," *Journal of Politics* 1 (May 1939), pp. 146–170; J. B. Shannon, "Presidential Politics in the South, 1938, II," *Journal of Politics* 1 (August 1939), pp. 278–300; and Charles M. Price and Joseph Boskin, "The Roosevelt 'Purge': A Reappraisal," *Journal of Politics* 28 (August 1966), pp. 660–70. Interview with Rep. Howard W. Smith, February 9, 1965.

11. John F. Manley, "The Conservative Coalition in Congress," *American Behavioral Scientist* 17 (November–December 1973), p. 236.

12. The coalition's astute antagonist Rep. Richard Bolling (D-Mo.) said: "There is nothing as tangible or dramatic as a . . . pact. . . . When a majority of each group votes together or in unison . . . the coalition is in operation" (*House Out of Order*, p. 80). In an interview with John Manley on August 19, 1970, coalition leader Howard Smith said:

Joe Martin was a very powerful partisan leader. He and Eugene Cox worked together on many issues. Our group—we called it our "group" for lack of a better term—was fighting appropriations. We did not meet publicly. The meetings were not formal. Our group met in one building and the conservative Republicans in another, on different issues. *Then Eugene Cox, Bill Colmer, or I would go over to speak with the Republicans, or the Republican leaders might come to see us. It was very informal.* [italics in text] Conservative southerners and Republicans from the northern and western states. A coalition did exist on legislation. But we met in small groups. There were no joint meetings of conservative Republicans and southern Democrats. (Manley, "The Conservative Coalition in Congress," pp. 231–32.)

See also Patterson, *Congressional Conservatism and the New Deal*; David W. Brady and Charles S. Bullock, III, "Is There a Conservative Coalition in the House?" *Journal of Politics* 42 (May 1980), pp. 549–59.

13. Martin continues:

Cox was the real leader of the southerners in the House. He was a good speaker and wielded considerable influence. He and I came to Congress the same year, and we became friends while serving together on the Rules Committee. After I was chosen leader he and I were the principal points of contact between the northern Republicans and the southern Democratic conservatives. A bushy-haired Georgia lawyer, Cox was a typical old-fashioned southern leader, who fought tirelessly for states' rights. (Joe Martin and Robert J. Donovan, *My First Fifty Years in Politics* [New York: McGraw-Hill, 1960], pp. 84–85.)

14. Ibid. Martin is referring to the 76th Congress, 1939–41.

15. Manley, "The Conservative Coalition in Congress," p. 235.

16. Howard Reiter's analysis of Poole and Rosenthal's roll- call data for the House of Representatives (see the figure) shows a divergence between southern and non-southern Democratic members of Congress on the "role of government in the economy" starting in 1937–38.

Keith T. Poole and Howard Rosenthal, *Congress: A Political-Economic History of Roll Call Voting* (New York: Oxford University Press, 1997).

Figure to Note 16: Conservatism of Democratic Representatives, 1933–44, by Section

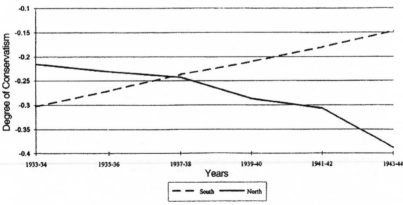

Source: Howard L. Reiter, "The Building of a Bifactional Structure: The Democrats in the 1940s," *Political Science Quarterly* 116 (Spring 2001), pp. 107–29.

17. Dewey W. Grantham, "The South and Congressional Politics," in Neil R. McMillen, ed., *Remaking Dixie: The Impact of World War II on the American South* (Jackson: University Press of Mississippi, 1997), pp. 21–22.

18. Carl Albert, with Danney Goble, *Little Giant: The Life and Times of Speaker Carl Albert* (Norman: University of Oklahoma Press, 1990), p. 217.

19. Thompson's statement said:

> During the war years, the coalition succeeded in passing the Smith antistrike bill, a states rights armed services' voting bill, established the Un-American Activities Committee as a permanent House committee, and watered down the price control program and the excess profits tax measures.
>
> By 1945, coalition voting alignments took place on 16 percent of all House roll calls, as a combination of Rules Committee power, seniority, and attrition among northern Democrats in off-year elections helped conservatives strengthen their grip on the legislative machinery of the House. [Manley's figures agree. See table 1.2.]
>
> In the immediate postwar period of the 79th Congress the coalition used its power to pass the Case strike-control bill, to exclude farm labor from NLRB jurisdiction, to turn over the U.S. Employment Service to the states, and to take the first steps toward gutting the price control program. This latter action soon resulted in a wave of speculation, profiteering, and inflation, costing the American public billions of dollars in lost purchasing power. . . .
>
> During the Eisenhower administration, the coalition has continued to play a dominant role. It has won a number of important victories, including those in which it turned over offshore oil resources to a few coastal states, reduced funds for the soil conservation program, blocked liberalization of the unemployment compensation system, watered-down several public housing bills, passed the natural gas bill, defeated school construction legislation, watered-down a minimum wage bill increasing the extent of coverage, blocked an investigation of administration fiscal and monetary policies, defeated the Kennedy-Ives labor reform bill, blocked consideration of the community facility loan program.
>
> The coalition has also appeared on such issues as antitrust legislation, water pollution control measures, civil rights, natural resource development, public works, foreign aid, H.E.W. appropriation measures, and legislation affecting the District of Columbia.
>
> After the election of the Republican 80th Congress in 1946, the coalition achieved its greatest numerical strength. It succeeded in passing the Taft-Hartley Act and in overriding President Truman's veto of the measure. It reduced coverage under the Social Security Act, overrode Truman's veto of the "rich man's" tax reduction bill, and further weak-

ened price and rent controls. (Statement inserted by Rep. Frank Thompson in the *Congressional Record*, January 27, 1960, pp. 135–38.)

20. Clem Miller, *Member of the House: Letters of a Congressman*, ed. John W. Baker (New York: Scribner, 1962), p. 91.

21. George B. Galloway, *The History of the House of Representatives*, 2d ed., revised by Sidney Wise (New York: Crowell, 1976), p. 180.

22. Cox and Sabath died within two months of one another in 1952.

23. Neil MacNeil writes:

> Rayburn cracked the Rules Committee's reluctance to report out bills the conservatives opposed by persuading his personal friends among the committee's conservatives to help him. He depended most, from 1937 to 1953, on his close personal friend Eugene Cox of Georgia. Later, Rayburn depended on his close friend Joseph Martin, the Republican leader, to help persuade one or two of the conservative Republicans to vote for the bills Rayburn felt he needed. Cox, long a member of the Rules Committee and long the leader of the Southern conservative bloc in the House, held great influence in the committee even though he never achieved the rank of chairman. He frequently called on Rayburn in the Speaker's office to discuss legislation. Rayburn, when he needed help in getting a bill through the Rules Committee, simply asked Cox for that help, even though Cox himself opposed the bill. "Do you really need this?" Cox asked Rayburn, on bill after bill. When Rayburn said he did, Cox, if he could, arranged for the bill to be cleared by the Rules Committee for a vote on the House floor. Why did Cox do it? Rayburn was his friend. "He was an ornery fellow," Rayburn said of him, and he was devoted to Rayburn. Cox once knocked down a newspaperman who wrote a disparaging story about Rayburn. "He loved me," Rayburn said. (*Forge of Democracy*, p. 106.)

William Colmer of Mississippi refers to "the indescribable and lovable Gene Cox of Georgia, who had a fine mind but a bigger heart" (William M. Colmer, Oral History Interview with Charles T. Morrissey for Former Members of Congress Project, Manuscript Division, Library of Congress, October 27, 1978, p. 7.)

24. Albert, *Little Giant*, p. 227.

25. Ibid., pp. 229–30. Tie votes defeat a motion to send a bill to the floor.

26. Bolling, *House Out of Order*, p. 80. The liberal journalist Richard L. Strout writing as T.R.B. describes a Rules Committee meeting on the 1962 Tax Bill submitted by the Ways and Means Committee:

> In a grating voice Smith throws 10 months' hearings out of the window. The bill doesn't balance, he says . . .

It is up to [Wilbur Mills, Ways and Means Committee chairman] to go back and tell his committee now that they must meet Smith's wishes. Unless they do the bill won't get an exit visa from Rules and can't reach the House floor. (You are probably going to see the same process repeated on the trade bill and particularly on the health bill.)

And so, 48 hours later, here we are again! Same place, same people, but changed bill. Mills sneeringly tells what has been done that morning in the Ways and Means Committee to meet the Smith ultimatum.

Reporters' jaws gape as he briskly drops tens of millions here, hundreds of millions there. ("T.R.B. from Washington," *New Republic*, April 2, 1962, p. 2.)

James A. Robinson reports an instance in which House Judiciary chairman Emanuel Celler (D-N.Y.) appeared before the Rules Committee to request a rule on a minor amendment relating to patent fees.

During Mr. Celler's ten- or fifteen-minute statement, Judge Smith was seen to motion to Clarence Brown (Republican, Ohio) to move up a seat so they could talk.

When Celler completed his testimony, Mr. Brown asked one question about the patent fees and then made an inquiry of a different kind. "Mannie," he prefaced his question, "you don't come up here as often as some of us would like to see you." He would like to take this opportunity, Brown continued, to ask about a bill the Chairman of the Rules Committee had pending before the Judiciary Committee. Judge Smith, Brown said, was too modest to inquire, but Celler ought to be told that there had been discussion in the Rules Committee about reporting H.R. 3 directly to the House floor, a rare and unusual action, but one within the Rules Committee's authority.

Celler said he hoped this would not happen, that no chairman likes to see his committee discharged. He had referred H.R. 3 to a subcommittee and thought it had reported the bill unfavorably. Smith intervened to say that the bill had been reported neither favorably nor unfavorably. Celler said he had asked Judge Smith to appear before the full Judiciary Committee, but had received no response to the invitation.

Brown spoke again to say that he did not believe in "horse-trading," but wondered what could be done to expedite H.R. 3. Celler admitted a liking for "horse-trading," and implied he might hasten action on Smith's bill if the Chairman of the Rules Committee could see his way clear to assist in granting a rule on the so-called pre-merger notification bill. Smith allowed that "I'm a horse-trader and the son of a horse-trader." When the laughter subsided, Celler asked Smith whether he wanted to meet with the Judiciary Committee, but the Judge declined, saying he just wanted the bill voted up or down.

A few days later Chairman Smith called up a rule but devoted his time not to the pending rule and bill, but to H.R. 3 instead. "I think this discussion may stimulate the thing a little bit in the Judiciary Committee," said Smith. "That was the purpose of it. They are very fine folks over there." (James A. Robinson, *The House Rules Committee* [Indianapolis, Ind.: Bobbs-Merrill Co., 1963], pp. 13–14.)

One of Judge Smith's great moments in opposition to civil rights illustrating his grasp of floor procedures was compellingly described by Rep. Sidney Yates (D-Ill) in his newsletter of March 17, 1960:

This week the House became a battleground for three determined contesting groups when the civil rights bill came to the floor. All had high hopes and well-laid plans. The first group was the liberal Democrats, led by friendly and experienced Congressman Celler of New York, Chairman of the House Committee on the Judiciary, whose discharge petition had forced the Rules Committee to clear the civil rights bill. Secondly, there were the Republican forces, led by Minority Leader Halleck of Indiana. Halleck, an able, aggressive tactician, has been planning his strategy for months, to capture the civil rights issue for the Republican Party. The third group, consisting of members from the South, who were led by shrewd old Judge Howard Smith of Virginia, Chairman of the House Committee on Rules, were opposed to passage of any bill.

Of the three leaders, Halleck's task was the most delicate and difficult. His proposal had to contain a sufficiently strong voting rights program to command the acquiescence, if not the approval, of the liberal Democrats, and at the same time it had to be weak enough to forestall the wrath of the Southerners with whom he had been allied so frequently in the past and whose support he needed on other legislation. It seemed to him that his purpose could best be accomplished in the bill filed by Republican Congressman McCulloch of Ohio, and when it appeared that Congressman Celler's petition would obtain the 219 signatures needed to bring the civil rights bill to the floor, Halleck and Smith drafted a restrictive rule which permitted the committee bill to emerge, but which gave special preference to McCulloch's bill as an amendment to it.

McCulloch offered his amendment on Monday and most members believed it would be approved as the final bill. However, on Tuesday, when Congressman Kastenmeier of Wisconsin offered an amendment to strengthen the McCulloch proposal, it was the opportunity that Judge Smith had been waiting for. Maneuvering his forces with the skill of General Robert E. Lee, he first joined with Celler's liberal group to accept the Kastenmeier amendment in preference to the McCulloch amendment, and then on the next vote, reversed his position and his group to vote with the Republicans to defeat the Kastenmeier amendment. After all the votes had been taken, Smith gazed in triumph at the wreckage on the battlefield. All that was left for consideration now was the original committee-approved bill which contained no voting rights section at all.

At this point, Smith expected to be able to prevent any further amendment to attach a voting rights section to the bill, on the ground that such proposals had already been voted on. When McCulloch again offered his amendment, Smith promptly made a point of order against it, but McCulloch replied that it was not the same amendment inasmuch as he had stricken a key paragraph from it. Smith's hopes crumbled when the chairman overruled his point of order. But then, consternation spread through the Republican ranks when it became clear during the Clerk's reading of the amendment that someone had slipped up, for the key paragraph had not been stricken. McCulloch's quick attempt to correct the error was prevented by Congressman Abernathy of Mississippi. Immediately Celler moved into the breach. He offered a substitute for the McCulloch amendment exactly like the one McCulloch had filed except that the objectionable paragraph had been deleted. The House approved the Celler substitute.

These events are also described by Clem Miller in his newsletter of April 1, 1960 and (with names suppressed) in Miller, *Member of the House*, pp. 126–29.

27. Walter Kravitz, "The Legislative Reorganization Act of 1970," *Legislative Studies Quarterly* 15 (August 1990), p. 376.

28. Richard W. Bolling, *Defeating the Leadership's Nominee in the House Democratic Caucus*, Inter-University Case Program, Inc., no. 91 (Indianapolis, Ind.: Bobbs-Merrill, 1965), p. 1.

29. Carl Elliott, Sr., and Michael D'Orso, *The Cost of Courage* (New York: Doubleday, 1992), pp. 131–33. Rep. Stewart Udall (D-Ariz.) said:

Graham Barden, the Education chairman from North Carolina, had the idea that a good session of Congress for his committee was to do nothing—I mean literally. I've heard him say that, "Some of the members complain as though if we do nothing we're failing the nation. I'm not sure but what the best thing we can do for the nation is do nothing." He wouldn't say that when the public was there, but he said it to us privately. (Stewart L. Udall, Oral History Interview with Charles T. Morrissey for Former Members of Congress, Inc., Manuscript Division, Library of Congress, March 15, 1979, p. 15.)

30. Frank J. Munger and Richard F. Fenno, Jr., *National Politics and Federal Aid to Education* (Syracuse, N.Y.: Syracuse University Press, 1962), p. 110. Fenno wrote the chapter in which this quote appears.

31. Ibid., p. 109.

32. John Jacobs, *A Rage for Justice: The Passion and Politics of Phillip Burton*

(Berkeley: University of California Press, 1995), p. 218. See also Jeffrey Biggs, with Tom Foley, *Honor in the House: Speaker Tom Foley* (Pullman: Washington State University Press, 1999), p. 35; and Stephen C. Sturgeon, *The Politics of Western Water: The Congressional Career of Wayne Aspinall* (Tucson: University of Arizona Press, 2002).

33. Richard F. Fenno, Jr., *Congressmen in Committees* (Boston: Little, Brown and Co., 1973), p. 61.

34. Ibid., p. 119. The Interior Committee's exemplary rules preceded Aspinall's chairmanship. In 1959 Stewart Udall, a committee member, described Aspinall's predecessor Clair Engle of California as largely responsible:

> I think I can say with considerable assurance that there is no committee of the House which operates more democratically or which operates more smoothly than does the House Interior Committee. I regard it as a model committee. If anyone were to ask me, "Point out a committee that operates and functions so that participation is encouraged and so that the member wherever he happens to sit at the committee table, if he has a contribution to make can make it." Senator Engle not only presided over that committee but was responsible in a rather large measure for the very excellent rules which that committee has. . . . And in presiding over that committee it was not his job nor has it been conceived as the job of the chairman of such a committee where Clair Engle had the gavel to ram through what he wanted, but rather to see that everyone was heard and to see that parliamentary rules were followed. ("School for Freshmen," transcript of five unofficial Congressional Seminars held January 13–21, 1959 in Washington, D.C. as an orientation program for 82 new members of the House of Representatives [Congressional Quarterly, Inc., 1959] p. 18.)

35. Fenno, *Congressmen in Committees*, pp. 120–121. Aspinall commented in an interview on his style as chairman:

> In some respects, I suppose I'm kind of a crank. I don't want the girls to smoke at their desks and they didn't smoke at their desks. I didn't want the girls to come in slacks and they didn't come in slacks. I didn't want the boys to go down to the coffee rooms and have coffee during their work hours and they didn't go down. They had coffee in my own private office and in my chairmanship office. I wasn't a hard task master. They didn't know the hours of the clock. They came in on time but, if the necessity demanded, they stayed late—they never watched the clock. When you have people like that you just get things done. (Interview with Wayne Aspinall by David McComb of the Oral History of Colorado Project, June 11, 1974. Archived at the Manuscript Division, Library of Congress.)

36. "Rep. Cannon Dies; Led Funds Panel," *New York Times*, May 13, 1964, p. 38.

37. Biggs, with Foley, *Honor in the House*, pp. 37–38. Foley first came to Congress in 1965. A decade later the trauma of his first committee meeting had evidently become a part of House folklore. His story is recounted by Norman Y. Mineta, who arrived in Congress in 1974, in "Update from Capitol Hill: Power and Seniority in the House of Representatives," *Public Affairs Report* 17 (December 1976), p. 3. A slightly less extreme story is told about Carl Vinson, Chairman of Armed Services:

> Utterly secure, he ran a committee with no tolerance at all for inter-ference. Lyndon Johnson used to tell the story of when he had served with Vinson on Naval Affairs and had tried to ask a question of an admiral who was testifying. The chairman slammed his gavel down and ruled the question out of order. Lyndon, no shrinking violet himself, got mad. Declaring that he had never once been allowed to speak, he shouted that "after three terms a fellow should be allowed to ask a simple ques-tion." "All right," Vinson gave in, "but just one." (Albert, *Little Giant*, p. 222.)

"Vinson . . . has been a committee chairman longer than any man in the history of Congress," the *New York Times* wrote in 1963. "[He] sits his com-mittee members on a horseshoe-shaped, two-tiered dais. Freshmen sit behind him, where he can not see them and hopes not to hear them" ("The Swamp Fox at 80," *New York Times*, November 19, 1963). See also Cecil Holland, "Senior Member of the House," *Sunday Star* (Washington, D.C.), January 7, 1962.

Clair Engle of California noted to the 1959 Freshman Class: "There is one committee of the House where the rule apparently is that your first term you get to ask one question. Your second term you get to ask two questions and your third term you get to ask three questions and no more" ("School for Freshmen," transcript of five unofficial Congressional Seminars held January 13–21, 1959 in Washington, D.C. as an orientation program for 82 new mem-bers of the House of Representatives [Congressional Quarterly, Inc., 1959] p. 19).

38. See Ira Katznelson, Kim Geiger, and Daniel Kryder, "Limiting Liberalism: The Southern Veto in Congress, 1933–1950," *Political Science Quarterly* 108 (Summer 1993), pp. 283–306; and Barbara Deckard Sinclair, "The Policy Con-sequences of Party Realignment: Social Welfare Legislation in the House of Representatives, 1933–54," *American Journal of Political Science* 22 (February 1978), pp. 83–105.

39. Frank Thompson said:

> The hand of the coalition was also seen in blocking such measures as an effective public housing program, Federal aid to education, civil

rights, an increase in the minimum wage, an adequate farm program, and other legislation which President Truman proposed to the 80th Congress . . .

The high frequency of coalition voting is at least partially explained by the change in House rules on the opening day of the session. The House Rules Committee was stripped of its power to pigeonhole bills reported by standing committees by adoption of the 21-day rule, which permitted committee chairmen to call up bills reported by his committee, if they were not acted upon by the Rules Committee within a 21-day period. This meant that many of the controversial administration bills reached the floor for debate and vote which otherwise would have been held up in the Rules Committee.

Among the measures brought to the floor under the new 21-day rule were Hawaiian and Alaskan statehood bills, a rivers and harbors bill, the National Science Foundation bill, an antipoll tax bill, a VA hospital bill, and a joint resolution providing for U.S. participation in international organizations. In addition, the threat of using the new rule forced a reluctant Rules Committee to act on minimum wage, social security, and public housing legislation, all of which were subsequently enacted into law.

The conservative coalition did succeed in defeating an attempt to repeal the Taft-Hartley Act; in rejecting the Brannan farm plan; in permitting "local option" decontrol of rents; in defeating the National Minerals Act; in watering down the minimum wage bill; in passing the natural gas and basing point bills (both vetoed); in reducing foreign aid funds and funds for public housing; in rejecting controls over commodity speculation; and in watering-down an FEPC bill.

A coalition attempt to repeal the 21-day rule early in the 2d session of the 81st Congress failed. However, the new rule was repealed by the coalition on the opening day of the 82d Congress. Since that time, the Rules Committee has tightened its hold over the legislative machinery of the House. (Thompson, *Congressional Record*, January 27, 1960.)

40. Sherman Adams, *Firsthand Report: The Story of the Eisenhower Administration* (New York: Harper, 1961), p. 314; Arthur Krock, "One Third and One," *New York Times*, May 1, 1960; "President Coins Slogan on Vetoes," *New York Times*, April 30, 1960; Matthew Jarvis, "Eisenhower's Veto Threats: Full of Nothing, Signifying Sound and Fury." Prepared for delivery at the 2002 Annual Meeting of the American Political Science Association, Boston, August 28–September 1.

41. In 1959, the Gallup Poll asked individuals, "If you had to re-register today, would you register as a Democrat or Republican?" Fifty-five percent indicated they would re-register as a Democrat, and only 37 percent indicated they would re-register as a Republican. George H. Gallup, *The Gallup Poll: Public*

*Opinion 1935–1971*, vol. 3 (New York: Random House, 1972), p. 1639. Data from the 1958 and 1960 University of Michigan surveys show a similar distribution of preferences (see the accompanying table).

42. The 22nd Amendment, limiting presidents to two terms, was ratified in 1951. Eisenhower was the first president to whom it applied.

43. Mark F. Ferber, "The Democratic Study Group: A Study of Intra-Party Organization in the House of Representatives" (Ph.D. diss., UCLA, 1964). Ferber dates the formation of the DSG to a meeting in mid-September 1959 (p. 1). *CQ* says:

> The Democratic Study Group is an outgrowth of a less formalized association in the House which existed in an effort to make the aims of liberal Democratic members felt more positively. These go back to a group of about 30 members formed around Rep. Eugene J. McCarthy (D-Minn.) ... in 1956. On January 8, 1957, 80 Democratic members signed a ... "liberal manifesto" which outlined major legislative goals. During 1957 and 1958 this group operated loosely through personal communication and a system of "whips"—about 12 members who alerted another 60 to 80 when a special vote was due. ("Liberal House Democrats Organize for Action," *Congressional Quarterly*, January 8, 1960, p. 39).

See also Kenneth Kofmehl, "The Institutionalization of a Voting Bloc," *Western Political Quarterly* 17 (June 1964), pp. 256–72.

44. Bolling, *House Out of Order*, pp. 205–7.

> Speaker Sam Rayburn (D-Texas) met Jan. 3 with Democratic Reps. Thompson [N.J.], Metcalf [Mont.], John A. Blatnik (Minn.), Chet Holifield (Calif.), Henry S. Reuss (Wis.) and George M. Rhodes (Pa.). They said in a joint statement following the meeting: "We have received assurances from Speaker Rayburn that legislation which has been duly considered and reported by legislative committees will be brought before the House

TABLE TO NOTE 41. Partisan Preferences of Voters, 1958 and 1960

| Party | 1958 | 1960 |
|---|---|---|
| Democrats (with leaners) | 56 | 52 |
| Republicans (with leaners) | 33 | 36 |

Source: The National Election Studies, Center for Political Studies, University of Michigan, *The NES Guide to Public Opinion and Electoral Behavior* (Ann Arbor: University of Michigan, Center for Political Studies, 1995–98, tables 2A.1 and 2A.2.

NOTES TO PAGE 22   185

for consideration within a reasonable period of time. Our confidence in
the Speaker is great, and we believe he will support such procedural steps
as may become necessary to obtain House consideration of reported bills
from legislative committees." (*Congressional Quarterly*, January 8, 1960,
p. 39.)

45. Ferber, "Democratic Study Group," pp. 43–45, 48. Joe Martin said:

If they didn't enlarge the committee the Republicans would be blamed
for every piece of legislation that died in the committee and of course
the Democrats would maneuver all the legislation in there to die in there.
Then the Republicans would be blamed. . . . When I led, I put Scott on
[the Rules Committee] and he would let legislation by for the good of
the cause sometimes. Henry Latham did too. But not now. (Interview
with Rep. Joe Martin, July 27, 1961.)

46. Ferber, "Democratic Study Group," p. 45.
47. "Party Caucuses Precede Session Opening," *CQ Weekly Report*, January
9, 1959, p. 43.
48. Bolling, *House Out of Order*, p. 206.
49. Budge was defeated in 1960, and in March 1961, Reece died. Leo Allen
did not run for reelection in 1960. They were replaced in 1961 by the equally
conservative Katharine St. George of New York, Elmer Hoffman of Illinois, and
Allen Smith of California. When Rayburn "packed" the committee with Carl
Elliott and B. F. Sisk in 1960, the Republicans added William Avery of Kansas.
50. "A Paradoxical Congress," September 19, 1959, p. 925. Quoted in Ferber,
"Democratic Study Group," p. 37. Political historian Sidney Hyman wrote in
the *New York Times Magazine* ("Inquiry into the 'Decline' of Congress," January
3, 1960, p. 5):

It mattered little that the Congressional Democrats held an impressive
majority of the seats. It mattered little that, in Mr. Eisenhower, they faced
a President of the opposition party who was nearing the end of his
tenure, specially marked as the first man to be barred by the constitution
from succeeding himself. In the controversy over the budget—central to
everything else—it was President Eisenhower who chose the field of battle, who held the initiative, and who won virtually every point at issue.
     The Congress for its part, failed to generate any real steam behind
major programs of its own. It showed little inventive power of its own
in matters of policy. More significantly, it failed even to subject the President's visions of the nation's needs and capabilities to a searching and
instructive public debate. The sum of the Congressional achievement was
some local "pork-barrel" victories, arranged mainly in the House of Rep-

resentatives, plus a few minimal votes and revisions of what the President himself wanted done.

For a description of the Landrum-Griffin labor bill, see Alan K. McAdams, *Power and Politics in Labor Legislation* (New York: Columbia University Press, 1964).

51. Bolling, *House Out of Order,* p. 208.

52. Ibid., p. 209.

53. Richard Bolling, "The House Committee on Rules," Paper delivered at Midwest Conference of Political Scientists, Columbia, Missouri, May 11, 1961, p. 6.

54. Clem Miller, *Member of the House: Letters of a Congressman* (New York: Scribner, 1962), pp. 90 and 91. This quotation is taken from Rep. Miller's newsletter of March 1, 1960.

55. "The Committee grants all but about twenty requests for hearings each Congress. It withholds rules from about twelve bills on which it holds hearings, while giving rules to more than a hundred" Robinson, *House Rules Committee* p. 41).

56. *Congressional Record* (perm.), June 30, 1960, p. 15187.

57. The accompanying table gives the *CQ* definition determining membership in the conservative coalition for 1959.

58. Rep. Gerald Flynn, *Congressional Record* (perm.), June 30, 1960, pp. 15189–90.

59. Chairman Graham Barden was not amused. In an interview Frank Thompson of New Jersey said:

> Chairman Barden motioned me to sit by him and asked in his old-boy voice, "Frank, what about these boys, who are they?"
>
> "Well, that first fellow on the end there is Roman Pucinski—that's spelled P-u-c-i-n-s-k-i. He's from Chicago, and he's a Roman Catholic. Then the next fellow there is Bob Giaimo, spelled G-i-a-i-m-o. He's an Italian-American from Connecticut. And he's a Roman Catholic. The next one is Dominick Daniels."
>
> Barden brightened and said, "Daniels. That sounds like a good Anglo-Saxon name."
>
> "No," I said, "he's of Italian background, too. And he's a Roman Catholic from New Jersey. And that last young fellow there, that's John Brademas, spelled B-r-a-d-e-m-a-s, from Indiana. He's the first Greek-American ever elected to Congress. And he used to teach at St. Mary's College."
>
> By this time, Barden's face was a vivid red, and the arteries were standing out above his shirt collar. It looked like apoplexy was on the point of overtaking him. "Goddammit," growled Barden. "It looks like they've given me the whole goddamned League of Nations and the Pope

TABLE TO NOTE 57.   The Conservative Coalition, 1959

---

A *conservative coalition roll call* is any roll call on which the majority of voting southern Democrats and the majority of voting Republicans oppose the stand taken by the majority of voting northern Democrats. A *member's conservative coalition support score* is the percentage of conservative coalition roll calls on which the member votes "yea" or "nay" in agreement with the position of the conservative coalition.

*1959 Conservative Coalition Roll Calls*

*RC 21, S 57.* Housing Act of 1959. Thomas (D-TX) amendment to make all additional funds authorized in the bill available only upon enactment of pertinent appropriation bills. Agreed to 222–201. (CC won)

*RC 22, S 57.* Kilburn (R-NY) motion to recommit the bill and substitute the Herlong (D-FL) bill (HR 7117), authorizing no public housing and cutting the total housing authorization to $1.3 billion. Rejected, 189–234. (CC lost).

*RC 44, HR 288.* Open rule for debate on bill HR 3, a bill to limit court application of the federal preemption doctrine. Adopted. (CC won)

*RC 46, HR 3.* Permit federal courts to strike down state laws under the federal preemption doctrine only if Congress had specified its intention to preempt the field of legislation involved or if a state and a federal law were in irreconcilable conflict, and to permit state enforcement of laws barring subversive activities against the federal government. Lindsay (R-NY) motion to recommit bill. Rejected, 191–227. (CC won)

*RC 47, HR 3.* Passage of federal preemption doctrine bill. Passed, 225–192.(CC won)

*RC 51, HR 4957.* "Mallory Rule" bill to amend the Federal Rules of Criminal Procedure to bar federal judges from disqualifying confessions of suspects solely because of delay in bringing suspects for arraignment. Lindsay (R-NY) motion to recommit the bill. Rejected, 138–261. (CC won)

*RC 52, HR 4957.* Passage of "Mallory Rule" bill. Passed, 262–138. (CC won)

*RC 58, HR 8342.* Labor–Management Reporting and Disclosure Act of 1959. Landrum (D-GA) and Griffin (R-MI) amendment to substitute for the committee bill the language of their bill, containing curbs on secondary boycotts and organizational and recognition picketing, and giving the states power to handle "no man's land" labor disputes. Agreed to, 229–201. (CC won)

*RC 59, HR 8342.* Kearns (R-PA) motion to recommit the substitute labor bill. Rejected, 149–279. (CC won)

*RC 60, HR 8342.* Passage of the substitute labor bill. Passed 303–125. (CC won)

*RC 61, HR 7040.* Independent Offices Appropriations for fiscal 1960. Thomas (D-TX) motion that the House disagree, for the second time, to a Senate amendment providing $25 million, instead of the $10 million approved by the House, for federal contributions to the states for the civil defense program. Agreed to 241–167. (CC won)

---

Source: *Congressional Quarterly Almanac*, 1959, pp. 140–41.

of Rome, too." (Andrée E. Reeves, *Congressional Committee Chairmen: Three Who Made an Evolution* [Lexington: University Press of Kentucky, 1993], p. 33.)

The fifth liberal freshman was James G. O'Hara of Michigan.

60. See, in addition to McAdams, *Power and Politics in Labor Legislation*, the excellent case study by Samuel C. Patterson, *Labor Lobbying and Labor Reform: The Passage of the Landrum Griffin Act*, Inter-University Case Program, Inc., no. 99 (Indianapolis, Ind.: Bobbs-Merrill, 1966).

61. See Ferber, "Democratic Study Group," pp. 55–155, 215–304 for details.

62. Miller, *Member of the House*, pp. 123–24.

63. Brady and Bullock, "Is There a Conservative Coalition in the House?" p. 558. Galloway, *History*, p. 180.

64. See Nelson W. Polsby, Miriam Gallaher, and Barry Spencer Rundquist, "The Growth of the Seniority System in the U.S. House of Representatives," *American Political Science Review* 63 (September 1969), pp. 787–807; and Nicholas Masters, "Committee Assignments in the House of Representatives," *American Political Science Review* 55 (June 1961), pp. 345–57.

65. Albert, *Little Giant*, pp. 220–21.

66. Raymond E. Wolfinger and Joan Heifetz, "Safe Seats, Seniority, and Power in Congress," *American Political Science Review* 59 (June 1965), pp. 337–49.

67. Randall Ripley, *Majority Party Leadership in Congress* (Boston: Little, Brown, 1969), pp. 61–62, 143–44. The rule was changed in 1975. For purposes of voting on the floor for Speaker and other officers of the House and for committee assignments, a majority vote in the caucus henceforth bound Democrats.

68. Hardeman and Bacon, *Rayburn: A Biography*, p. 346. Hardeman was present at this meeting.

69. Neil MacNeil, personal papers, January 1959. The influential Wilbur Mills (D-Ark.) says flatly: "We didn't have caucuses back in those days. Sam Rayburn didn't believe in them anymore than I would allow them now if I were in his position. They do nothing but split the party and cause a lot of confusion and ill will" (Wilbur D. Mills, Oral History Interview with Charles T. Morrissey for Former Members of Congress, Inc., Manuscript Division, Library of Congress, April 5 and June 7, 1979, p. 48).

Carl Albert recalled:

[Rayburn] deliberately allowed the Democratic Caucus to atrophy as an instrument of party discipline. Previous Speakers, most conspicuously Champ Clark and John Nance Garner, had regularly assembled all Democratic members into caucus to define and mobilize official party positions on major issues. Fearful of an eruption between our various factions, Speaker Rayburn limited the caucus to big biennial assemblies, their only purpose to ratify the party's slate of House leaders. (Carl Albert, "The Speakership in My Time," in Ronald M. Peters, Jr., ed., *The Speaker* [Washington, D.C.: CQ Press, 1995], p. 185.)

Neil MacNeil, in a background memo dated January 31, 1961, pp. 10–11, notes an instructive exception. At the start of the 81st Congress, the Democratic caucus adopted the 21-day rule by 176 to 48. This rule permitted a legislative committee's chairman to call up for House action any bill reported by his committee that the Rules Committee had ignored for 21 legislative days. "Rayburn made the caucus a binding caucus . . . requiring that every Democrat vote for the rule on the floor unless (1) he held the change unconstitutional or (2) he had actively campaigned for re-election against the change." Thirty-one Democrats, all from the South, refused to be bound anyway. The rule was adopted, but it only lasted two years. It was killed at the beginning of the 82nd Congress.

70. See the accompanying table. Rutgers political scientist Ross K. Baker was a consultant to the House Democratic caucus in 1983. His "Short History of the House Democratic Caucus" (mimeo, January 1983) says, "In the years between 1939 and 1969, the caucus acted intermittently on matters relating to membership and specific policy questions." He gives two examples during the Rayburn years: in 1942 the caucus voted to bar the seating of Vito Marcantonio of New York as a Democrat, thus preventing Marcantonio from receiving a committee assignment for the 78th Congress. In 1949 the caucus instructed the chairman of the Banking and Currency Committee to offer amendments to a Republican-sponsored housing bill (p. 15).

71. See Rowland Evans and Robert Novak, *Lyndon B. Johnson: The Exercise of Power* (New York: New American Library, 1966), pp. 264–65; Robert Dallek, *Lone Star Rising: Lyndon Johnson and His Times, 1908–1960* (New York: Oxford University Press, 1991), p. 570. Paul T. David, "The Presidential Nomination," in David, ed., *The Presidential Election and Transition 1960–61* (Washington, D.C.: Brookings, 1961), p. 25.

72. Stanley Kelley says:

That Lyndon Johnson's primary assignment was to hold the South for the Democrats shows up clearly in the way he allocated his campaign time (of course, that this was his assignment was evident from the moment he was chosen to be Kennedy's running mate). Nixon, Lodge, and Kennedy devoted roughly equal portions of their time to the Southern states (from about 15 to 20 per cent). Johnson devoted about 44 per cent of his time to the region. He gave about half of his campaign in the final three weeks to the South, about one quarter of it to Texas alone. (Stanley Kelley, Jr., "The Presidential Campaign," in David, ed., *The Presidential Election and Transition* pp. 71–72.)

TABLE TO NOTE 70. Democratic House Caucus Meetings, 1921–60

| Year | Democratic caucuses (month, purpose) | Speaker |
|------|--------------------------------------|---------|
| 1921 | | Frederick H. Gillett (R-MA) |
| 1922 | | |
| 1923 | December, organizational | |
| 1924 | | |
| 1925 | March, organizational | Nicholas Longworth (R-OH) |
| 1926 | February, policy | |
| 1927 | | |
| 1928 | | |
| 1929 | March, organizational | |
| | May, policy | |
| 1930 | | |
| 1931 | December, organizational | John N. Garner (D-TX) |
| 1932 | | |
| 1933 | March, organizational | Henry T. Rainey (D-IL) |
| | March, policy | |
| 1934 | March, policy | |
| | March, policy | |
| 1935 | | Joseph W. Byrns (D-TN) |
| 1936 | December, organizational | William B. Bankhead (D-AL) |
| 1937 | January, organizational | |
| | August, discipline | |
| 1938 | | |
| 1939 | January, organizational | |
| | January, policy | |
| | February, discipline[a] | |
| | July, discipline[a] | |
| 1940 | September, organizational | Sam T. Rayburn (D-TX) |
| 1941 | January, organizational | |
| 1942 | | |
| 1943 | January, organizational | |
| 1944 | | |
| 1945 | January, organizational | |
| 1946 | November, organizational | |
| 1947 | January, organizational | Joseph W. Martin (R-MA) |
| 1948 | | |
| 1949 | January, organizational | Sam T. Rayburn (D-TX) |
| 1950 | January, organizational | |
| 1951 | | |
| 1952 | | |
| 1953 | January, organizational | Joseph W. Martin (R-MA) |
| 1954 | | |
| 1955 | January, organizational | Sam T. Rayburn (D-TX) |
| 1956 | | |
| 1957 | January, organizational | |
| 1958 | | |
| 1959 | January, organizational | |
| 1960 | | |

[a]From George B. Galloway, *History of the House of Representatives* (New York: Crowell, 1976), p. 182.

Note: Shaded areas indicate that Democrats held majority in the House.

Source: Data compiled from *New York Times Index*, 1921–60.

Also Theodore H. White, *The Making of the President 1960* (New York: Atheneum Publishers, 1961), pp. 172–77, on why LBJ was selected.

73. The rump session was convened on August 8, 1960, and adjourned on September 1, 1960. *Congressional Quarterly Almanac,* 1960, p. 65. See Tom Wicker, "Again That Roadblock in Congress," *New York Times Magazine,* August 7, 1960, p. 14; "The Congress: The Democratic Debacle," *Time,* September 5, 1960, p. 12. Paul T. David in David, ed., *The Presidential Election and Transition,* p. 25 says:

> One of the oddities of the Johnson strategy was his decision, in collaboration with Speaker Sam Rayburn, to bring Congress back into session again after the conventions were over. Apparently, this was intended to strengthen the position in seeking support for the Johnson candidacy at the convention, as well as to give him a favorable forum in which to begin the campaign if nominated. To the extent that these were indeed the motivations, they seem to have reflected an erroneous judgment in both respects.

74. Ferber, "Democratic Study Group," passim.

75. Larry Hufford, *D.B.: Reminiscences of D. B. Hardeman* (Austin, Tex.: AAR/Tantalus, 1984), p. 145.

76. Tip O'Neill's memoirs say: "When he first became Speaker [Rayburn] knew plenty of congressmen, but as the years went on, he became increasingly isolated in the party. By the time I came along [1953] he was dealing almost exclusively with the committee chairmen" (*Man of the House* [New York: St. Martins, 1987] p. 153).

77. *Congressional Quarterly Almanac,* 1961, p. 1025.

78. The rule of the caucus at the time was:

> In deciding upon action in the House involving party policy or principle, a two-thirds vote of those present and voting at a Caucus meeting shall bind all members of the Caucus: *Provided* The said two-thirds vote is a majority of the full Democratic membership of the House: *And provided further,* That no member shall be bound upon questions involving a construction of the Constitution of the United States or upon which he made contrary pledges to his constituents prior to his election or received contrary instructions by resolutions or platform from his nominating authority. ("Preamble and Rules Adopted by the Democratic Caucus," U.S. Government Printing Office [no date].)

On September 9, 1975, the caucus repealed the two-thirds rule but added this rule: "With respect to voting for Speaker and other officers of the House, for each committee chairman or ranking minority member, and for membership of committees, a majority of those present and voting at a Democratic Caucus shall bind all members of the Caucus." I am grateful to Walter Oleszek of the Library of Congress for this information.

79. MacNeil, *Forge of Democracy*, p. 420.

80. The other was to be the affable middle-of-the-roader B. F. Sisk of California's central valley, originally a Texan.

81. MacNeil, *Forge of Democracy*, pp. 412–48; William R. MacKaye, "A New Coalition Takes Control: The House Rules Committee Fight of 1961," *Eagleton Institute Cases in Practical Politics* 29 (New Brunswick, N.J.: Rutgers, The State University, 1963); Bolling, *House Out of Order*, pp. 210–20; Robert L. Peabody, "The Enlarged Rules Committee," in Robert L. Peabody and Nelson W. Polsby, eds., *New Perspectives on the House of Representatives* (Chicago: Rand McNally and Company, 1963), pp. 129–64; Milton C. Cummings, Jr. and Robert L. Peabody, "The Decision to Enlarge the Committee on Rules: An Analysis of the 1961 Vote," in ibid., pp. 167–94.

82. Elliott, *Cost of Courage*, p. 205.

83. B. F. Sisk, with A. I. Dickman, *A Congressional Record: The Memoir of Bernie Sisk* (Fresno, Calif.: Panorama West, 1980), pp. 106–9. Carl Albert writes: "Fearful of a bloody fight to purge Colmer and of its even bloodier consequences, the Swamp Fox [Vinson] made the Speaker an offer. If Mr. Rayburn would drop the purge motion, Vinson would get him enough Southern Democratic votes to add three new members to the Rules Committee" (Albert, *Little Giant*, p. 240). On the roll call Rayburn got the southern votes as shown in the accompanying table.

84. Walter Kravitz, *A Short History of the Development of the House Committee on Rules*, revised by Walter J. Oleszek (Washington, D.C.: Congressional Research Service, Library of Congress, 1975).

85. *Congressional Quarterly*, October 13, 1961, p. 1728.

86. See H. Douglas Price, "Race, Religion and the Rules Committee," in Alan F. Westin, ed., *The Uses of Power: 7 Cases in American Politics* (New York: Harcourt, Brace & World, 1962), pp. 1–71; Frank J. Munger and Richard F. Fenno, Jr., *National Politics and Federal Aid to Education, The Economics and Politics of Public Education* 3 (Syracuse, N.Y.: Syracuse University Press, 1962); and Robert Bendiner, *Obstacle Course on Capital Hill* (New York: McGraw-Hill, 1964). Kravitz indicates nine education bills hung up. The only other major failure was on the creation of a Department of Urban Affairs, first proposed as a bill, then disapproved as a reorganization.

## 2. Toward Liberalization

1. Bascom Timmons, "Rayburn," part 4, p. 1 (ditto, no date: supplied to newspapers at the time of Speaker Rayburn's death). D. B. Hardeman and Donald C. Bacon, *Rayburn: A Biography* (Austin: Texas Monthly Press, 1987), pp. 165–66.

2. "Second Session: The New Speaker," *Newsweek*, January 15, 1962, p. 15.

TABLE TO NOTE 83. Southern Democrats Voting for
Expansion of Rules Committee

| *Alabama* | *Louisiana* | *Texas* |
|---|---|---|
| Elliott | Boggs | Brooks |
| Jones | Brooks | Casey |
| Rains | Morrison | Ikard |
| Rob- | Thompson | Kilday |
| erts | Willis | Mahon |
| *Arkansas* | *North Carolina* | Patman |
| Alford | Bonner | Poage |
| Harris | | Rutherford |
| Mills | *Tennessee* | Teague |
| | Bass | Thomas |
| *Florida* | Davis | Thompson |
| Fascell | Evins | Thornberry |
| | Loser | Wright |
| *Georgia* | | Young |
| Pilcher | | |
| Vinson | | *Virginia* |
| | | Jennings |

Note: 35 of 95 southern Democrats (excluding Rayburn),
37%, voted to expand the Rules Committee.

Source: Data come from *Congressional Quarterly Almanac*,
1961, pp. 508–9.

From June through September 1961 and again in December 1961 and January
and February 1962, I spoke informally in Washington with more than 100
members of Congress, congressional staff members, journalists, and others on
the succession to Rayburn. In addition, during the latter period, I conducted
formal interviews with 26 Democratic congressmen from all parts of the country. Interviewees were given a pledge of anonymity, and so quotations have
occasionally been slightly altered in order to mask the identity of the informant.
My work in the summer of 1961 was supported by a grant in aid from the
Social Science Research Council, whose assistance is gratefully acknowledged.

3. Thomas P. O'Neill and William Novak, *Man of the House* (New York: St.
Martin's Press, 1987), pp. 140–41.

4. See comments by H. Douglas Price, "Race, Religion and the Rules Committee," in A. Westin, ed., *The Uses of Power* (New York: Harcourt, Brace &
World, 1962), p. 30. There is no biography of McCormack. Garrison Nelson,
who is working on one, has turned up fascinating evidence that McCormack
routinely misrepresented important details of his background in interviews in
order to conform his personal history to the Horatio Alger norms presumed to
be attractive to his South Boston constituency. Nelson, "Irish Identity Politics:
The Reinvention of Speaker John W. McCormack of Boston," *New England Journal of Public Policy* 15 (Fall/Winter 1999/2000), pp. 7–34; "In the Shadow of

John McCormack's Past Lie New Truths about His Life," *Boston Globe*, July 25, 1999.

5. Paul Duke, "House to Install McCormack, Albert Today Amid Lack of Enthusiasm by Democrats," *Wall Street Journal*, January 10, 1962, p. 2. Memories are very long in the House. Richard Bolling told me a story about a McCormack tactical error that had taken place a dozen years previously:

> In the 80th Congress [William] Colmer was the junior man and got tossed out of the Rules Committee when the Republicans took over. At the time of the 81st (1949) he didn't need to have gotten back on again, but Colmer wrote a letter to John McCormack asking to be put back on the committee . . . and McCormack made a big mistake. He wrote Colmer a letter and said of course everybody would get their committee assignments back and he assumed Colmer would get the Rules committee back. McCormack had to honor his word and this inadvertent act of McCormack's . . . changed the history of many subsequent Congresses. (Bolling (D-Mo.) interview, July 28, 1961).

6. "A Voluble Speaker," *New York Times*, January 11, 1962, p. 16.

7. James Reston, "A Happy New Year and All That," *New York Times*, December 31, 1961.

8. "The Congress: Mr. Speaker," *Time*, January 19, 1962, p. 16.

9. Neil MacNeil, "The House Confronts Mr. Kennedy," *Fortune*, January 1962, p. 172.

10. Morris Udall (D-Ariz.) interview, January 19, 1962.

11. See Arthur Krock, "Rayburn's Successor," *New York Times*, November 19, 1961. Krock was very close to the Kennedy family (he wrote the introduction to the book made of the President's Harvard senior thesis, *Why England Slept*). Hence, it is possible to give more than the usual credence to the following statement that appeared in his column and, to my knowledge, nowhere else: "Weeks before the Speaker went home to die of cancer, Mr. Kennedy passed the word that if the House wanted to elect Representative McCormack as its presiding officer this was agreeable to him." See also John Morris, "McCormack Leads for Rayburn Post," *New York Times*, November 17, 1961; Richard L. Lyons, "The Speakership," *Washington Post*, October 7, 1961.

12. Clem Miller (D-Calif.) interview, January 12, 1962.

13. A good theoretical treatment of the strategic situation faced by Democrats can be found in Thomas C. Schelling's *Strategy of Conflict* (Cambridge, Mass.: Harvard University Press, 1960), esp. pp. 53–80. This essay explores how actors differently situated can settle on outcomes when preliminary communication is impossible.

14. Nelson W. Polsby, Miriam Gallaher, and Barry S. Rundquist, "The Growth of the Seniority System in the U.S. House of Representatives," *American*

*Political Science Review* 63 (September 1969), p. 789. Also Nicholas A. Masters, "Committee Assignments in the House of Representatives," *American Political Science Review* 55 (June 1961), pp. 345–57. Masters says, "Continuous service . . . insures a member of his place on a committee but seniority may have very little to do with transfers to other committees, and it has virtually nothing to do with the assignment of freshman members" (p. 345). "When two or more members stake a claim to the same assignment, on the ground that it is essential to their electoral success, both party committees [that control assignments] usually, if not invariably, will give preference to the member with longer service" (p. 354).

15. A Richard Bolling newsletter to his constituents, January 25, 1963, said:

Action by the 88th Congress to keep the committee at 15 members means the Rules Committee will likely be more in tune with the Democratic leadership than with a handful of conservatives. As a member of Rules for eight years, I have been all too aware of how this coalition has frustrated efforts to pass major legislation. Instead of serving as a traffic cop to clear bills to the floor, the Rules Committee has too often been a jailer.

But another change, perhaps less generally known, is one which I foresaw would mean far more this year to the success of measures such as medical care for the aged through Social Security and tax reduction. This was the selection of House Democrats of two proven Administration supporters for the Committee on Ways and Means. This committee has jurisdiction over revenue matters and Social Security. The election of Representatives Ross Bass of Tennessee and W. Pat Jennings of Virginia will mean this vital committee will be manned by Congressmen disposed to a fair hearing for these major bills.

16. See Richard W. Bolling, *Defeating the Leadership's Nominee in the House Democratic Caucus*, Inter-University Case Program, Inc., no. 91 (Indianapolis, Ind.: Bobbs-Merrill Company, 1965).

17. Richard Bolling commented:

One of the reasons why I think about [Landrum] is he worries me. He's got a lot of ability. He's as tough as anybody I've seen around here, got a lot of courage, flexible. He would do as Smith does, he would calculate pretty carefully. He wouldn't make the mistake of going for 100% when he could only get 50. He'd be pretty sharp on getting 50, not 49; he wouldn't make the mistake of going for 52. Now that's the kind of person I consider dangerous as an opponent. (Transcript of Seminar at Wesleyan University, Middletown, Connecticut, December 10, 1962.)

The Committee on Political Education (COPE) of the AFL-CIO rated members of the Education and Labor Committee on 13 floor votes during the previous Congress (1957–58). Landrum's score sticks out like a sore thumb (see accopanying table).

18. "The Congress: Escape from Emasculation?" *Time*, January 18, 1963, p. 18. "The Congress: Quid Pro Nothing," *Time*, January 25, 1963, p. 16. During this era, the main *Time* magazine Capitol Hill correspondent was Neil MacNeil, a notably well-informed and capable journalist.

19. "The Congress: Quid Pro Nothing," *Time*, January 25, 1963, p. 16.

20. A contest in the caucus for a Ways and Means seat, though quite rare, was not entirely unprecedented. Back in 1951 Burr Harrison was elected to the committee in a six-way race for three open seats, beating out Winfield K. Denton, of Indiana, who had the endorsement of the leadership. This was also the year the conservative coalition killed off the two-year-old 21-day rule that weakened the stranglehold of the Rules Committee. In 1963, in contrast, it was the liberals who won. See Clayton Knowles, "House Rules Unit May Regain Power," *New York Times*, January 3, 1951, p. 19.

21. "Ways and Means Posts," *Congressional Quarterly*, January 18, 1963, p. 46.

22. Bolling, *Defeating the Leadership's Nominee*, p. 12.

23. "Smith decided that even a liberal might be preferable to an apostate,

TABLE TO NOTE 17. Pro- and Anti-Labor Votes, 1957–58 by Returning Democratic Members of the Committee on Education and Labor

| Returning Democratic member | Pro-Labor | Anti-Labor |
| --- | --- | --- |
| Graham A. Barden (NC), chairman | 4 | 9 |
| Adam C. Powell (NY) | 12 | 0 |
| Cleveland M. Bailey (WV) | 7 | 4 |
| Carl D. Perkins (KY) | 9 | 3 |
| Roy W. Wier (MN) | 11 | 2 |
| Carl Elliott (AL) | 11 | 2 |
| Phil M. Landrum (GA) | 4 | 9 |
| Edith Green (OR) | 12 | 1 |
| James Roosevelt (CA) | 13 | 0 |
| Herbert Zelenko (NY) | 12 | 0 |
| Frank Thompson, Jr. (NJ) | 13 | 0 |
| Stewart L. Udall (AZ) | 13 | 0 |
| Elmer J. Holland (PA) | 13 | 0 |
| Ludwig Teller (NY) | 11 | 0 |
| John H. Dent (PA) | 3 | 1 |

Source: Alan K. McAdams, *Power and Politics in Labor Legislation* (New York: Columbia University Press, 1964), p. 142.

and he led 25 or 30 Southern Conservatives into the liberals' camp" ("The Congress: Quid Pro Nothing," *Time*, January 25, 1963, p. 16). Phil Landrum said:

> The leadership decided to endorse me and Mr. Bass, leaving Mr. Jennings to scramble on his own. Under other circumstances, that would have been it—Mr. Jennings would have withdrawn. Without the leadership support, that would have been it. But this time it was different.
>
> There are three sets of Democrats in the House. There is one group who are joined together, it's called the [Democratic] Study Group, the reformists. They want to change everything and do it yesterday, instead of tomorrow. I don't like the terms "liberal" and "conservative," but in the common parlance, they are the extreme liberals, and they number about 75 to 100.
>
> Then there are the party Democrats—less liberal—they come from places where the party organization is important. Mr. McCormack, bless his soul, he's making a fine Speaker, and he's a good friend of mine. The party is important—now that's a somewhat smaller group.
>
> Then, you have a third kind of group. They come from the Southeast and the Southwest, all across the South. They support the party when it suits them, and they tell them to go to hell when it doesn't suit them. There is a little more in the Southwest than in the Southeast supporting the Democratic Party. But that's the third group.
>
> Now the first group, the Democratic Study Group, I got almost no votes there. There were three or four votes for me, but not many more than that. Jennings was their candidate—I was *non gratis* to them. One of them told me, "Phil, you're a damn good hunting companion, and I like you personally, but to hell with you, I don't want you sitting on that committee." So their vote was for Jennings and Bass and Bass got 169. Bass wasn't what those people liked, but he was better than Landrum.
>
> The second group—they followed the party and their vote was Landrum and Bass.
>
> Then you came to the South. The South split badly between Jennings and Bass. But the week before, I counted 129, and I got 126, so I figure I'm not a bad vote counter. I lost a scattered vote in two or three delegations, but for the most part I got a solid vote across the Southeast and Southwest. I lost a couple in Kentucky, Tennessee.
>
> Q: What about Virginia?
>
> A: Yes, a couple in Virginia. I might have lost one or two Mississippi votes. Know I lost one—the fellow came up and wanted his letter back endorsing me. I said, "Take your letter and your vote; your friendship means more to me than either of them." The whole Alabama delegation was gone—the governor's inauguration. In two states, Jennings got practically all the votes, and Bass got none.

> They asked me about Medicare and other issues. I said I wouldn't
> be an obstructionist, that I would work to get the best bill out of
> committee.
>
> I have no doubt as to the genuine sincerity of the leadership sup-
> port. I got up at the end of the caucus and I moved to make it unan-
> imous for Mr. Bass and Mr. Jennings. You have to have a thick hide
> in this business. (Interview, March 27, 1963.)

After the landslide election of 1964, the Democrats were entitled to two new
seats on the Ways and Means Committee. One of them went to the thick-
skinned Mr. Landrum who in the meantime had greatly improved his party
support score in voting on the floor of the House. Once safely on the committee,
however, he reverted to voting predominantly in opposition to the majority of
his party. See Kenneth A. Shepsle, *The Giant Jigsaw Puzzle: Democratic Committee
Assignments in the Modern House* (Chicago: University of Chicago Press, 1978),
pp. 147–148.

24. This section and the next draw on Paul D. O'Brien's fine Wesleyan
honors thesis, "Party Leadership and the Committee Selection Process in the
House of Representatives" (Middletown, Conn.: Wesleyan University Honors
College, June 1964).

25. Norman J. Ornstein, Thomas E. Mann, and Michael J. Malbin, *Vital
Statistics on Congress* (Washington, D.C.: Congressional Quarterly Inc., 1998),
table 2–7, p. 61.

26. "The Congress: I Love This House," *Time*, February 2, 1959, p. 14.

27. Rowland Evans, Jr., "Louisiana's Passman: The Scourge of Foreign Aid,"
*Harper's*, January 1962, pp. 76–83. Elizabeth Brenner Drew, "Mr. Passman
Meets His Match," *Reporter*, November 19, 1964, pp. 40–45.

28. Perhaps the most striking example of this influence—because the substantive committee was capably led and ideologically uncontentious—was the
House Appropriations Subcommittee on the Department of Defense. It was in
the appropriations hearings where military policy, as proposed by the executive
branch, received the most serious examination given by Congress. For a specific
instance of oversight by the Appropriations Committee of defense policy, see
Edith T. Carper, *The Defense Appropriations Rider*, Inter-University Case Program,
Inc., no. 59 (University: University of Alabama Press, 1960). Carper describes
the successful attempt of the Department of Defense subcommittee to attach
a rider on the appropriations bill limiting executive discretion in maintaining
(or not maintaining) local facilities and installations under the Defense Department's jurisdiction.

29. Rowland Evans and Robert Novak, "Inside Report: King Clarence,"
*Washington Post*, June 5, 1963.

30. Richard F. Fenno, Jr., *The Power of the Purse: Appropriations Politics in
Congress* (Boston: Little, Brown, 1966), p. 450. Also Fenno, "The Appropriations

Committee as a Political System," *American Political Science Review* 56: 2 (June 1962), pp. 310–24, p. 323.

31. Masters, "Committee Assignments in the House of Representatives," p. 352.

32. Julia Butler Hansen (D-Wash.) interview, July 14, 1963. This was one of a series of interviews on committee packing conducted in Washington in the summer of 1963 by Michael Leiserson and Paul D. O'Brien under my direction, some of which were used by Paul O'Brien in his 1964 Wesleyan honors thesis.

33. Fenno, "The Appropriations Committee as a Political System," p. 314.

34. In one case the member, Tom O'Brien of Illinois, was personally requested by Speaker Rayburn to leave Appropriations and move to Ways and Means. The other, Hamer Budge (R-Idaho), was chosen by a caucus of regional congressmen to be that region's representative on the Rules Committee (Fenno, "The Appropriations Committee as a Political System," p. 313).

35. Ibid., p. 312.

36. Ibid., p. 312.

37. Ibid., p. 320.

38. Ibid.

39. The "mean liberalism" score is calculated by taking the average of the Kennedy Domestic Support Indices of 1961 and 1962 (in *Congressional Quarterly*) and subtracting from that the average of the Kennedy Domestic Opposition Indices of 1961 and 1962.

40. Charles S. Joelson (D-N.J.) interview, July 16, 1963.

41. Julia Butler Hansen (D-Wash.) interview, July 14, 1963.

42. Charles S. Joelson (D-N.J.) interview, July 16, 1963.

43. Gary was the victim of a new Cannon rule: no committee member could serve as chairman of more than one subcommittee. The beneficiary was Otto Passman, who said "I didn't ask for the job. I didn't know I had the job until I read about it in the papers" (Fenno, *The Power of the Purse*, p. 146).

44. "I have sat under ten speakers," he said, "but I have never seen such biased and inept leadership" (*Congressional Record* 108 [October 13, 1962], p. 23486). See Jeffrey L. Pressman, *House vs. Senate: Conflict in the Appropriations Process* (New Haven, Conn.: Yale University Press, 1966); and a *Washington Post* editorial, "Trouble in the House," October 14, 1962.

45. Clem Miller (D-Calif.) interview, January 12, 1962.

46. The phrase comes from James MacGregor Burns, *The Deadlock of Democracy: Four-Party Politics in America* (Englewood Cliffs, N.J.: Prentice-Hall, 1963).

47. These included the creation of the Office of War Mobilization (and later Reconversion), the creation of the Defense Department and the CIA, the Employment Act of 1946, and the transfer of the Bureau of the Budget to the

Executive Office of the President in 1939. See Nelson W. Polsby, *Political Innovation in America* (New Haven, Conn.: Yale University Press, 1964).

48. Clarence Brown (R-Ohio) interview, August 4, 1961.

49. Alvin E. O'Konski (R-Wis.) interview, August 23, 1963.

50. Richard L. Lyons, "Old Guard Picks 6 for House Unit," *Washington Post,* January 24, 1963, p. A6.

51. E. Y. Berry (R-S. Dak.) interview, August 19, 1963.

52. Vernon W. Thomson (R-Wis.) interview, July 23, 1963.

53. Lyons, "Old Guard Picks 6 for House Unit," p. A6.

54. Robert K. Walsh, "Seat Scramble Poses Problem for Halleck," *Washington Evening Star,* January 11, 1963, p. A4.

55. Interview, August 28, 1963. On May 19, Gross gave a televised interview to Roger Mudd of CBS News. The transcript read, in part:

> MUDD: Well, now that you're on Foreign Affairs, Mr. Gross, are you going to be taking a lot of overseas junkets?
>
> GROSS: I have never taken one yet and have no plans to take a junket.
>
> MUDD: Wouldn't it be good for you to inspect overseas what our foreign aid money is doing?
>
> GROSS: Well, you know, you really don't have to go overseas to find out what's happening. The newspaper reporters and others provide us with enough information of the . . . failures in the foreign aid program.
>
> MUDD: When was the last time you were outside the United States?
>
> GROSS: Well, I took a trip overseas in 1918.
>
> MUDD: 1918?
>
> GROSS: Yes.
>
> MUDD: As a doughboy?
>
> GROSS: As a dog face, yes.
>
> MUDD: Have you ever voted for a foreign aid program, Mr. Gross?
>
> GROSS: No.
>
> [ . . . ]
>
> MUDD: Mr. Gross, is it true that you read every piece of legislation and every Committee report that comes before the House?
>
> GROSS: I try to know something about every bill that comes to the House floor, whether it's on a consent calendar, the private calendar, or whether it comes in under a rule. I try to know something about every bill before it comes in.
>
> MUDD: How do you have time to do all this?
>
> GROSS: Well, you don't go to the beach or play golf. You take the bills home at the end of the week and spend most of your waking hours reading bills and hearings and reports on bills. This you have to do if you are going to keep up with this thing.
>
> MUDD: You don't play golf or go to the beach?

GROSS: No, I don't.

MUDD: Do you have any form of recreation once you leave the Hill?

GROSS: No, I don't, unfortunately.

MUDD: What do you do on Saturday and Sunday?

GROSS: Read bills, and reports and hearings.

(Transcript, "Washington Report," CBS News, May 19, 1963, pp. 23, 19–20.)

Walter Trohan, of the *Chicago Tribune*, wrote:

Gross does his homework. He studies every bill. Then, armed with a rule book, he goes to the floor of the House to battle for the taxpayer, poised to leap to his feet, the bird dog of economy. He is the dread of proponents of legislation who rise to speak without preparation. His points of order, parliamentary inquiries, and questions have tied the House in knots, demolished pretentious champions of spending legislation, forced bills back to committee for revision, and frequently knocked them out altogether. (Extension of Remarks of Hon. Frank T. Bow, "The Honorable H. R. Gross," *Congressional Record* Appendix, October 13, 1963, p. A7693.)

See also Norman C. Miller, "Iowa's Mr. Gross Wins Fame by Viewing Life with Jaundiced Eye," *Wall Street Journal*, May 28, 1969.

56. Interview, August 23, 1963.

57. Leslie C. Arends (R-Ill.) interview, August 22, 1963.

58. James F. Battin (R-Mont.) interview, July 18, 1963.

59. John V. Lindsay (R-N.Y.) interview, August 19, 1963. Lindsay emphasized the role of the Committee Chairman Clarence Brown of Ohio: "Brown this year was determined to use the Committee on Committees to achieve political aims. . . . They put on a bunch of Neanderthals."

60. Bipartisanship scores were calculated by subtracting members' administration opposition scores on foreign policy from their administration support scores, as calculated by *Congressional Quarterly*. Data from *Congressional Quarterly Almanac*, 1961, pp. 624–25, and 1963, pp. 720–21.

61. The literature on this issue is voluminous. For a sampling of work on some of its dimensions and its historical foundations, see: J. Morgan Kousser, *The Shaping of Southern Politics: Suffrage Restrictions and the Establishment of the One-Party South, 1880–1910* (New Haven, Conn.: Yale University Press, 1974); Lester M. Salamon and Stephen Van Evera, "Fear, Apathy and Discrimination: A Test of Three Explanations of Political Participation," *American Political Science Review* 67 (December 1973), pp. 1288–1306; U.S. Commission on Civil Rights, *Political Participation* (Washington, D.C.: U.S. Commission on Civil Rights, 1968); V. O. Key, Jr., *Southern Politics in State and Nation* (New York:

Knopf, 1949) (new edition, Knoxville: University of Tennessee Press, 1984); Michael Perman, *Struggle for Mastery: Disenfranchisement in the South, 1888–1908* (Chapel Hill: University of North Carolina Press, 2001).

62. A notable Republican exception was the ranking member of the House Judiciary Committee in the 1960s, William McCulloch of Ohio. He supported

> all the civil rights bills beginning with the first major one in 1957, a voting rights act. He also supported the Civil Rights bill of 1959, an anti-bombing bill in 1960, the omnibus 1964 act that desegregated public accommodations and many other aspects of American life, the tough Voting Rights Act of 1965 and the Open Housing Act of 1968.
>
> In 1970, when the act that allowed federal officials to register black southerners to vote came up for renewal, Mr. McCulloch fought efforts by the Nixon administration to weaken the measure. He accused the administration of trying to "create a remedy where there is no wrong and leaving wrongs without a remedy."
>
> In 1971, when McCulloch announced plans to retire for reasons of health, Rep. Emanuel Celler (D-N.Y.), his long-time friend and ally in the civil rights field, said it was "tragic that a man of his great competence and integrity" was forced to leave Congress.
>
> In an interview in 1972, Mr. McCulloch said there were few votes to be won for a civil rights advocate back home in Piqua, Ohio. (J. Y. Smith, "Former Rep. William McCulloch Dies," *Washington Post*, February 23, 1980, p. C8.)

Occasionally, the Ohio connection took precedence. McCulloch voted with Judge Smith and the conservative coalition and against Sam Rayburn in the 1961 Rules Committee fight. To have voted otherwise would have meant pitting himself against his senior Ohio colleague Clarence Brown, ranking Republican on the Rules Committee and on the Republican Committee on Committees. Clarence Brown's influence may help to explain why Ohio freshman Charles Mosher, who usually voted with McCulloch in favor of civil rights, voted with him on the conservative coalition side in the Rules fight. Republican committee assignments were not made until after the vote on the Rules Committee. Out of 16 Ohio Republicans, all but William Ayres of Akron voted with Brown and Judge Smith.

See Charles Whalen and Barbara Whalen, *The Longest Debate: A Legislative History of the 1964 Civil Rights Act* (New York: New American Library, 1985). Charles Whalen (R-Ohio), a liberal Republican, served in Congress 1967–79.

63. See Theodore H. White, *Making of the President 1964* (New York: Atheneum Publishers, 1965).

64. See Robert L. Peabody, *Leadership in Congress: Stability, Succession, and Change* (Boston: Little, Brown, 1976), pp. 100–148.

65. *Congressional Quarterly* (*CQ*) commented that this was the first time a

House Democrat had been punished for party disloyalty since 1911. "House Mavericks Disciplined; New Rules Approved," *CQ Weekly Report*, January 8, 1965, p. 33. The caucus action took place on January 2, prior to the opening of Congress. When Congress convened on January 4, one censured member, Albert Watson of South Carolina, did not vote for McCormack for Speaker thus making him eligible for censure under Rayburn's criterion.

66. "DSG Strategy Meeting," *CQ Weekly Report*, December 11, 1964, p. 2793.

67. "House Rules Changes Enhance Majority Rule," *Congressional Quarterly Almanac*, 1965, p. 587.

68. "89th Congress Convenes: House Adopts Rules Changes; Senate Rules Fight Begins; President Sends Up State of the Union, Health Messages," *CQ Weekly Report*, January 8, 1965, p. 31.

69. "Congress, 1965—The Year in Review," *Congressional Quarterly Almanac*, 1965, p. 65.

70. "Congress, 1966—The Year in Review," *Congressional Quarterly Almanac*, 1966, p. 69.

71. To replace Smith and James Trimble of Arkansas, a mainstream Democrat, who was defeated in the general election.

72. "House Conservative Coalition," *Congressional Quarterly Almanac*, 1967, p. 76.

73. Ford gave a speech rejecting the "southern strategy" at Bowling Green University on May 10, 1967 that attracted some comment in the House. See remarks of Omar Burleson, *Congressional Record, House*, May 15, 1967, p. 12611. John Herbers, "House GOP Cutting Ties with Southern Democrats," *New York Times*, May 15, 1967; John Herbers, "Coalition in the House: South's Democrats Voting with GOP Despite Ford's Rejecting Such Tactics," *New York Times*, August 10, 1967.

74. "House and Senate Key Votes for 1967," *Congressional Quarterly Almanac*, 1967, p. 96.

75. See *Powell v. McCormack*, 395 U.S. 486 (1969). By then Powell had been reelected to the next Congress from his Harlem constituency and seated. This weakens the view that the Supreme Court does not accept cases rendered moot by events.

76. Norman J. Ornstein, "Causes and Consequences of Congressional Change: Subcommittee Reforms in the House of Representatives, 1970–73," in id., ed., *Congress in Change: Evolution and Reform* (New York: Praeger Books, 1975), p. 90

77. Larry L. King, "The Road to Power in Congress," *Harper's*, June 1971. Reprinted in Robert L. Peabody, ed. *Education of a Congressman: The Newsletters of Morris K. Udall* (Indianapolis, Ind.: Bobbs-Merrill, 1972), pp. 291–328. Morris Udall had succeeded to his brother Stewart's Arizona seat in a special election when Stewart became John Kennedy's Secretary of the Interior in 1961.

78. "House Seats Adam Clayton Powell; Greatly Boosts Education Funds; Votes to End Electoral College," *Congressional Quarterly Almanac*, 1969, p. 102.

Later the same year, the 77-year-old McCormack was embarrassed by his legislative assistant, Martin Sweig, who was accused of influence peddling and suspended in October 1969. "Legislative Branch: McCormack Aide," *Congressional Quarterly Almanac*, 1969, p. 1023. Sweig was later indicted and convicted. See also Richard Harwood and Laurence Stern, "Influence Case Points Up House Ills under McCormack's Speakership," *Washington Post*, January 14, 1970.

79. A 1972 poll of members of Congress conducted by Common Cause showed that congressional reform sentiment was also prevalent among junior and liberal Republicans. See Eric Schickler, Eric McGhee, and John Sides, "Remaking the House and Senate: Personal Power, Ideology, and the 1970s Reforms," Paper presented at the Annual Meeting of the Midwest Political Science Association, Chicago, April 25–28, 2001. Two decades earlier, reformers could also be found on both sides of the aisle. Stewart Udall said:

> There was a group of us—I think most of us came in in the 1950s who tended to talk reform and who were rather restive. We mostly wrote and talked, we didn't accomplish a great deal. But I do think we set the stage for things that happened later. . . . The Democratic Study Group, I think, would have to be exhibit A. My mentors, if I had any in those days, were Dick Bolling, Lee Metcalf from Montana, and Gene [Eugene J.] McCarthy. My friends on the Republican side were people like Perkins Bass [R-N.H.] and John Lindsay [R-N.Y.]. . . . We saw how much there was a need for change; so whether we were Republicans or Democrats, we talked about reform and worked on it. (Stewart L. Udall, Oral History Interview with Charles T. Morrissey for the Modern Congress in American History Project of Former Members of Congress, Inc., Manuscript Division, Library of Congress, March 15, 1979, pp. 5–6.)

80. Wolfinger and Heifetz, "Safe Seats and Seniority."

81. Bolling, *House Out of Order*, pp. 60–61.

82. Ibid., p. 244.

83. MacNeil, *Forge of Democracy*, p. 258.

84. Nelson W. Polsby, "Two Strategies of Influence in the House of Representatives: Choosing a Majority Leader, 1961," in Robert L. Peabody and Nelson W. Polsby, eds., *New Perspectives on the House of Representatives* (Chicago: Rand McNally, 1964), p. 256. I did extensive interviewing in the House in early 1961 (from which several of these quotes are drawn) and sat in with Bolling during his 1961 battle to become majority leader. John Blatnik of Minnesota said, "I would rate Dick an able guy, one of the ablest in the House. [But he] isolated himself too much from the membership and from the liberal group. Some of the guys felt that he went beyond the Speaker's wishes and was most unfair when he gave the impression to the press that he would be crown prince apparent." (Interview, January 9, 1962).

85. Stewart L. Udall, Oral History Interview with Charles T. Morrissey for Former Members of Congress, Inc., Manuscript Division, Library of Congress, March 15, 1979, p. 6.

86. Polsby, "Two Strategies of Influence in the House of Representatives," p. 255.

87. See John Jacobs, *A Rage for Justice* (Berkeley: University of California Press, 1995), p. 300: At the time of the 1976 battle "one member said he liked Bolling, but found him arrogant, self-important, and too quick to play the know-it-all . . . [Tip] O'Neill [D-Mass.] . . . served on Rules for years with Bolling and could not tolerate his arrogance. 'Jesus, Dick made a lot of enemies,' O'Neill said." See also Tip O'Neill, with William Novak, *Man of the House* (New York: St. Martins, 1987), p. 161. In 1976, when he ran again for majority leader, Bolling told his colleague Mo Udall, "I think I'm too arrogant to win" (reported by John M. Barry, *The Ambition and the Power* [New York: Viking, 1989], p. 20).

Rayburn's 1961 death triggered a series of changes in Bolling's life. He in effect gave himself a sabbatical, uncharacteristically playing hooky from the Rules Committee during the rush of legislation following John Kennedy's assassination. "In December, 1963," he said, "decisions were made about what issues would be dealt with before Christmas, and I had an understanding that I would not be needed at the Rules Committee. Then [President] Johnson changed his mind and wanted more legislation, so he decided he needed me back. He sent a private plane to the Caribbean, but I wouldn't come back" (Richard E. Cohen, "The House Loses Its Foremost Student of How to Make the Institution Work," *National Journal*, October 2, 1982, p. 1682). Bolling withdrew to the Center for Advanced Study at Wesleyan University in Connecticut and attempted—unsuccessfully—to write his book, which later appeared with the collaboration of Wes Barthelmes, *House Out of Order* (New York: E. P. Dutton, 1965). See esp. p. 9. He terminated his marriage of long standing and took up with the Washington lobbyist who in January 1964 became his second wife. "Bolling of Missouri Wed to Texan after Divorces," *New York Times*, January 17, 1964. He emerged a little later as an activist for the liberal causes he had always favored, but with a difference. While Rayburn was alive he espoused get-along-go-along strategies; thereafter he openly advocated institutional reform. See also Adam Clymer, "Richard Bolling, Missouri Liberal and U.S. House Insider, Dies at 74," *New York Times*, April 23, 1991, p. C20.

88. Ornstein, "Causes and Consequences of Congressional Change," p. 92.

89. Ibid., p. 112.

90. Ibid., p. 92. Conlon was staff director of the Democratic Study Group from 1971 until his untimely death in a boating accident in June 1988. A shrewd and cheerful former journalist from the middle west, he came to Washington in 1968 on the Congressional Fellowship program of the American Political Science Association and worked for three years in the office of Senator Walter Mondale of Minnesota before joining the staff of the DSG. At the time

of his death, Rep. David Obey of Wisconsin, a longtime DSG activist, said, "I don't think it would be possible to find any congressman or staff member on the Hill who had as much of an impact as Dick did" (Chris Adams, "Hill Aide Missing after Sailboat Accident," *Washington Post*, June 21, 1988). Linda Greenhouse in the *New York Times* quoted Rep. Tony Coelho (D-Calif.), himself a former congressional staffer, as saying that Conlon "enjoyed such credibility with so many House members that virtually no major legislation could pass without his personal support" ("Richard Conlon Dies in Accident: Head of Democratic Unit Was 57," June 23, 1988).

91. Walter Kravitz of the Library of Congress summarizes:

> It began to curb the abuse of power by committee chairs, opened committee deliberations a little more to the public, and eliminated some flagrant dilatory tactics in the House. Its procedural changes gave members and others more time to study legislation before bills came to the floor for action, protected the House from overzealous conference committees, and took a first step toward providing the House with a method for dealing with nongermane Senate amendments.
>
> It provided a more equitable distribution of committee assignments and chair positions in the Senate. It gave the House a time-saving mechanism for recording votes and quorum calls. It enhanced the minority party's right to committee staff. It gave Congress greater access to fiscal information, laying a foundation upon which a new congressional budget process was eventually built.
>
> And it resolved many institutional problems little noticed by, and of little interest to, most outsiders but of considerable consequence inside the place. The Congressional Research Service was strengthened and revitalized; GAO was thrust further into valuable investigations for committees and members; the Legislative Counsel's Office in the House received a statutory base that protected its priorities; the pay system of House employees was rationalized; the administrative officers of Congress were protected from unqualified or incompetent employees, improving the institution's administrative staff support; and tourists were granted free tours of the Capitol, a modest but useful blessing of which most current visitors are unaware. ("Legislative Reorganization Act of 1970," *Legislative Studies Quarterly* 15 [August 1990], pp. 396–97.)

92. Ornstein, "Causes and Consequences of Congressional Change," pp. 111–12.

93. The Hansen Committee's recommended changes to the seniority system were adopted by the House Democratic caucus on January 20, 1971. *CQ* reports that the changes to the caucus rules were:

The Democratic Committee on Committees would recommend to the caucus nominees for the chairmanship and membership of each committee, and such recommendations need not necessarily follow seniority. The Committee on Committees would make recommendations to the caucus, one committee at a time; upon the demand of 10 or more members, nominations could be debated and voted on. If a nomination was rejected, the Committee on Committees would submit another nomination. ("The House: New Leaders of Democratic Majority," *Weekly Report*, January 22, 1977, p. 177.)

The March 15, 1972 rules of the Democratic caucus say: "Upon the written request of 10 Democratic Members of any committee or upon the written request of a majority of the Democratic Members, whichever is less, addressed to the chairman thereof to hold a Caucus of the Democratic Members, said chairman shall call such Caucus within 10 days of such a request. Said request shall contain the subject matter for discussion at such Caucus." My source for this is Dr. Stanley Bach of the Library of Congress Congressional Research Service, who comments, "The Caucus rules dated March 19, 1969, say nothing at all about committee caucuses" (personal communication, March 20, 2001). Evidently this new rule was adopted April 21, 1971.

94. Jeffrey R. Biggs, with Thomas Foley, *Honor in the House: Speaker Tom Foley* (Pullman: Washington State University Press, 1999), p. 37.

95. Ornstein, "Causes and Consequences of Congressional Change," p. 110.

96. Ibid., p. 106.

97. Michael Malbin, "Congress Report: New Democratic Procedures Affect Distribution of Power," *National Journal*, December 1974, p. 1883.

98. Ibid.

99. Norman Y. Mineta, "Update from Capitol Hill: Power and Seniority in the House of Representatives," *Public Affairs Report* 17 (December 1976), p. 4.

100. There was thorough news coverage of these events. See, e.g., Mary Russell, "Freshmen-led Drama Yet to be Played Out," *Washington Post*, January 19, 1975; Richard L. Lyons and Mary Russell, "Democrats Strip Hebert, Poage of Unit Chairs," *Washington Post*, January 17, 1975; Richard D. Lyons, "House Democrats Oust 3 Chairmen but Retain Hays," *New York Times*, January 23, 1975.

101. Barbara Hinckley, "Seniority 1975: Old Theories Confront New Facts," *British Journal of Political Science* 6 (1976), pp. 383–99.

102. Rowland Evans and Robert Novak, "Something Worse Than Seniority," *Washington Post*, January 25, 1975.

103. Common Cause, "Report on House Committee Chairmen," mimeo (Common Cause: 2030 M Street NW, Washington, D.C., January 13, 1975), p. 30.

104. Common Cause found considerable fault with Mahon's conservatism (see Report) but consider the testimony of liberal member Stewart Udall:

George Mahon was a man who was cut out of the old mold, and I had great respect for him. He had some of the qualities that were a lot like my father. He was very hard-working, very fair. He commanded respect in a way that few did in the House, because of his command of issues. He worked very hard. And, they were doing it then with small staffs. The congressmen themselves had to do an enormous amount of work. George, as conservative as he was, when he said something to you, when he presented a defense budget on the floor, you knew he had put the military on the pan. You could count on his judgment. He was one of the stalwarts, one of the people who put the House in a good light and proved that the House could do just as good a job as the Senate. I think that in all those years, that was true of George Mahon. He was one of the strongest, most effective people in the House. (Stewart L. Udall, Oral History Interview with Charles T. Morrissey for Former Members of Congress, Inc., Manuscript Division, Library of Congress, March 15, 1979, p. 13.)

105. Joseph K. Unekis and Leroy N. Rieselbach write: "the House Armed Services Committee is . . . a reelection-oriented committee. Though its jurisdiction covers military matters of great policy significance, particularly the Pentagon's basic defense programs, Armed Services has not often challenged the professional military's expertise. It has consistently supported the services' call for larger budgets . . . without subjecting defense programs to substantial scrutiny" (*Congressional Committee Politics: Continuity and Change* [New York: Praeger, 1984], pp. 11–12). This was even true during the extended chairmanship (on the Naval Affairs Committee, 1931–46, and then the consolidated Armed Services Committee, 1949–53 and 1955–65) of Hebert's predecessor but one, the venerable Carl Vinson of Georgia, who served in Congress from 1914 to 1965 and was widely regarded as an authoritative figure on all aspects of defense policy. When Lewis A. Dexter in the late 1950s questioned one member of the Armed Services Committee on the role of Congress in military policy-making, the member snapped back:

What the hell is the point of that? What would you do with it? I don't see that any public service would be performed by it. You can't find anything particular to say. In fact, how do we know what should be considered? We mostly reflect what the military people recommend; military policy is made by the Department of Defense. Our committee is a real estate committee. (Lewis Anthony Dexter, "Congressmen and the Making of Military Policy," in Robert L. Peabody and Nelson W. Polsby, eds., *New Perspectives on the House of Representatives* [Chicago: Rand McNally, 1963], p. 311.)

A second member of Armed Services compared his committee with the Appropriations Committee: "Our committee accepts the reports of the Department of Defense more completely than does Appropriations. We never question opinions about personnel, et cetera. We kid Appropriations members about this, say we aren't military experts, but they are, et cetera" (ibid., p. 316).

The Armed Services Committee exercised very little oversight over decisions of the Defense Department concerning the procurement of the missiles, aircraft, and the related modern delivery systems critical to the execution of contemporary military policy. See Bernard K. Gordon, "The Military Budget: Congressional Phase," *Journal of Politics* 23 (November 1961), p. 691. See also Raymond H. Dawson, "Congressional Innovation and Intervention in Defense Policy: Legislative Authorization of Weapons Systems," *American Political Science Review* 56 (March 1962), pp. 42–57.

106. Common Cause, "Report on House Committee Chairmen."

107. Jacobs, *Rage for Justice*, pp. 267–68. See also Biggs, with Foley, *Honor in the House*, p. 56. Hebert had already given ample indications of his inflexibility. For example, Berkeley, California's, representative Ron Dellums wrote in his 2000 memoir:

> The successful 1973 effort by the Congressional Black Caucus to secure me a seat on the House Armed Services Committee was not greeted with warmth by committee chairman F. Edward Hebert. Having called every member of the Democratic Party Committee on Committees to prevent the appointment of a "black male bomb-thrower from Berkeley"—a security risk and a radical—he was personally affronted at the fact that Speaker Albert and the leadership had forced my appointment on him.
>
> Representative Pat Schroeder, elected in 1972 as a peace candidate, also secured an appointment to Armed Services. Hebert called her "the white woman bomb-thrower from Denver." He was clearly distressed at the idea of both of us being on the committee. On the day the body met to organize, adopt its rules, and pick its subcommittee chairs, Schroeder and I arrived in the hearing room early. As we looked at the nameplates we noticed that there was only one chair available for the two of us at our adjoining places on the dais. . . .
>
> I turned to Schroeder. "Let's not give these guys the luxury of knowing they can get under our skin. . . . Let's sit here and share this chair as if it's the most normal thing in the world. If it's all right with you, it's all right with me." And we did, sitting through the entire organizational meeting of the committee cheek to cheek. . . . At the next meeting of Armed Services, we both had chairs, but our lack of welcome at the committee had been made abundantly clear.
>
> In light of Hebert's belligerent attitude toward me, I attended com-

mittee meetings armed with the book of House rules. Normally members should not have to fight for their rights. Decency, mutual respect, and comity are the necessary ingredients of a successful legislative process. A chair who fails to recognize the requirement for these elements of fair play is, in my opinion, a poor chair, and Hebert was such a chair. (Ronald V. Dellums, with H. Lee Halterman, *Lying Down with the Lions: A Public Life from the Streets of Oakland to the Halls of Power* [Boston: Beacon Press, 2000], pp. 149–150.)

Pat Schroeder tells this story in a way that implies that she and Dellums shared the same chair for the entire session of Congress (see Pat Schroeder, *24 Years of House Work . . . And the Place is Still a Mess: My Life in Politics* (Kansas City: Andrews McMeel, 1998), pp. 41–43.

108. Norman J. Ornstein and David W. Rohde, "Shifting Focus, Changing Rules, and Political Outcomes: The Impact of Congressional Change on Four House Committees," in Robert L. Peabody and Nelson W. Polsby eds., *New Perspectives on the House of Representatives*, 3rd ed. (Chicago: Rand McNally, 1977), p. 206.

109. Biggs, with Foley, *Honor in the House*, p. 56.

110. "Report on Committee Chairmen." Dick Conlon of the Democratic Study Group staff also noted, in an interview, that Poage had denied staff to subcommittees (Interview, January 17, 1975).

111. Unekis and Rieselbach, *Congressional Committee Politics*, p. 9.

112. Ornstein and Rohde report very substantial turnover among Democrats serving on the Agriculture Committee between the 91st and 94th Congresses (elected in 1968 and 1974, respectively). Twenty-one out of 27 Democrats in 1975 were new since 1970. Before the turnover, southern members had eight of the nine senior positions; after, five of 10. In the earlier period, the committee was extremely conservative. In the 94th Congress, it was much more liberal, though still more conservative than the average for House Democrats (see the accompanying tables).

113. Richard Bolling served with Patman on the Joint Committee on the

TABLE I TO NOTE 112. Mean Conservative Coalition Support Scores

|  | Congress | |
| --- | --- | --- |
|  | 91st | 94th |
| Agriculture | 70 | 45 |
| All House Members | 41 | 37 |

Source: Ornstein and Rohde, "Shifting Focus, Changing Rules," p. 262, table 9–23.

TABLE 2 TO NOTE 112. Subcommittee Chairmen: Region of Origin

| Subcommittee Chairmen | Congress | | | |
|---|---|---|---|---|
| | 91st | 92nd | 93rd | 94th |
| Southern | 8 | 8 | 7 | 7 |
| Non-southern | 2 | 2 | 3 | 3 |

Source: Ornstein and Rohde, "Shifting Focus, Changing Rules," p. 208, table 9–7.

Economic Report. In an interview with Kenneth Underwood (April 10, 1956) he said:

> I have reflected for a long time upon the career of [Rep.] Patman. His views in my judgment have some validity for the people he represents— he is an agrarian, populist reformer representing people who are mainly debtors. But he no longer can communicate effectively in Congress be- cause he has become identified with a fanatical allegiance to a particular issue position. (Ditto, Wesleyan University, Middletown, Conn., p. 10.)

The *Wall Street Journal* wrote, "After his defeat, Rep. Patman said he had been done in by the big banks" ("Reuss Beats Patman for Chairmanship of House Bank Panel, Maps Bold Course," January 23, 1975).

114. Carl Albert, with Danney Goble, *Little Giant: The Life and Times of Speaker Carl Albert* (Norman: University of Oklahoma Press, 1980), p. 368. Unekis and Rieselbach describe Patman as "irascible, elderly and autocratic" (*Congressional Committee Politics*, p. 13). For a scholarly account of Patman's early career as a grass-roots populist, see Nancy Beck Young, "Wright Patman's Entrepreneurial Leadership in Congress, 1929–1941," in Thomas P. Wolf, William D. Pederson, and Byron W. Daynes, eds., *Franklin D. Roosevelt and Congress: The New Deal and its Aftermath*, Vol. 2 (Armonk, N.Y.: Sharpe, 2001), pp. 79–97. For his later career, as chairman, see John E. Owens, "Extreme Advocacy Leadership in the Pre-Reform House: Wright Patman and the House Banking and Currency Committee," *British Journal of Political Science* 15 (April 1985), pp. 187–206.

115. See Henry S. Reuss, *When Government Was Good: Memories of a Life in Politics* (Madison: University of Wisconsin, 1999). Walter Taylor, "Patman Fights to Hold Key Post," *Washington Star-News*, January 19, 1975. Paul Duke, "A Crusader Goes Down," *Washington Post*, January 25, 1975.

116. Hays was by all accounts a difficult man to do business with. Typical stories at the time included Mary McGrory, "It's Like Having Your Own Hit Man," *Washington Star-News* January 20, 1975: "perhaps the most notorious bully in Congress." Compared to Hebert:

Connoisseurs of congressional tyranny, hard put to choose, rank Hays the winner by a hair. Although both treated members of their own committees like serfs, Hays' reign of terror has a wider range, extending to House pages, elevator operators, waiters, and cooks. . . .

"If you promise not to use my name [said one older liberal], I'll tell you I voted for Hays. I barely speak to the guy, but you've got to remember, he talks back to the lobbies . . . who screech every time we get a new allowance and call our recesses 'vacations.' "

Laurence Stern and Walter Pincus describe Hays's "famous cobra bites of caustic insult," which his colleagues put up with because of his control over "the bread-and-butter needs of many members" through his chairmanship of the House Administration Committee ("Hays Holds Many Colleagues' IOUs," *Washington Post*, June 8, 1976, p. A1).

Warren Weaver, Jr., "Wayne Hays Says———and———to Critics," *New York Times*, February 22, 1976, commented:

The committee that the crusty Democrat has ruled for the last five years has absolute authority over allowances for members' office and travel expenses, allocation of typewriters and parking spaces, and, most important of all, the operating budgets of all the other House committees. . . . These housekeeping matters . . . are critically important personally to each of the 434 other Representatives, who manage their offices and conduct their committee business . . . at the sufferance of the House Administration Committee, which means its chairman.

See also Mary Russell, "Hays Has Clout to Go with Bluster," *Los Angeles Times*, May 26, 1976, and "Power Detailed," *Washington Post*, May 25, 1976. Common Cause said: "Chairman Hays is known for his abusive treatment of House service workers: barbers, waiters, elevator operators, and other . . . support staff" ("Report on House Committee Chairmen"). The equable Carl Albert remarked that as a new Speaker he could have worked with any of the people putting themselves forward as majority leader "except maybe Hays, whom no one could work with in any capacity" (Albert, with Goble, *Little Giant*, p. 326). To some of his Republican colleagues Hays was evidently a figure of fun. The diary of a Republican member from Virginia reports:

According to Peter [Frelinghuysen, of New Jersey] Hays showed up [at an official Anglo-American meeting in Bermuda] with two girls, either from his staff or from the Foreign Affairs Committee, one of them a platinum blonde. He was apparently just as abrasive and sarcastic at the conference as he is on the floor of the House, leaving the British somewhat nonplused and the Americans fuming.

Hays after a dust-up caused by a *Washington* Post exposé in May 1976 admitted to a "relationship" with a "typist" on his staff who claimed to be unable to type (G. William Whitehurst, *Diary of a Congressman* [Norfolk, Va.: Donning, 1983], pp. 12, 202–3). See also, John M. Goshko, "FBI Begins Hays Inquiry," *Washington Post*, May 25, 1976; *Washington Post* editorial, "The Case of the Chairman's Clerk," May 26, 1976; David S. Broder, "Hays' Abuse of Power," *Washington Post*, June 16, 1976, p. A27.

117. Jacobs, *Rage for Justice*, pp. 269–71. Just as Hays was allied with Burton, Thompson was allied with Burton's rival Richard Bolling. A year later, in the bruising contest over the majority leadership, these alliances would reappear. And many years after that close observers could still discern aftershocks of the Bolling–Burton rivalry. See David Rogers, "New Democratic Leadership of House is Guided by Memories of Rival Reformers Bolling, Burton," *Wall Street Journal*, June 22, 1989, p. A16.

118. "New Congress Organizes: No Role for Mills," *CQ Weekly Report*, December 7, 1974, p. 3250.

119. See John F. Manley, *The Politics of Finance* (Boston: Little, Brown and Company, 1970). Tom Curtis (R-Mo.), a Republican member of the committee, remembered that Mills's predecessors

Dan Reed, (R, N.Y.) . . . always had subcommittees; so did Jere Cooper (D, TN) who was chairman . . . after Dan Reed. Mills became chairman on Cooper's death. Wilbur Mills was the one who came along and knocked off all the subcommittees. . . . His argument was, that with a relatively small committee of twenty-five, particularly on very important, basic, fundamental issues like taxation, and social security, it ought to be done by the full committee. I thought he could have preserved his values and done the other things as well. I think the real reason was that Wilbur knew that Hale Boggs would claim Foreign Trade, reciprocal trade legislation, and he didn't want Boggs to have that subcommittee chairmanship. Now I'm just saying this, but I think it's true. (Oral History Interview with Thomas B. Curtis by Fern S. Ingersoll for Former Members of Congress Inc. Manuscript Division, Library of Congress, December 9, 1978, pp. 83–84.)

Mills's conservatism was a matter not only of substance, but also of style. Manley (p. 151) comments: "Chairman Mills's idea of going on the offensive is to lean forward in his foxhole."

120. Albert, with Goble, *Little Giant*, p. 266.

121. Julian E. Zelizer, *Taxing America: Wilbur D. Mills, Congress, and the State, 1945–1975* (Cambridge: Cambridge University Press, 1998), p. 349.

122. Ibid., p. 350.

123. Ibid., p. 351.

124. See Roy Reed, "Mills Puzzles the Folks Back Home," *New York Times*, December 5, 1974.

125. Albert R. Hunt, "Mills May Lose His Ways and Means Post as Committee Democrats Look to Ullman," *Wall Street Journal*, December 3, 1974, p. 2.

126. Mary Russell, "House Units Feel Impact of Freshmen," *Washington Post*, January 22, 1975.

127. Mary Russell and Richard Lyons, "Staggers, Sullivan are Deposed from House Subcommittee Chairs," *Washington Post* January 29, 1975.

128. Ornstein, "Causes and Consequences of Congressional Change."

### 3. Causes of Liberalization

1. "Dixiecrats" are defined as members of the Democratic Party from the 11 former Confederate states who have a party support to party opposition ratio of less than 2:1. The term is used interchangeably with "conservative Democrats" when referring to southerners.

2. In retrospect Albert portrayed himself as less hesitant. Carl Albert, "The Speakership in My Time," in Ronald M. Peters, Jr., *The Speaker* (Washington, D.C.: CQ Press, 1995), pp. 189 ff. The earliest DSG initiative of McCormack's Speakership was a proposal to form a party steering committee advisory to the Speaker. Jack Steele, "McCormack Accepts Steering Committee," *Washington Daily News*, January 13, 1962:

> Publicly, at his first news conference yesterday as Speaker, Mr. McCormack was only lukewarm to the idea. "I would have no objection if the Democratic caucus decides to do it," he said, but added he would take no active part himself in setting up such a steering committee. Mr. McCormack previously had said, "A policy committee is out."

See also "House Liberals Expect to Get Steering Unit," *Evening Star* (Washington), January 13, 1962.

3. V. O. Key, Jr., *Southern Politics in State and Nation*, with the assistance of Alexander Heard [1st ed.] (New York: A. A. Knopf, 1949). A later edition was published in 1984 by the University of Tennessee Press, Knoxville.

4. See Hugh Douglas Price, *The Negro and Southern Politics* (New York: New York University Press, 1957), which discusses these effects in Florida and Milton C. Cummings, "Southern Congressional Elections," Paper prepared for the 1964 Annual Meeting of the American Political Science Association, Chicago, September 9–12, 1964.

5. The only exception was Harry M. Wurzbach of Seguin who served the 14th District of Texas from 1921 to 1931, preceding the next Texas Republican, Bruce Alger of Dallas, by a quarter century.

6. *Almanac of American Politics 1988* (Washington, D.C.: National Journal, 1997), pp. 1386–88.

7. Key, *Southern Politics*, pp. 280–285 (1984 edition).

8. For the story of agriculture-induced migration in the South, see Jack Temple Kirby, *Rural Worlds Lost: The American South, 1920–1960* (Baton Rouge: Louisiana State University Press, 1987). If we were discussing the Southwest, presumably the agricultural products would not be cotton, sugar, tobacco, peanuts, or poultry but rather cattle, and the relevant technologies would be barbed wire, railroads, and refrigerated railroad cars.

9. See Nicholas Lemann, *The Promised Land: The Great Black Migration and How It Changed America* (New York: A. A. Knopf, 1991); Neil Fligstein, *Going North: Migration of Blacks and Whites from the South, 1900–1950* (New York: Academic Press, 1981); Chad Berry, *Southern Migrants, Northern Exiles* (Urbana: University of Illinois Press, 2000).

10. Adam D. Sheingate, *The Rise of the Agricultural Welfare State* (Princeton, N.J.: Princeton University Press, 2001), p. 245.

11. Raymond Arsenault, "The End of the Long Hot Summer: The Air Conditioner and Southern Culture," *Journal of Southern History* 50 (November 1984), p. 610. Like the telephone, the commercial uses of air conditioning preceded the spread of the innovation to household use. Factories, railroad cars, government offices, banks, and movie theaters were air conditioned long before air conditioning was generally available in private homes. On the telephone, see Claude Fischer, *America Calling: A Social History of the Telephone to 1940* (Berkeley: University of California Press, 1992).

12. See James G. Gimpel and Jason E. Schuknecht, "Interstate Migration and Electoral Politics," *Journal of Politics* 63 (February 2001), pp. 207–231, for some prudent estimates.

13. U.S. Census of the Population, vol. 1, 1960, table 100, shows over half of the inhabitants of Florida who had lived outside the region five years before were over the age of 50 in 1960. For Arkansas the percentage is 15.6 percent.

14. Cramer served in Congress from 1955 to 1971. His father, he wrote, was a "Jeffersonian Democrat." Cramer became a Republican in 1948, on his return from World War II and the Harvard Law School. In 1950 he was elected to the state legislature and in 1951 became minority leader of the Florida House. He ran for an open congressional seat in 1952 and lost, and in the next election (1954) he beat Courtney Campbell narrowly. He attributes his victory in part to Dwight Eisenhower's showing at the presidential level in 1952 and to the "hidden" Republican sympathizers who had moved down from the North as well as to his record as a state representative and to successful campaigning (personal communication from William C. Cramer, February 8, 2000).

15. Donald S. Strong, *Urban Republicanism in the South* (University: Bureau of Public Administration, University of Alabama, 1960), p. 38.

16. "1972 Urban–Rural Characteristics of Southern Republican Districts," *Congressional Districts in the 1970s*, 2d ed. (Washington, D.C.: CQ Press, 1974), p. 144.

17. In 1964 Milton Cummings pointed out that southern districts with the

strongest Republican votes both for Congress and the president were districts with the fewest black inhabitants. Cummings reports:

> It was in 1956 that the first large gains were registered by GOP House candidates in the South. . . . The great majority of the southern districts where the GOP made a respectable showing in 1962 were located either in the Appalachian plateau region . . . or in rapidly growing industrial and urban enclaves scattered from Richmond, Virginia, to Miami, Florida, and Dallas, Texas. . . . The emergence of Republicanism with mass support among the professional and middle classes of the region's economically expanding urban centers . . . is a . . . recent phenomenon. ("Southern Congressional Elections," p. 11.)

By 1967 Malcolm Jewell found similar patterns—especially Republican gains in metropolitan areas—in voting for representatives in state legislatures (Malcolm E. Jewell, *Legislative Representation in the Contemporary South* [Durham, N.C.: Duke University Press, 1967], esp. pp. 105–21).

18. Ileana Ros-Lehtinen was elected in a special election following Claude Pepper's death in 1989. Lincoln Diaz-Balart was elected to what was once part of Fascell's district in 1992. Both still serve in Congress. Between 1961 and 1970 about 226,800 Cuban immigrants entered the United States with approximately 276,800 more coming in 1971–79 (U.S. Bureau of the Census, *Statistical Abstract of the United States: 1984*, 104th ed. [Washington, D.C.: U.S. Government Printing Office, 1985], table 126). By 1990, there were over 737,000 Cuban-born residents in the United States (U.S. Bureau of the Census, *Statistical Abstract of the United States: 1995*, 116th ed. [Washington, D.C.: U.S. Government Printing Office, 1996], table 55). In 1990 in Miami-Dade county, there were 953,407 residents of Hispanic origin (U.S. Bureau of the Census, *City and County Data Book: 1994* [Washington, D.C.: U.S. Government Printing Office, 1994], table B). The accompanying table shows the percentages of Hispanic and foreign-born residents in south Florida congressional districts in 2000.

19. Bernard Cosman, "The Republican Congressional Results from Dallas, Texas: An Analysis of Urban Republicanism in the South" (M.A. thesis, Department of Political Science, University of Alabama, 1958).

20. Ibid., tables 43 and 78, pp. 105–108, 166–69.

21. Ibid., p. 177.

22. Calculated from *Congressional Districts in the 1970s*, 2d ed., September 1974 (Washington, D.C.: Congressional Quarterly, 1974).

23. See the accompanying table.

24. See the first accompanying table. In the 99th Congress (1985–86) three of the 10 districts in the nation with the highest incomes (see the second table) were in the South and all three were represented by Republicans (Steve Bartlett of the Third District of Texas, Bill Archer of the Seventh District of Texas, and

TABLE TO NOTE 18. South Florida Congressional Districts, 2000 (Hispanic voters)

| District | Member (party) | % Hispanic | % Foreign born |
|---|---|---|---|
| 21 | Lincoln Diaz-Balart (R) | 69.6 | 55.8 |
| 18 | Ileana Ros-Lehtinen (R) | 66.7 | 56.8 |
| 17 | Carrie P. Meek (D) | 23.0 | 29.5 |
| 22 | E. Clay Shaw, Jr. (R) | 12.8 | 20.9 |
| 20 | Peter Deutsch (D) | 12.3 | 14.0 |
| 23 | Alcee Hastings (D) | 9.4 | 18.1 |
| 19 | Robert Wexler (D) | 6.2 | 12.1 |

Source: Deirdre A. Gaquin and Katherine A. DeBrandt, eds., *2000 County and City Extra: Annual Metro, City, and County Data Book,* 9th ed. (Lanham, Md.: Bernan Press, 2000), table E.

TABLE TO NOTE 23. Six Southern Seats with Highest Percentage of Population Age 65+ (93rd Congress)

| District | Percent of population 65+ | Representative (party) |
|---|---|---|
| FL-6 | 29.6 | C. W. Bill Young (R) |
| FL-10 | 19.1 | L. A. "Skip" Bafalis (R) |
| FL-11 | 19.1 | Paul G. Rogers (D) |
| FL-8 | 18.6 | James A. Haley (D) |
| FL-5 | 18.5 | William D. Gunter, Jr. (D) |
| FL-12 | 16.5 | J. Herbert Burke (R) |

Source: U.S. Dept. of Commerce, Bureau of the Census, *United States Congressional District Data Book for the Ninety-Third Congress, 1973* [Computer file], ICPSR ed. (Ann Arbor, Mich.: Inter-university Consortium for Political and Social Research [producer and distributor], 1999).

Frank Wolf of the Tenth District of Virginia). The nine congressional seats in the nation with the largest percentage of residents over the age of 65 were all located in Florida, and six of them including the top two were held by Republicans (see the third table). Eight of the 10 districts in the nation with the most population growth were in the South (three in Texas and five in Florida), five of which were represented by Republicans (see the fourth table).

25. Phil Duncan, *Politics in America* (Washington, D.C.: CQ Press, 1993), p. 94.

26. See G. William Whitehurst, *Diary of a Congressman* (Norfolk, Va.: Donning, 1983).

27. See the accompanying table.

TABLE I TO NOTE 24. Sixteen Southern Seats with Highest Percentage of Population Born out of State (93rd Congress)

| District | Percent born out of state | Representative (party) |
|---|---|---|
| VA-8 | 29.1 | Stanford E. Parris (R) |
| VA-10 | 25.8 | Joel T. Broyhill (R) |
| FL-14 | 25.7 | Claude Pepper (D) |
| VA-2 | 25.2 | G. William Whitehurst (R) |
| FL-12 | 24.1 | J. Herbert Burke (R) |
| FL-6 | 23.9 | C. W. Bill Young (R) |
| FL-15 | 23.8 | Dante B. Fascell (D) |
| FL-9 | 23.7 | Louis Frey, Jr. (R) |
| AR-2 | 23.2 | Wilbur D. Mills (D) |
| AR-3 | 22.4 | John Paul Hammerschmidt (R) |
| FL-10 | 22.3 | L. A. "Skip" Bafalis (R) |
| FL-11 | 22.2 | Paul G. Rogers (D) |
| FL-1 | 22.0 | Robert L. F. Sikes (D) |
| FL-5 | 20.6 | William D. Gunter, Jr. (D) |
| AR-1 | 20.0 | Bill Alexander (D) |
| GA-4 | 17.7 | Ben B. Blackburn (R) |

Source: See table to note 23 for source.

TABLE 2 TO NOTE 24. Ten Congressional Districts with Highest Income (99th Congress)

| District | Income index | Representative (party) |
|---|---|---|
| NY-15 | 214.4 | Bill Green (R) |
| CA-23 | 180.4 | Anthony C. Bielenson (D) |
| TX-7 | 178.0 | Bill Archer (R) |
| TX-3 | 170.0 | Steve Bartlett (R) |
| MD-8 | 167.5 | Michael Barnes (D) |
| MI-18 | 167.2 | William S. Broomfield (R) |
| IL-10 | 163.2 | John Edward Porter (R) |
| VA-10 | 162.6 | Frank Wolf (R) |
| CA-40 | 158.0 | Robert Badham (R) |
| CA-42 | 157.0 | Dan Lungren (R) |

Source: Linda F. Williams, ed., *The JCPS Congressional District Fact Book*, 2d ed. (Washington, D.C.: Joint Center for Political Studies, 1986), p. 24.

TABLE 3 TO NOTE 24. Ten Congressional Districts with Most Elderly (99th Congress)

| District | Percent 65+ | Representative (party) |
|---|---|---|
| FL-8 | 34.1 | C. W. Bill Young (R) |
| FL-13 | 33.1 | Connie Mack (R) |
| FL-14 | 30.7 | Daniel A. Mica (D) |
| FL-9 | 30.4 | Michael Bilirakis (R) |
| FL-18 | 29.9 | Claude Pepper (D) |
| FL-15 | 28.3 | E. Clay Shaw, Jr. (R) |
| FL-12 | 25.2 | Tom Lewis (R) |
| FL-10 | 24.1 | Andy Ireland (R) |
| FL-6 | 24.0 | Buddy MacKay (D) |
| KS-5 | 23.4 | Bob Whittaker (R) |

Source: Linda F. Williams, ed., *The JCPS Congressional District Fact Book*, 2d ed. (Washington, D.C.: Joint Center for Political Studies, 1986), p. 28.

TABLE 4 TO NOTE 24. Ten Congressional Districts with Most Population Growth (99th Congress)

| District | Percent population change | Representative (party) |
|---|---|---|
| FL-14 | 126.3 | Daniel A. Mica (D) |
| TX-7 | 103.6 | Bill Archer (R) |
| CA-43 | 103.2 | Ron Packard (R) |
| FL-9 | 91.6 | Michael Bilirakis (R) |
| AZ-3 | 90.8 | Bob Stump (R) |
| TX-26 | 87.3 | Dick Armey (R) |
| FL-13 | 86.5 | Connie Mack (R) |
| TX-22 | 76.9 | Tom DeLay (R) |
| FL-16 | 74.6 | Larry Smith (D) |
| FL-6 | 70.9 | Buddy MacKay (D) |

Source: Linda F. Williams, ed., *The JCPS Congressional District Fact Book*, 2d ed. (Washington, D.C.: Joint Center for Political Studies, 1986), p. 26.

28. Strong, *Urban Republicanism*, and James Prothro et al. report Republican voting for president in the Eisenhower elections was concentrated among more affluent southerners. Strong's chapter 2 is headed "Prosperous City Dwellers Liked Ike Most." See James W. Prothro, Ernest Q. Campbell, and Charles M. Grigg, "Two-Party Voting in the South: Class vs. Party Identification," *American Political Science Review* 52 (March 1958), pp. 131–139. This is a study of 1956 voting in Tallahassee, Florida. Also Raymond E. Wolfinger and Robert B. Ar-

TABLE TO NOTE 27. Eleven Southern Seats with Lowest Percentage of Population Living in Same State and House (93rd Congress)

| District | Percent in same state and House | Representative (party) |
|----------|--------------------------------|------------------------|
| FL-12 | 36.7 | J. Herbert Burke (R) |
| FL-15 | 36.2 | Dante B. Fascell (D) |
| FL-9 | 36.0 | Louis Frey, Jr. (R) |
| FL-14 | 35.7 | Claude Pepper (D) |
| GA-4 | 35.1 | Ben B. Blackburn (R) |
| TX-7 | 35.0 | Bill Archer (R) |
| TX-24 | 34.6 | Dale Milford (D) |
| VA-2 | 34.5 | G. William Whitehurst (R) |
| AR-3 | 34.5 | John Paul Hammerschmidt (R) |
| TX-3 | 34.1 | James M. Collins (R) |
| VA-8 | 29.7 | Stanford E. Parris (R) |

Source: See table to note 23 for source.

seneau, "Partisan Change in the South, 1952–1976," in Louis Maisel and Joseph Cooper, eds., *Political Parties: Development and Decay* (Beverly Hills, Calif.: Sage Publications, 1978), pp. 179–210; Raymond E. Wolfinger and Michael G. Hagen, "Republican Prospects: Southern Comfort," *Public Opinion* 8 (October/November 1985), pp. 8–13; and Cummings, "Southern Congressional Elections."

29. Rebecca Carr, "Lott's House Apprenticeship," *Congressional Quarterly*, June 8, 1996, pp. 1572–73.

30. Joe Cannon (Speaker, 1903–10) was born in North Carolina in 1836 and moved with his family in the 1840s to a new Quaker settlement in Indiana as a small boy. After six months in law school, he settled in Illinois and started a law practice at age 22. It is a curiosity that the famously foul-mouthed Cannon was raised in a Quaker family. See Donald R. Kennon, ed., *The Speakers of the U.S. House of Representatives: A Bibliography, 1789–1984* (Baltimore: Johns Hopkins University Press, 1985), p. 197. The second was Champ Clark (Speaker, 1911–18) born in Kentucky in 1850. He reached Missouri, which he represented (1893–95; 1897–1921), at age 26 after law school. The third was Sam Rayburn, born in 1882 in Roane County, Tennessee. Rayburn joined the migration from Tennessee to a more or less empty Texas at the age of 5. When he arrived there, Texas had a population density of 6.1 inhabitants per square mile (1,592,000 people). By the time he was first elected to Congress in 1912—after serving as Speaker of the Texas House—Texas had roughly doubled its population to 14.8 inhabitants per square mile (3,897,000 people.) In short, until Gingrich, most Speakers did not move out of their state of birth. Those few who did were following the leading edge of the American frontier (see accompanying table).

TABLE TO NOTE 30. Speakers of the House of Representatives, 1900–2001

| Speaker | Speaker | Born (Date) | Represented |
|---|---|---|---|
| Joseph G. Cannon (R) | 1903–11 | North Carolina (1836) | Illinois (1873–91; 1893–1913) |
| Champ Clark (D) | 1911–19 | Kentucky (1850) | Missouri (1893–95; 1897–1921) |
| Frederick H. Gillett (R) | 1919–25 | Massachusetts (1851) | Massachusetts (1893–1925) |
| Nicholas Longworth (R) | 1925–31 | Ohio (1869) | Ohio (1903–13; 1915–31) |
| John N. Garner (D) | 1931–33 | Texas (1868) | Texas (1903–33) |
| Henry T. Rainey (D) | 1933–34 | Illinois (1860) | Illinois (1903–21; 1923–34) |
| Joseph W. Byrns (D) | 1935–36 | Tennessee (1869) | Tennessee (1909–36) |
| William B. Bankhead (D) | 1936–40 | Alabama (1874) | Alabama (1917–40) |
| Samuel T. Rayburn (D) | 1940–47, 1949–53, 1955–61 | Tennessee (1882) | Texas (1913–61) |
| Joseph W. Martin (R) | 1947–49, 1953–55 | Massachusetts (1894) | Massachusetts (1925–67) |
| John W. McCormack (D) | 1962–71 | Massachusetts (1891) | Massachusetts (1928–71) |
| Carl Albert (D) | 1971–77 | Oklahoma (1908) | Oklahoma (1947–77) |
| Thomas (Tip) P. O'Neill, Jr. (D) | 1977–87 | Massachusetts (1912) | Massachusetts (1953–87) |
| James C. Wright, Jr. (D) | 1987–89 | Texas (1922) | Texas (1955–89) |
| Thomas S. Foley (D) | 1989–95 | Washington (1929) | Washington (1965–95) |
| Newton (Newt) L. Gingrich (R) | 1995–99 | Pennsylvania (1943) | Georgia (1979–99) |
| J. Dennis Hastert (R) | 1999–current | Illinois (1942) | Illinois (1987–current) |

31. They were 4.1 percent of the southern electorate in the 1950s, 12.3 percent in the 1960s, 16.0 percent in the 1970s, and 21.8 percent in the 1980s. Byron E. Shafer and Richard G. C. Johnston, "The Transformation of Southern Politics Revisited: The House of Representatives as a Window," *British Journal of Political Science* 31 (October 2001), p. 611.

32. Ibid., p. 613.

33. Ibid.

34. Richard F. Fenno, Jr., *Congress at the Grassroots: Representational Change in the South, 1970–1998* (Chapel Hill: University of North Carolina Press, 2000).

35. Fenno, ibid., writes on page 97:

Ronald Reagan captured the district (with 69 percent of the vote) in 1984, and it has gone Republican in presidential elections ever since. George Bush carried it by 47 percent and Bob Dole by 50 percent, both in three-way races. A strong Democratic district had become a strong Republican district. . . . Nowhere was the change more prominent than in the district's suburbs. Between 1976 and 1996, the Third District had become steadily more suburban. In the 1970s it was still classified as more nonmetropolitan (52 percent) than suburban (43 percent), according to a *Congressional Quarterly* study. By the 1990s, however, it was classified as solidly suburban. The district's four suburban counties (Clayton, Coweta, Fayette, and Henry) had grown from a population of 84,000 with 35,000 registered voters, in the 1950s, to a population of 282,000 with 182,000 registered voters, in the 1990s.

36. Ibid., p. 142.

37. Ibid., p. 97.

38. Tape recorded interviews took place on Capitol Hill the week of June 21, 1993, unless otherwise indicated, and were conducted by Jonathan Bernstein, Sharon Kaye, and me, and transcribed by Sharon Kaye, with the assistance of Jonathan Bernstein. They generally lasted between half an hour to an hour.

39. Tim Hutchinson interview.

40. Lamar Smith interview, February 18, 1993.

41. Michael Barone and Grant Ujifusa, *The Almanac of American Politics* (Washington, D.C.: National Journal, 1988), p. 1182.

42. Barone and Ujifusa, *Almanac of American Politics*, 1992, pp. 1236–38.

43. Thurmond switched in 1964. See Earl Black and Merle Black, *The Rise of Southern Republicans* (Cambridge, Mass.: Harvard University Press, 2002), p. 1.

44. The Appendix gives a brief discussion of ideological ratings. ACU stands for American Conservative Union, ADA for Americans for Democratic Action, a liberal group.

45. Data come from *Politics in America*, 1996 edition.

46. There is another story about air conditioning and politics much better known than (and largely irrelevant to) my argument. It is compactly told by Joe Martin of Massachusetts in his 1960 memoir. When he came to Congress in 1925, he said:

Of course there was no air conditioning. Summers seemed even hotter in Washington then than they do now. Many of the committee rooms were ill-ventilated, and members could sometimes come to the verge of fainting during long hearings. The installation of air conditioning in the 1930s did more, I believe, than cool the Capitol: it prolonged the sessions.

The members were no longer in such a hurry to flee Washington in July. The southerners especially had no place else to go that was half as comfortable. (Joe Martin, as told to Robert J. Donovan, *My First Fifty Years in Politics* [New York: McGraw-Hill, 1960], p. 49.)

For an elaboration, see Marsha E. Ackermann, *Cool Comfort: America's Romance with Air-Conditioning* (Washington, D.C.: Smithsonian Institution, 2002), pp. 62–76.

### 4. Consequences: Toward a More Responsible Two-Party System?

1. American Political Science Association, Committee on Political Parties, *Toward a More Responsible Two-Party System: A Report* (New York: Rinehart, 1950).

2. Fiona M. Wright argues, plausibly, that the use of the caucus to remove three committee chairs in 1975 was influential in improving the party unity scores of all chairmen. See, "The Caucus Reelection Requirement and the Transformation of House Committee Chairs, 1959–94," *Legislative Studies Quarterly* 25 (August 2000), pp. 469–80; also Sara Brandes Crook and John R. Hibbing, "Congressional Reform and Party Discipline: The Effects of Changes in the Seniority System on Party Loyalty in the US House of Representatives," *British Journal of Political Science* 15 (April 1985), pp. 207–26.

3. See, e.g., Marjorie Hunter and David E. Rosenbaum, "Defeats Split Bitter House Democrats," *New York Times*, July 2, 1975:

> [T]he role of leadership has been changed drastically by recent changes that weakened the seniority system and diffused power within the House Democratic party structure.
>
> Speaker Albert believes that the leadership has become even stronger
> . . .
> The Democratic Caucus has become more active, he said. The Steering Committee that he heads "is no longer just cosmetic." And the Rules Committee—which controls the flow of legislation to the floor—now "follows the Speaker as it never did before."
>
> But his assessment of a stronger leadership is disputed by many of his colleagues.
>
> "He's absolutely balmy," Les Aspin exclaimed when told of the Speaker's views. "He's got no carrots or sticks. Albert's got no levers."
>
> [Majority leader] O'Neill, too, disputes the Speaker's assertion that the leaders of today hold a stronger hand than those of the past such as the almost legendary strong man, Speaker Sam Rayburn of Texas. . . .
>
> "It probably is true that the leadership is ineffectual," said Represen-

tative Jim Wright, an experienced and respected Texan. "But if it were ... the way it was in Sam Rayburn's day the same people would be saying that the leader was a czar."

4. This was notably true of Carter's de facto Chief of Staff, Hamilton Jordan, whom O'Neill took to calling Hannibal Jerken:

He was supposed to be the president's top man, but I remember seeing him only about three times in four years. To this day, I can't understand why the closest man to Jimmy Carter, the key staff guy at the White House, didn't even join us at the White House breakfast meetings where we discussed upcoming legislation with the president. This was unprecedented. People used to say that Jordan was the most brilliant guy around, but you couldn't prove it by me. (Tip O'Neill, with William Novak, *Man of the House* [New York: St. Martins, 1987], p. 372.

5. Eric Davis, "Legislative Liaison in the Carter Administration," *Political Science Quarterly* 94 (Summer 1979), pp. 287–301.

6. Albert R. Hunt, "Tipping the Balance: How O'Neill Guides Carter's Energy Plan toward House Passage," *Wall Street Journal*, August 5, 1977; Spencer Rich, "Tip O'Neill: A Legend Being Born," *Washington Post*, August 7, 1977.

7. Barbara Sinclair, "The Emergence of Strong Leadership in the 1980s House of Representatives," *Journal of Politics* 54 (August 1992), pp. 657–84.

8. Tip O'Neill, "Rules for Speakers," in Ronald M. Peters, Jr., ed, *The Speaker* (Washington, D.C.: Congressional Quarterly Press, 1995), pp. 204–5. As majority leader, O'Neill once observed, "We Democrats are all under one tent. In any other country, we'd be five splinter parties." Richard L. Lyons, "Vetoes Frustrate Democrats," *Washington Post*, June 17, 1975; see also Steven V. Roberts, "Eroding Loyalty Weakens House Leaders," *New York Times*, June 4, 1979; Martin Tolchin, "House Democrats Seek a Return to Strong Leadership," *New York Times*, October 24, 1979; Mary Russell, "O'Neill Rebounds from Setbacks in Party and on Floor," *Washington Post*, November 22, 1979.

9. See Alan Ehrenhalt, "The Campaign against Tip O'Neill," *CQ Weekly Report* 39 (July 25, 1981), p. 1367.

10. John A. Farrell, *Tip O'Neill and the Democratic Century* (Boston: Little, Brown, 2001), pp. 551, 574–75, 620–21. There is no doubt about the official line, but Gary Hymel, O'Neill's assistant says, "That was a myth. I think he had Tip and Millie for dinner once. Tip never liked Reagan because he thought Reagan forgot whence he came" (personal communication, April 8, 2002).

11. Carl Albert, with Danney Goble, *Little Giant: The Life and Times of Speaker Carl Albert* (Norman: University of Oklahoma Press, 1990), p. 267.

12. And for some years more was de facto ranking member owing to the disinclination of Noah Mason (R-Ill). who was senior to him, to act as ranking member. See John W. Byrnes, Oral History Interview, January 17, 1979, re-

corded by Charles Morrissey for Former Members of Congress, Inc., Manuscript Division, Library of Congress. Mason was famous for going home each summer regardless of whether the House remained in session on the principled ground that the Legislative Organization Act of 1946 declared that Congress must adjourn by July 31 of each year. Mason's colleague and party whip Les Arends (R-Ill.) referred to this practice as "a good illustration of Noah's 'rugged individualism.' " ("The Late Hon. Noah Mason," *Congressional Record,* March 30, 1965, pp. H6077–79). See also Charles Adams Mosher, *Reinterpreting Congress and Its Works: A Speculative Theory Essayed: The Reflections, Confessions and Credo of Charles Adams Mosher* (Oberlin, Ohio: C. A. Mosher, 1984), p. 69.

13. John W. Byrnes interview, pp. 19–22. Wilbur Mills fully reciprocated Byrnes's feelings. In his interview with Charles Morrissey for the Former Members of Congress Project:

> Morrissey: Many people have spoken about the good relationship between yourself and John Byrnes.
> Mills: Oh it was terrific. . . . It was just that John and I could get along, and he was a very wonderful individual with a tremendous mind. (Mills, Oral History Interview, recorded by Charles Morrissey for Former Members of Congress, Inc., Manuscript Division, Library of Congress, April 5 and June 7, 1979, p. 63.)

See also John F. Manley, *The Politics of Finance: The House Committee on Ways and Means* (Boston: Little, Brown, 1970), pp. 88–90.

14. Julian E. Zelizer, *Taxing America: Wilbur D. Mills, Congress, and the State, 1945–1975* (New York: Cambridge University Press, 1998), p. 350. Byrnes saw the handwriting on the wall a good bit earlier, manifested in Democratic objections to the automatic awarding of a closed rule to Ways and Means bills. In his 1979 interview he says:

> Well, toward the end, you had the growth of this feeling that now predominates, almost, but these things move in gradually. There were four or five who said, "What the hell, the House ought to be able to work its will. We want a democracy. We don't want these people telling us that we have to have this or nothing." Then there were . . . the reformers on the Democratic side, who had their targets out for Wilbur. He was, in their view, too conservative for them, and not social-minded enough, or whatever it was they wanted. So they made the attack indirectly on him through the Rules Committee. . . . Back in the fifties, in the early sixties, I don't recall that you ever had the issue raised. . . . On the trade bills, we always painted this horrendous scene—special interests with their special duties, reports that will take place if you have an open rule, and the same way with the tax bills. . . . It got kind of nasty towards—oh, I'd say, starting about '66-'67-'68, in through there—this

drive of the reformists. They were going to get Wilbur and his conservatism, take some of his power away. It would be part of the reform process. So we used to have some hassles over the closed rule. (John W. Byrnes interview, pp. 22–23.)

15. Allen Schick, "The Ways and Means of Leading Ways and Means," *Brookings Review*, Fall 1989, p. 20.

16. Randall Strahan, *New Ways and Means: Reform and Change in a Congressional Committee* (Chapel Hill: University of North Carolina Press, 1990), p. 99.

17. Catherine E. Rudder, "Committee Reform and the Revenue Process," in Lawrence C. Dodd and Bruce I. Oppenheimer, eds., *Congress Reconsidered* (New York: Praeger, 1977), p. 127. Richard L. Lyons, "House Feels Clout of New Rules," *Washington Post*, March 2, 1975.

18. Rudder, "Committee Reform," 131.

19. Richard E. Cohen, *Rostenkowski: The Pursuit of Power and the End of Old Politics* (Chicago: Ivan R. Dee, 1999) p. 137. See also, Schick, "The Ways and Means of Leading Ways and Means," pp. 16–23.

20. Richard F. Fenno, Jr., *The Power of the Purse: Appropriations Politics in Congress* (Boston: Little, Brown, 1966).

21. Fenno amasses a lot of testimony in this vein. He continues:

Two subcommittee chairmen described situations in which they had exchanged positions while maintaining internal harmony through cooperation:

"When I have served as chairman of this committee [he] has given me the utmost cooperation and support. I have tried to reciprocate and together we have carried on the work of the committee without any friction, without any partisan politics."

"One thing that has impressed me about [him] is that at all times during these ten years he has shown a great disposition to cooperate with the leadership of the committee, and by virtue of that fact [he] received cooperation when he served as chairman."

A Republican chairman testified to the considerable sharing of information and skill which takes place when he said of the Democrat he had just succeeded,

"He has been very generous with his knowledge and experience in assisting and counseling me during my first year as chairman . . . it has been a pleasure to work with him and I hope to continue to draw on his knowledge and guidance in the future, as I have in the past."

And a Democratic chairman referred to his ranking minority member as "my old professor who trained me how to handle the bill."

Still another pair of senior Committee men who traded official positions for fifteen years painted a picture of substantial role reciprocity resulting in integration. Said Tweedledum, "I have served under [his] chairmanship and it has been said that it did not make much difference which of us happened to be presiding officer of the subcommittee." Said Tweedledee, "He and I have worked together . . . many members say we have worked so closely that seldom if ever do our views differ." These comments, related to five different subcommittees, depict considerable success in the minimization of partisanship. (Ibid., pp. 201–2).

22. Ibid., pp. 200–203.

23. John Hersey, *The President* (New York: Alfred A. Knopf, 1975), p. 60. Hersey, unfamiliar with the ways of Congress, could barely contain his incredulity: "The prospects are bleak. It is hard to understand why the President, who has made so much of the need . . . is not upset" (p. 39).

24. Richard F. Fenno, Jr., *Congressmen in Committees* (Boston: Little, Brown, 1973) and Frank J. Munger and Richard F. Fenno, *National Politics and Federal Aid to Education: The Economics and Politics of Public Education* (Syracuse, N.Y.: Syracuse University Press, 1962). Mickey Edwards, a conservative Republican from Oklahoma, served on the Education and Labor Committee (1977–81). He wrote that work there was "for most Republicans a lot like the first circle of Dante's Inferno . . . the . . . committee is so unbalanced, so out of sync even with a House that is two-to-one Democratic, that it invariably sends to the floor legislation that goes far beyond what other members of the House are willing to support" (*Behind Enemy Lines* [Chicago: Regnery Gateway, 1983], p. 37).

25. John Brademas, Address at a symposium "Citizenship and Partisanship: Educating the Enlightened America," Hunter College, New York, October 19, 2002, p. 7.

26. Holbert N. Carroll, *The House of Representatives and Foreign Affairs* (Pittsburgh: University of Pittsburgh, 1958), p. 96.

27. Fenno, *Congressmen in Committees*, p. 93.

28. Ibid.

29. Interview with Wayne Aspinall by Nancy Whistler for Former Members of Congress, Inc., Library of Congress, Manuscript Division, February 15, 1979, p. 8.

30. P.L. 92–484.

31. Mosher, *Reinterpreting Congress*, pp. 136–37, 148–51.

32. Ibid., p. 150. Congressional staff members now and again become members of Congress (e.g. Trent Lott, Tom Foley, Bob Michel, Tony Coelho), and once in a great while a member becomes an official in the House administrative bureaucracy. Pat Jennings of Virginia was Clerk of the House from 1967 to 1975. Gilbert Gude of Maryland was Director of the Congressional Research Service of the Library of Congress from 1977 to 1985. Emilio Daddario left Congress in 1971 after being drafted by the Connecticut Democratic Party to run—unsuccessfully—for governor in 1970. He was appointed Director of the

Office of Technology Assessment, an agency he had helped to create, and served from 1973 to 1977. In at least one other instance, a member of Congress became a working member of a congressional committee staff: Laurie Battle, Democrat of Alabama, was staff director of the House Rules Committee (1966–76), working for his fellow Democrats, Chairmen William Colmer (Miss.) and Ray Madden (Ind.), not, as in Mosher's case, for a committee controlled by the opposite party.

33. Even this committee later on became a "battleground marking the lengths to which partisan rancor . . . advanced in the 104th Congress" (Dan Carney, "Committee Clamor Illustrates Extent of Partisan Divide," *Congressional Quarterly*, May 11, 1993, pp. 1291–92).

34. Bruce Keith, "A Comparison of the House Armed Services Committees in the 91st and 94th Congresses: How They Differed and Why". Ph.D. diss., University of California, Berkeley, 1982), vol. 2, p. 353.

35. Farrell, *Tip O'Neill*, pp. 654–655.

36. Wayne Biddle, "Push in House Military Panel to Depose Price is Reported," *New York Times*, January 3, 1985, p. A19.

37. See the comments of Keith, "a Comparison of the House Armed Services Committees," vol. 2, pp. 366–68. Also Ralph K. Huitt, "The Outsider in the Senate," *American Political Science Review* 55: 3 (September 1961), pp. 566–75. Early reports on Aspin's dissenting style on the committee include Carol H. Falk, "Rep. Aspin's Secrets in Battling Pentagon Are No Secrets at All," *Wall Street Journal*, May 10, 1973; Constance Holden, "Congressman Les Aspin: Bee in the Brass's Bonnet," *Science* 181 (August 3, 1973), pp. 424–427; and Daniel Rapoport, "The Revolution of Private Aspin," *Washington Post*, March 2, 1975.

38. Margaret Shapiro, "Democrats Remove Price as Chairman; Rep. Aspin to Head Armed Services," *Washington Post*, January 5, 1985, p. A1.

39. Ronald V. Dellums, with H. Lee Halterman, *Lying Down with the Lions: A Public Life from the Streets of Oakland to the Halls of Power* (Boston: Beacon Press, 2000), pp. 153–154.

40. Edward Walsh, "Leaders Endorse Bennett for Armed Services," *Washington Post*, January 9, 1987, p. A4.

41. Edward Walsh, "Aspin Regains Chairmanship of Armed Services Committee," *Washington Post*, January 23, 1987, p. A1.

42. He continued to have difficulties in checking what a colleague described as "his Lone Ranger instincts" but made sufficient headway at reorganizing the way he did business to become Bill Clinton's first Defense Secretary in 1993—a job he did not hold for long. See especially an article by the exceptionally well-informed Pat Towell, "Aspin Moves to Avoid Reruns of His Political Missteps," *Congressional Quarterly*, April 14, 1990, pp. 1141–45.

43. Edward Walsh wrote in the *Washington Post*, January 23, 1987:

Although Aspin had alienated many colleagues by . . . votes [on aid to the Nicaraguan contras and deployment of MX missiles] and by a style that was described as aloof and cocky, Leath proved too conservative for a majority of House Democrats. In the final days of intense campaigning, Aspin's supporters circulated a detailed analysis of Leath's voting record that they said showed him to be "completely out of step with the vast majority of House Democrats."

44. Albert R. Hunt, "Ways and Means Unsung Mr. Conable," *Wall Street Journal*, July 9, 1973.

45. William F. Connelly, Jr., and John J. Pitney, Jr., *Congress' Permanent Minority? Republicans in the U.S. House* (Lanham, Md.: Rowman and Littlefield, 1994), p. 8.

46. Timothy J. Burger and Jim O'Connell, "Michel Quits after 38-Year Career Filled with Bipartisanship, Congress-Boosting, and Song," *Roll Call*, October 7, 1993, p. 12. The story continues: "The leader recalled what was often a 'rancorous, cantankerous' partisan atmosphere in the 102nd Congress and thought 'My gosh, will it get any better?' "

47. "The Hill Interview: Former House Minority Leader Bob Michel," *The Hill*, February 14, 2001, p. 26.

48. Connelly and Pitney, *Congress' Permanent Minority?*, p. 26.

49. Ibid., p. 27.

50. O'Neill, in Tip O'Neill, with William Novak, *Man of the House* (New York: St. Martin's Press, 1987) recalls:

Toward the end of Reagan's first term, several of these right-wing Republicans started taking advantage of a procedure known as "special orders" to attack their Democratic colleagues. After the House has finished its business for the day, a member is entitled to take the floor and to speak for up to an hour on any subject of his choosing. By then the House chamber is empty, and these special-order speeches have traditionally been made for home consumption. But in recent years there's been a whole new national audience on the C-Span cable TV network.

What really infuriated me about these guys is that they had no real interest in legislation. As far as they were concerned, the House was no more than a pulpit, a sound stage from which to reach the people at home. If the TV cameras were facing the city dump, that's where they'd be speaking.

I happened to be watching in my office one afternoon as Newt Gingrich was taking advantage of special orders to attack Eddie Boland's voting record and to cast aspersions on his patriotism. The camera focused on Gingrich, and anybody watching at home would have thought that Eddie was sitting there, listening to all of this. Periodically, Gingrich would challenge Boland on some point, and would then step back, as if waiting for Eddie to answer. But Boland had left hours ago, along with everybody else in the place.

The next day, when Robert Walker of Pennsylvania tried something similar, I called Charlie Rose, the member in charge of television in the House and told him I thought the cameras should pan the entire chamber. Charlie informed the camera crew, and when they showed the empty hall, Walker looked like a fool . . .

A few days later, I rebuked Newt Gingrich on the floor of the House: "You deliberately stood in that well before an empty House and challenged these people when you knew they would not be there," I said. "It is the lowest thing that I have ever seen in my thirty-two years in Congress."

Trent Lott, the Republican whip, objected to my language, and on the advice of the House parliamentarian, the word lowest was ruled out of order and stricken from the record. I had done my best to control my temper, but harsher thoughts were on my mind. (pp. 423–24).

This was an extremely rare event. The Annenberg Public Policy Center of the University of Pennsylvania searched the Record from 1936 to 1998 for occasions when words were requested to be taken down or actually taken down and found virtually nothing except for three small blips: nine requests for a ruling and five rulings in 1940, 15 requests and seven rulings in 1946, and 14 requests and six rulings in 1994.

It is notable that the two largest blips occurred when Republicans interrupted the long-term control by the Democrats of the House. *Civility in the House of Representatives: The 106th Congress* (Philadelphia: Annenberg Public Policy Center, 2001), p. 7.

51. Steven V. Roberts, "Mired in Fractiousness with Eye on Voters . . . ," *New York Times*, January 26, 1984, p. 10.

52. A general nonpartisan discussion of strategies of disagreement can be found in John B. Gilmour's thoughtful book *Strategic Disagreement: Stalemate in American Politics* (Pittsburgh: University of Pittsburgh Press, 1995). He says, "The success of Newt Gingrich in rising through the Republican party in the House of Representatives illustrates some of the reasons to avoid compromise" (p. 24).

53. David Rogers, "Assault from the Right: Rep. Gingrich Fights Democrats," *Wall Street Journal*, May 23, 1984, p. 58.

54. Keith T. Poole and Howard Rosenthal, *Congress: A Political-Economic History of Roll Call Voting* (New York: Oxford University Press, 1997). NOMINATE scores are computed by taking a set of votes by each Member of Congress and estimating a multidimensional ideology score for each member underlying those votes. The first dimension, which Poole and Rosenthal argue is a measure of liberalism/conservatism, can explain most of the variation in congressional voting. Issues such as abortion, taxes, and welfare spending fit into this di-

mension such that liberalism means supporting abortion, taxes, and welfare spending, and conservatism means opposing them.

55. In the 1989 fight for Republican whip between Gingrich and Edward Madigan, which Gingrich won by two votes, analysis shows that conservative coalition scores for the 87 Gingrich supporters averaged 85.99 and for the 85 Madigan backers was 83.52. See Douglas L. Koopman, *Hostile Takeover* (Lanham, Md.: Rowman and Littlefield, 1996), p. 17.

56. David Cohen, personal communication, March 31, 2002.

57. An excellent overview is Joe Klein, "The Town That Ate Itself," *New Yorker*, November 23, 1998, pp. 79–87.

58. This is a reference to the ratios of Democrats to Republicans on committees.

59. Under the Constitution, the House determines who its own members will be. In the nineteenth century disputed elections were frequently overturned by the House, usually in highly partisan actions. But disputed elections are nowadays quite rare. (Polsby, "Institutionalization of the House of Representatives.")

The facts in this case were as follows:

On election night 1984, McCloskey held a 72-vote lead over Republican Richard D. McIntyre. The Indiana Secretary of State, a Republican, certified McIntyre the winner based on a state-ordered recount putting McIntyre ahead by 34 votes. When Congress convened on January 3, 1985, Democrats in the House demanded a recount before McIntyre was sworn in or seated. A three-member panel (two Democrats, one Republican) was established to supervise another recount, conducted by auditors from the General Accounting Office. They excluded 32 absentee ballots that either had arrived late or lacked notarization, giving the election to McCloskey by four votes out of some 230,000 cast. Republicans argued that these ballots should have been counted. Leon Panetta (D-Calif.), chairman of the panel, argued that the decision not to count them was valid under House precedent and the laws of every state. He said, "Do we want the election to turn on illegal ballots? I don't think so." Republicans advocated a special make-up election, but did not prevail. Steven V. Roberts, "Indiana Democrat Seated, GOP Walks Out," *New York Times*, May 2, 1985. David Shribman, "House Clears Way to Seat McCloskey but GOP Pledges to Continue Protests," *Wall Street Journal*, May 1, 1985. David Shribman, "Longest Election Night Continues in Indiana as Washington Holds Key to Vacant Seat," *Wall Street Journal*, January 17, 1985.

60. Norman J. Ornstein, "Washington: Minority Report," *Atlantic*, December 1985, pp. 30–38.

61. William S. White, *The Taft Story* (New York: Harper, 1954), p. 85. James T. Patterson, *Mr. Republican* (Boston: Houghton Mifflin, 1972), p. 446.

62. White, *Taft Story*, pp. 84–85. See also Patterson, *Mr. Republican*, pp. 447–49.

63. On Everett Dirksen, see Neil MacNeil, *Dirksen: Portrait of a Public Man* (New York: World, 1970), pp. 88ff. On p. 95: "The Republican ranks in Congress were swept with bitterness and partisanship against the Democratic administration, and Dirksen joined vociferously in the political caterwauling."

64. Nelson W. Polsby, "Toward an Explanation of McCarthyism," *Political Studies* vol. 8, October 1960, pp. 250–271.

65. Richard Rovere, *Senator Joe McCarthy* (New York: Harcourt, Brace, 1959), p. 37. Rovere never identified the eight. Doing an independent count, I could come up with only five. One of them, I assumed, was William Benton of Connecticut. I believe I demonstrated that Benton was not beaten by McCarthy, but by Dwight Eisenhower's coattails. Polsby, "Toward an Explanation."

66. Fred I. Greenstein, *The Hidden Hand Presidency: Eisenhower as Leader* (New York: Basic Books, 1982), pp. 155–227.

67. Michael W. Straight, *Trial by Television* (Boston: Beacon Press, 1954).

68. See Robin Toner, "Tired of Cooling Their Heels, the Republicans Turn Up Heat," *New York Times*, January 16, 1989.

69. John Jacobs, *A Rage for Justice: The Passion and Politics of Phillip Burton* (Berkeley: University of California Press, 1995); Bruce I. Oppenheimer and Robert L. Peabody, "The House Majority Leadership Contest, 1976," Paper prepared for delivery at the 1977 annual meeting of the American Political Science Association, Washington, D.C., September 1–4, 1977; Richard Bolling, "Learn from My Losses: How Not to Run for Speaker," *Washington Post*, July 27, 1986.

70. John M. Barry, *The Ambition and the Power* (New York: Viking, 1989), p. 5. Barry's book is a 768-page chronicle of Wright's two-year Speakership in which he had "daily, routine access to virtually all meetings in which Wright participated. . . . Other members of the Democratic leadership also granted me access to many of their private meetings, and several other members of Congress invited me to theirs as well, even when their purpose was to defeat Wright. Most of the events related in this book [he wrote] I personally observed" (p. 765).

71. Coelho was the first elected Democratic whip. Before 1986, the whip was appointed by the Speaker and hence responsible to him. O'Neill (*Man of the House*, p. 266) never liked the idea of an elected whip but agreed to the change on his way out the door, and thus the whip became responsible to the caucus (see Barry, *Ambition and Power*, pp. 34, 77–79). On p. 81, Barry says, "Wright . . . neither consulted nor informed Coelho about the selection of the ten Deputy Whips . . . Coelho might be the Whip, but the whip organization belonged to Wright." Gary Hymel comments, "What happened was Coelho had leaked he was going to appoint [Steny] Hoyer [Md] so Wright, to prove the appointment was his, had to pick someone else, although Hoyer was his first choice" (personal communication, April 8, 2002; Janet Hook, "Despite Whip's Political Role, Personal Ties Matter Most," *Congressional Quarterly*, July 6, 1991, pp. 1818–19).

72. Chapman had been elected in a special election to the previous Congress to replace the deceased Wright Patman.

73. Barry, *Ambition and Power*, p. 76.

74. Steven V. Roberts, "Wright's Style: Both a Strength and a Weakness," *New York Times*, October 25, 1988; Robin Toner, "Congress: Jim Wright Is Respected, but Colleagues are Concerned about His Tendency to Go It Alone," *New York Times*, April 3, 1989.

75. Susan F. Rasky, "Everyone Has Something to Say about Wright," *New York Times*, December 18, 1987.

76. Janet Hook, "GOP Chafes under Restrictive House Rules," *Congressional Quarterly*, October 10, 1987, pp. 2449–52.

77. Armey's remarks are in the *Congressional Record*, May 24, 1988, p. H3579; Cheney's in James A. Barnes, "Partisanship," *National Journal*, November 7, 1987, p. 2825. Also John Gregg, "Concessions Follow House Wrangling," *Roll Call*, November 15, 1987, p. 3. Elizabeth Wehr, "Wright Finds a Vote to Pass Reconciliation Bill," *Congressional Quarterly*, October 31, 1987, pp. 2653–55; Janet Hook, "Bitterness Lingers from House Budget Votes," *Congressional Quarterly*, November 7, 1987, pp. 2712–13.

78. On occasion Democrats also bridled at the lack of opportunity to offer amendments. See Patrick J. Knudsen and Julie Rovner, "Fight Erupts over Restrictive Rules: Amid Democratic Dissension, Welfare Bill is Delayed Again," *Congressional Quarterly*, December 12, 1987, pp. 3036–37. On May 24, 1988 under a special order, the Republican leadership laid out in detail its complaints on issues of House management including information about restrictions on debate. The attack was somewhat blunted by the inclusion of numerous other gripes, some of which made no sense at all. For example, there were complaints that the increased size of House staff was not adequately reflected in legislative "productivity." "The First Congress," Jerry Lewis of California said, "by most accounts the most productive Congress ever, managed to obtain that distinction without any committee staff at all." *Congressional Record-House*, May 24, 1988, pp. H3576–92. The Lewis quote is at p. H3580. A more incisive critique going over some of the same ground is Richard B. Cheney, "An Unruly House: A Republican View," *Public Opinion* 11 (January/February 1989), pp. 41–44. See also Connelly and Pitney, *Congress' Permanent Minority?*, pp. 72–74.

79. Jonathan Fuerbringer, "A House Divided by Political Rancor," *New York Times*, March 16, 1988, p. 28. See also Eric Pianin, "The Wrath of House Republicans Is on Jim Wright's Head," *Washington Post Weekly*, January 3, 1988, p. 15; Janet Hook, "Jim Wright: Taking Big Risks to Amass Power," *Congressional Quarterly*, March 12, 1988, pp. 623–26; Irvin Molotsky, "House Republicans Rail at Democrats," *New York Times*, May 25, 1988; "GOP Snipes at How Democrats Run House," *Congressional Quarterly*, May 28, 1988, p. 1437.

80. Eleanor Clift and Tom Brazaitis, *War Without Bloodshed: The Art of Politics* (New York: Scribner, 1996), p. 238.

81. Newspaper comment at the time on the merits of these changes varied. On one hand, Brooks Jackson, the *Wall Street Journal*'s corruption specialist, wrote that even more than the 69 charges adopted by the committee were justified. On the other hand, John Barry, the freelance journalist who was shadowing Wright for an independent book, publicly doubted the probity of the committee's prosecution. Brooks Jackson, "Many Additional Charges could have been Lodged," *Wall Street Journal*, June 1, 1989. John Barry, "Distinguishing between Wright and Wrong," *Washington Post Weekly*, May 8–14, 1989, p. 24. For a level-headed evaluation by a specialist in professional ethics, see Dennis F. Thompson, *Ethics in Congress* (Washington, D.C.: Brookings, 1995).

82. Michael Oreskes, "Coelho to Resign His Seat in House in Face of Inquiry," *New York Times*, May 27, 1989.

83. Richard E. Cohen, "The Unhappy Few Lose Another Chief," *National Journal*, March 18, 1989, p. 693.

84. Jeffrey H. Birnbaum, "Bitter Fight for Republican House Whip Places Division in Party Thinking in Stark Contrast," *Wall Street Journal*, March 21, 1989; Phil Duncan, "House GOP: No More Mr. Nice Guy," *Congressional Quarterly*, February 9, 1991, p. 394.

85. See Koopman, *Hostile Takeover*, pp. 11–29; Janet Hook, "Battle for Whip Pits Partisans against Party Pragmatists," *Congressional Quarterly*, March 18, 1989, pp. 563–65; Jeffrey H. Birnbaum, "Gingrich to Be House GOP Whip; Madigan Edged out in 87–85 Vote," *Wall Street Journal*, March 23, 1989; Robin Toner, "House Republicans Elect Gingrich of Georgia as Whip," *New York Times*, March 23, 1989; Janet Hook, "Gingrich's Selection as Whip Reflects GOP Discontent," *Congressional Quarterly*, March 25, 1989, pp. 625–27.

86. Dan Balz, "These Republicans Aren't about to Hang Up Their Gloves," *Washington Post Weekly*, June 26–July 2, 1989, p. 14; E. J. Dionne, Jr., "Attack Shows GOP Strategy Shift," *New York Times*, June 11, 1989; Michael Oreskes, "War Drums in the House: Republicans Vow to Press Attack on Ethics while Digging in for Democratic Reprisals," *New York Times*, May 28, 1989.

87. E. J. Dionne, Jr., "GOP Keeping Up Ethics Pressure on the Democrats," *New York Times*, May 29, 1989.

88. The fair-minded and thoughtful Foley held what by most criteria should have been a Republican seat in eastern Washington state from 1965 to 1994. See John E. Yang, "House Speaker Foley, Very Much the Product of His State, Hasn't Fallen Far from the Tree," *Wall Street Journal*, August 23, 1989. Also John Newhouse, "Profile: The Navigator," *New Yorker*, April 10, 1989, pp. 45–84; David Rogers and John E. Yang, "Foley Steps in as New Speaker of House, Casting Himself as a Healer for 2 Parties," *Wall Street Journal*, June 7, 1989. Even his low-key and gentlemanly demeanor did not insulate Foley from attempts in June 1989 by the Republican National Committee with the cooperation of a Gingrich staff member to repeat their success with Wright by launching a nasty personal attack on him. See Biggs, with Foley, *Honor in the House*, pp. 116–17. Also James M. Perry and David Rogers, "GOP Aide Dismissed

as Attack on Foley Misfires; Imbroglio May Trim Party's Edge on Ethics Issue," *Wall Street Journal*, June 8, 1989.

89. Readers wishing to follow the story in detail can consult newspapers in February and March of 1992. For example: Thomas W. Lippman and Guy Gugliotta, "Political Furor Grows over House Bank," *Washington Post*, March 16, 1992; Clifford Krauss, "The House Bank: Gingrich Takes No Prisoners in the House's Sea of Gentility," *New York Times*, March 17, 1992: "Unlike the non-confrontational Republicans who have led the minority party in the House, Mr. Gingrich says the best way to save Congress is to destroy its reputation by any means necessary."

90. See Committee on Standards of Official Conduct, "Inquiry into the Operation of the Bank of the Sergeant-at-Arms of the House of Representatives," Report 102–452, together with Minority Views, March 10, 1992 (Washington, D.C.: U.S. Government Printing Office, 1992).

91. *Congressional Quarterly Almanac*, 1992, "House Bank Scandal," pp. 34–35. Also Clifford Krauss, "GOP Success in House Splits Party Leadership," *New York Times*, March 20, 1992.

92. *Congressional Quarterly Almanac*, 1992, "House Bank Scandal," p. 39. For a detailed analysis, see Gary C. Jacobson and Michael A. Dimock, "Checking Out: The Effects of Bank Overdrafts on the 1992 House Elections," *American Journal of Political Science* 38 (August 1994), pp. 601–24.

93. The story was picked up and reported in *Roll Call*. Timothy J. Burger, "Bob Michel Defends Statement Labeling Frosh as 'Hard-Line' ", August 16, 1993.

94. David S. Broder, "Another Team Player Retires," *Washington Post Weekly*, October 18–24, 1993, p. 4.

95. Jackie Calmes, "As Michel Leaves Top House GOP Post, Young Generation Flexes for Fights," *Wall Street Journal*, October 5, 1993; Grover C. Norquist, "Whipped into Shape," *American Spectator*, February, 1995, p. 57.

96. Eleanor Clift and Tom Brazaitis report:

At the least, GOPAC provided seed money to further Gingrich's goal of ending the war between right-wingers and moderates by downplaying issues that divided them, like abortion, and enlisting Republicans in a crusade they could all support—the dismantling of "the corrupt liberal welfare state." To recruit young activists, Gingrich and his allies recorded instructional tapes—more than two thousand of them over ten years—and GOPAC sent them to Republican candidates around the country. The motivational tapes disseminated Gingrich's views and insured that a new breed of Republicans would be created in his likeness. One flyer—"Language: A Key Mechanism of Control"—offered a word list for candidates who wanted to "Speak Like Newt." It recommended sixty-four words and phrases to define Democrats, such as "pathetic," "sick," "corrupt," "bizarre," and "traitors." (*War Without Bloodshed*, p. 238).

97. Frank Newport, "Gingrich an Unpopular Figure during His Tenure as Speaker," *Gallup Poll Monthly* 398 (November 1998), pp. 12–13, 51. Daniel J. Palazzolo writes, "From January to December 1995, public unfavorable ratings of Gingrich went from 29 percent to 56 percent. By December, while 61 percent of Americans had a favorable opinion of Clinton, only 24 percent had a favorable opinion of Gingrich. By 51 percent to 34 percent, the public believed Clinton's proposals for the budget were better for the country than Republican plans" ("The Two Speakerships: Newt Gingrich's Impact on Budget Policy," *Extensions* [Carl Albert Center, University of Oklahoma] [Fall 2000], p. 17).

98. Gary C. Jacobson, "The 1994 House Elections in Perspective," *Political Science Quarterly* 111 (Summer 1996), pp. 203–23. Jacobson wrote:

> The New York Times/CBS News Poll of 29 October–1 November found that 71 percent of respondents had never heard of the Contract and another 15 percent said it would make no difference in how they voted. Only 7 percent said it would make them more likely to vote for the Republican House candidate, while 5 percent said it would make them less likely to do so. (p. 209.)

99. See, "GOP, to Its Own Great Delight, Enacts House Rules Changes," *CQ Weekly Report*, January 7, 1995, pp. 73–75; "Republicans Lay out New Hill Rules," *Congressional Quarterly Almanac*, 1994, pp. 18–21.

100. Asra Q. Nomani, "End of the Ice Age Has Congress Staffers Carrying Their Own," *Wall Street Journal*, August 5, 1997.

101. Forrest Maltzman makes the point that many of the practices adopted by Gingrich vis-à-vis committees did not require changes in the rules (*Competing Principals: Committees, Parties, and the Organization of Congress* [Ann Arbor: University of Michigan Press, 1997], esp. p. 159).

102. "Statement of Thomas J. Craren, CPA, Engagement Partner Price Waterhouse LLP before the Committee on House Oversight of the US House of Representatives, July 18, 1994," *Lexis Nexis Congressional Federal Document Clearing House*, July 18, 1995. R. H. Melton, "Independent House Audit Finds Millions Wasted, Controls Limited," *Washington Post*, July 18, 1995, p. A4; AP, "Outside Auditors Find Vast Disarray in the House's Finances," *New York Times*, July 19, 1995, p. A16; Raymond R. Coffey, "Congress Needs to Get Finances and House in Order," *Chicago Sun-Times*, July 20, 1995, p. 6.

103. A trenchant argument emphasizing Republican inexperience is Richard Fenno's *Learning to Govern: An Institutional View of the 104th Congress* (Washington, D.C.: Brookings, 1997). Also Alan Ehrenhalt, "Hijacking the Rulebook," *New York Times*, December 20, 1998.

104. Nicol C. Rae, *The Decline and Fall of the Liberal Republicans from 1952 to the Present* (New York: Oxford University Press, 1989), pp. 157–95.

105. See, e.g., the contrast between John Taber (R) and Clarence Cannon

(D) on Appropriations. Richard F. Fenno, Jr., *The Power of the Purse* (Boston: Little, Brown, 1966), p. 55.

106. David Maraniss and Michael Weisskopf, *Tell Newt to Shut Up* (New York: Simon and Schuster, 1996), pp. 87–88. It took a couple of years for Livingston to rebel. His declaration of independence was an extraordinary letter to the Speaker making a bid to take back quite a lot of the turf Gingrich had seized at the beginning of his Speakership. It was sent on November 6, 1998, three days after the election, marked "Personal and Confidential" and promptly leaked. Here is the text, from *Roll Call* on November 9:

In consideration of the deep respect and friendship that I hold for you, I have set forth herewith a list of requirements that I believe are critical and vital to the success of the 106th Congress. In order for the majority to complete its work and demonstrate that we can properly govern, I believe it is imperative that you acknowledge and agree to these suggested changes in house procedure, without exception:

1. I, as Chairman of the Appropriations Committee, shall run the Committee as I see fit and in the best interest of the Republican majority with full consultation with the Leadership, but without being subject to the dictates of any other Member of Congress.

2. That I be the final authority to determine content of legislation within the Appropriations Committee, and the schedule under which legislation is produced, without interference.

3. That all future budget resolutions be completed for House approval between April 15 and April 30, and that thereafter all Appropriations bills are free to proceed with or without a Budget Resolution, for completion in the House of Representatives by the end of June of every calendar year. The Senate will be urged to do likewise so that all conferences can be completed before the August break of each calendar year.

4. I, as Appropriations Chairman, shall be present in all Leadership discussions of the budget affecting Appropriations matters. No decisions on Appropriations issues will be made within the context of budget negotiations without consultation (not necessarily approval) with me.

5. There will be no amendment in Rules or Law affecting Appropriations jurisdiction without my approval.

6. No member or Subcommittee Chairmen will be removed from my Committee or from their post on my Committee without my approval.

7. [Text illegible] affecting Appropriations bills will be issued in [text illegible] with the Leadership, but no such rule or provision thereof will be issued over my objections.

8. It has become apparent that Members are assigned too many Committees and that the work product of such Committees and Subcommittees is suffering for lack of attendance at meetings. Committee sizes are

out of proportion to any sense of reality and power is adversely distributed accordingly. Therefore all Committees should be limited to 55 Republican and Democrat Members, with an absolute maximum of 60
Members. These goals can be attained by attrition.

9. Members should not be assigned to Committees "because of their
districts." Fragile members are afraid to cast tough votes, and that in-
hibits the passage of credible legislation.

10. No Republican will be assigned to the Appropriations Committee
without my approval.

11. No Member should be on more than 5 subcommittees without
waivers, and waivers should never be issued except under the strictest
of conditions of dire emergency or importance. No Member of the Appropriations Committee shall serve on any Committee or Subcommittee
other than that of the Budget Committee.

12. The legislation schedule requires substantial revision. We should
have longer work weeks and many fewer holidays. The work schedule
should in most cases begin at 12:00 noon on Monday with votes after
5:00 pm on Monday and continue each day between 10:00 am and
6:00 pm through Friday with no afternoon votes on Friday. Members
should understand that at peak times, they may be required to work late
hours, but that on most occasions they may make plans at night without
fear of cancellation.

13. I, as Chairman of the Appropriations Committee, during last minute negotiations with Democrats or with representatives of the White
House on all Appropriations bills, will make final decisions, but with full
consultation with the leadership.

14. There should be weekly meetings with Democrats to last no more
than one hour, and I as Chairman of the Appropriations Committee
should be included.

16. [sic] The Speaker shall insist that the Senate concur and conform
to our expedited schedule on Appropriations and budget, with the understanding that should either House fail to pass an Appropriations bill
by July 30, that the respective bill which has been passed by the remaining House of Congress will become the actionable vehicle for conference.

107. Fenno, *Learning to Govern*, p. 31. See also Jackie Koszczuk, "Gingrich
Puts More Power into Speaker's Hands," *CQ Weekly Report*, October 7, 1995,
pp. 3049–53; David Rogers, "General Newt: GOP's Rare Year Owes Much to
How Gingrich Disciplined the House," *Wall Street Journal*, December 18, 1995.

108. Brett Lieberman, "After Their Retreat, Legislators Pledge Civility," *Plain
Dealer* (Cleveland), March 23, 1999. For the earlier retreat, see Jennifer Bradley,
"Hershey Kisses All Around as House Members Head to Bipartisan Retreat,"

*Roll Call*, March 6, 1997; David S. Broder, "A Two-Party Retreat?" *Washington Post National Edition*, July 29–August 4, 1996, p. 4.

109. Richard E. Cohen, "Chaos Still Prevailing over Civility," *National Journal*, July 5, 1997, p. 1382.

110. A good account of Gingrich's tribulations can be found in Peter Baker, *The Breach* (New York: Scribner, 2000).

111. Jason DeParle, "Listen, Learn, Help, Lead," *New York Times Magazine*, January 28, 1996, p. 34 ff.; Jackie Koszczuk, "Gingrich under Fire as Discord Simmers from Rank to Top," *Congressional Quarterly*, June 21, 1997, pp. 1415–18.

112. Newt Gingrich, *Lessons Learned the Hard Way* (New York: Harper-Collins, 1998), pp. 149–50.

113. See Jackie Calmes, "Paxon Resigns House Leadership Post after Failed Attempt to Oust Gingrich," *Wall Street Journal*, July 18, 1997; Jerry Gray, "Gingrich Removes a Lieutenant for Role in Failed Coup Attempt," *New York Times*, July 18, 1997; Jackie Koszczuk, "Party Stalwarts will Determine Gingrich's Long-Term Survival," *Congressional Quarterly*, July 26, 1997, pp. 1751–55; Richard E. Cohen, "Beginning of the End," *National Journal*, July 26, 1997, pp. 1516–17.

114. Jim VandeHei, "Gingrich Quits," *Roll Call*, November 9, 1998.

115. Ibid. That Gingrich and Gephardt had virtually no communication for four years was not much commented upon, but was a very significant fact of life in Washington. See David S. Broder, "The Next Speaker of the House," *Washington Post National Edition*, November 23, 1998.

116. For historical perspective, see Garrison Nelson, "Partisan Patterns of House Leadership Change, 1789–1977," *American Political Science Review* 71 (September 1977), pp. 918–39.

117. On John Rhodes, see Mary Russell, "Rhodes Will Step Down as House Republican Leader Next Year," *Washington Post*, December 13, 1979. Russell reports:

He . . . has been under pressure from a hard-charging class of 37 freshman Republicans. They have been critical of Rhodes' leadership, calling him too passive and low-key in taking on the Democrats. By last summer, their disillusionment amounted to "near insurrection" as one member put it.

Rhodes has taken steps to quell the criticism . . . and was considering running again for minority leader. But he was told by [Robert] Michel and others he would have to fight off challengers to keep the post. "I didn't want him blind-sided like Charlie Halleck was," Michel said.

On his way out, Rhodes sounded a lot like Bob Michel. "The truth is," he told Marjorie Hunter of the *New York Times*, "Tip and I had a good relationship in that we trusted one another. If Tip ever told me something was going to happen, I knew it would. He has always been a dear friend." As for his junior colleagues, he wrote in his 1976 book *The Futile System* (McLean, Va.: EPM Publications), p. 7: "Today a large number of Congressmen are cynical, abrasive, frequently uncommunicative and ambitious to an inordinate degree. In their eagerness to draw attention to themselves, and advance politically, they frustrate the legislative process." In a mellow moment in his exit interview with Hunter he pulled back from this characterization, but not all the way (Marjorie Hunter, "After 30 Years, Era Ending in House with Departure of a GOP Loyalist," *New York Times*, December 18, 1982). See also Irwin B. Areiff, "House Freshmen Republicans Seek Role as Power Brokers," *CQ Weekly Report*, July 7, 1979, and other stories in the package, pp. 1339–45, especially "John Rhodes: 'Loose Reins' Leadership," p. 1345; Martin Tolchin, "Rhodes to Quit House GOP Post," *New York Times*, December 13, 1979.

118. Bob Livingston, Gingrich's designated successor, withdrew in disarray and resigned from the House before even taking the oath of office. He decided that in view of the impeachment charges then pending against President Clinton his own record of marital infidelity could not withstand scrutiny. Damon Chappie, "Bob Livingston's Stunning Rise and Fall," *Roll Call*, December 21, 1998; Jim VandeHei, "House Impeaches President: Hastert Likely New Speaker," *Roll Call*, December 21, 1998.

119. This is one of those famous phrases that migrates readily into famous mouths. It is also attributed to the Boston Brahmin president of Harvard (1908–33) A. Lawrence Lowell, referring to university administration (Morton Keller and Phyllis Keller, *Making Harvard Modern* [New York: Oxford University Press, 2001] p. 17).

120. See Robin Toner, "Atmosphere in the House Becomes Personal and Mean and Nasty," *New York Times*, November 19, 1995.

## 5. Overview: How Congress Evolves

1. A preliminary version of this chapter appears as "Political Change and the Character of the Contemporary Congress," in Anthony King, ed., *The New American Political System*, 2d ed. (Washington, D.C.: AEI Press, 1990), pp. 29–46.

2. For discussions of these various achievements, see E. Pendleton Herring, *Presidential Leadership* (New York: Farrar and Rinehart, 1940); Arthur M. Schlesinger, Jr., *The Coming of the New Deal* (Boston: Houghton Mifflin, 1958); William E. Leuchtenburg, *Franklin D. Roosevelt and the New Deal, 1932–1940* (New York: Harper & Row, 1963); James T. Patterson, *Congressional Conservatism and the New Deal* (Lexington: University of Kentucky Press, 1967); and David M. Kennedy, *Freedom from Fear: The American People in Depression and War, 1929–1945* (New York: Oxford University Press, 1999).

3. See Herman Somers, *Presidential Agency* (Cambridge, Mass.: Harvard University Press, 1950); Stephen K. Bailey, *Congress Makes a Law: The Story behind the Employment Act of 1946* (New York: Columbia University Press, 1950); Nelson W. Polsby, *Political Innovation in America* (New Haven, Conn.: Yale University Press, 1984); and Paul Hammond, *Organizing for Defense* (Princeton, N.J.: Princeton University Press, 1961), esp. pp. 131–59, 249–87.

4. Much of this legislation passed in the 89th Congress. See *Congressional Quarterly Almanac*, 89th Congress, 1st Session, 1965, vol. 21, pp. 65–112; and *Congressional Quarterly Almanac*, 89th Congress, 2d Session, 1966, vol. 22, pp. 69–94, 99–115.

5. Kennedy, *Freedom from Fear*, esp. pp. 381–564.

6. James MacGregor Burns, *The Deadlock of Democracy: Four Party Politics in America* (Englewood Cliffs, N.J.: Prentice-Hall, 1963). See also Eleanor Bontecou, *The Federal Loyalty-Security Program* (Ithaca, N.Y.: Cornell University Press, 1953).

7. This discussion may seem to contradict (but does not) the argument in David Mayhew's elegant book *Divided We Govern* (New Haven, Conn.: Yale University Press, 1991), in which he shows that split partisan control of the political branches of government does not cause a noticeable slackening of legislative productivity. According to Mayhew's figures, which cover 1947–89, in the Great Society period (1964–68) there were on average a dozen "important enactments" a year; in the 1947–63 and 1969–89 periods, annual productivity of "important enactments" was at the rate of five or six a year, or half speed compared with the highly productive period.

8. Genesis: chapter 11. Liberals should take note that in the Bible, God (or in a secularist rendition, human nature) is firmly on the side of confusion.

9. On crisis and its effects on innovation, see Polsby, *Political Innovation*, esp. pp. 167–72.

10. For authoritative commentary on the Legislative Reorganization Act of 1946, see George Galloway, *Congress at the Crossroads* (New York: Crowell, 1946).

11. On Johnson, see Ralph K. Huitt, "Democratic Party Leadership in the Senate," *American Political Science Review* 55 (June 1961), pp. 331–44. On the packing of the Rules Committee, see Neil MacNeil, *Forge of Democracy: The House of Representatives* (New York: McKay, 1963), pp. 412–47; and William MacKaye, *A New Coalition Takes Control: The House Rules Committee Fight of 1961* (New York: McGraw-Hill, 1963). On 1970s reforms of the House, see Norman Ornstein, "The Democrats Reform Power in the House of Representatives, 1969–1975," in Allan Sindler, ed., *America in the Seventies: Problems, Policies, and Politics* (Boston: Little, Brown, 1977), pp. 2–48; Roger H. Davidson and Walter J. Oleszek, *Congress Against Itself* (Bloomington: Indiana University Press, 1977); and Leroy N. Rieselbach, *Congressional Reform in the Seventies* (Morristown, N.J.: General Learning Press, 1977).

12. Nelson W. Polsby, Miriam Gallaher, and Barry Spencer Rundquist, "The Growth of the Seniority System in the U. S. House of Representatives," *American Political Science Review* 63 (September 1969), pp. 787–807.

13. Nicholas Masters, "Committee Assignments in the House of Representatives," *American Political Science Review* 55 (June 1961), pp. 345–57.

14. See Barbara Deckard Sinclair, "Determinants of Aggregate Party Cohesion in the U.S. House of Representatives, 1901–1956," *Legislative Studies Quarterly* 2 (May 1977), pp. 155–75, esp. p. 160; and Barbara Deckard and John Stanley, "Party Decomposition and Region: The House of Representatives, 1945–1970," *Western Political Quarterly* 27 (June 1974), pp. 249–64, esp. pp. 250, 257. Also see Julius Turner and Edward V. Schneier, Jr., *Party and Constituency: Pressures on Congress* (Baltimore: Johns Hopkins University Press, 1970), esp. pp. 41–106 and 165–89; Nelson W. Polsby and William G. Mayer, "Ideological Cohesion in the American Two-Party System," in Nelson W. Polsby and Raymond E. Wolfinger, eds., *On Parties: Essays Honoring Austin Ranney* (Berkeley: Institute of Governmental Studies Press, 1999), pp. 219–54; and David Mayhew, *Party Loyalty among Congressmen: The Difference between Democrats and Republicans, 1947–1962* (Cambridge, Mass.: Harvard University Press, 1966).

15. See Thomas Mann and Norman Ornstein, eds., *The New Congress* (Washington, D.C.: American Enterprise Institute, 1981), esp. chapters by Roger Davidson and Michael Malbin, pp. 99–177; Leroy Rieselbach, *Congressional Reform in the Seventies* (Morristown, N.J.: General Learning Press, 1977) ; and Ornstein, "The Democrats Reform Power."

16. See Clem Miller, in John Baker, ed., *Member of the House* (New York: Scribner, 1962), esp. pp. 116–31.

17. See Mark Ferber, "The Democratic Study Group: A Study of Intra-Party Organization in the House of Representatives" (Ph.D. diss. University of California at Los Angeles, 1964).

18. Five of the last six Republican leaders (Martin, Halleck, Rhodes, Michel, Gingrich) were either overthrown or left office in anticipation of being replaced. Only Ford, appointed vice president, escaped unscathed.

19. See, e.g., David B. Truman, ed., *The Congress and America's Future* (Englewood Cliffs, N.J.: Prentice-Hall, 1965), pp. 1–31.

20. Nelson W. Polsby, "Institutionalization of the U.S. House of Representatives," *American Political Science Review* 62 (March 1968), pp. 144–68.

21. Raymond E. Wolfinger and Joan Heifetz, "Safe Seats, Seniority, and Power in Congress," *American Political Science Review* 59 (June 1965), pp. 337–49. Nicholas Lemann, *The Promised Land: The Great Black Migration and How It Changed America* (New York: A. A. Knopf, 1991).

22. David W. Brady, *Critical Elections and Congressional Policy Making* (Stanford, Calif.: Stanford University Press, 1988).

23. Norman Ornstein, Thomas Mann, and Michael Malbin, *Vital Statistics*

*on Congress 1997–1998* (Washington, D.C.: American Enterprise Institute, 1998), pp. 135–39; John Hart, *The Presidential Branch* (New York: Pergamon Press, 1987).

24. Nelson W. Polsby, *Consequences of Party Reform* (New York: Oxford University Press, 1983).

25. The main decisions were *Baker v. Carr,* 369 U.S. 186 (1962), which took jurisdiction in state apportionment cases; *Wesberry v. Sanders,* 376 U.S. 1 (1964), which required substantial equality of populations within U.S. House districts; and *Reynolds v. Sims,* 377 U.S. 533 (1964), which required the apportionment of both houses of bicameral state legislatures on the same proportional basis. For a thorough discussion of these and other cases, see Robert G. Dixon, *Democratic Representation* (New York: Oxford University Press, 1968). In *Wells v. Rockefeller,* 389 U.S. 421 (1969), the Court defined more exactly—and more narrowly—what "substantial equality" meant. See Nelson W. Polsby, ed., *Reapportionment in the 1970s* (Berkeley: University of California Press, 1971). The line of cases continues to grow. For more recent commentary, see Bernard Grofman, Arend Lijphardt, Robert McKay, and Howard Scarrow, *Representation and Redistricting Issues* (Lexington, Mass.: Lexington Books, 1982). In *Mahan v. Howell,* 410 U.S. 315 (1973), the Court pressed the state of Virginia closer to "one person, one vote" in state districts. In *Karcher v. Daggett,* 462 U.S. 725 [103 S.Ct. 2653] (1983), the Court demanded that congressional districts be more exactly equal in population than the U.S. Census is capable of warranting. In *Shaw v. Reno,* 509 U.S. 630 (1993), the Court held that while race could be considered in drawing congressional district lines it could not be a decisive factor.

26. David Lublin conservatively estimates that from seven to 11 congressional seats were held by Republicans after the 1994 elections that Democrats would have occupied had not minority voters been subtracted from them (*The Paradox of Representation: Racial Gerrymandering and Minority Interests in Congress* [Princeton, N.J.: Princeton University Press, 1997], pp. 111–14).

## Appendix: Methods and Sources

1. Ivor Crewe and Anthony King, *SDP: The Birth, Life and Death of the Social Democratic Party* (Oxford: Oxford University Press, 1995).

2. Hugh Heclo and Aaron Wildavsky, *The Private Government of Public Money* (Berkeley: University of California Press, 1974); Peter Hennessy, *The Hidden Wiring: Unearthing the British Constitution* (London: Gollancz, 1995), *Whitehall* (London: Secker & Warburg, 1989); Noel Annan, *Our Age: Portrait of a Generation* (London: G. Weidenfeld and Nicolson, 1990), *Changing Enemies: The Defeat and Regeneration of Germany* (London: HarperCollins, 1995), and *The Dons: Mentors, Eccentrics, and Geniuses* (Chicago: University of Chicago Press, 1999).

3. Crewe and King, *SDP*, p. 53.

4. See, e.g., James Sterling Young, *The Washington Community, 1800–1828* (New York: Columbia University Press, 1966).

5. Among the works on one or another aspect of Congress that I have written, I include: "Two Strategies of Influence in the House of Representatives: Choosing a Majority Leader," in Nelson W. Polsby and Robert L Peabody, eds., *New Perspectives on the House of Representatives* (Chicago: Rand McNally, 1963), pp. 324–54; *Congress and the Presidency* (Englewood Cliffs, N.J.: Prentice-Hall, Foundations of Political Science Series, 1964) (revised 1971, 1976, 1986); "The Institutionalization of the U.S. House of Representatives," *American Political Science Review* 62 (March 1968), pp. 144–68; "Thoughts on Congress, National Security, and the Rise of the Presidential Branch," *Atlantic Community Quarterly* 26 (Spring 1968), pp. 97–104; "Goodbye to the Inner Club," *Washington Monthly* 1 (August 1969), pp. 30–34; "The Growth of the Seniority System in the U.S. House of Representatives," with Miriam Gallaher and Barry S. Rundquist, *American Political Science Review* 63 (September 1969), pp. 787–807; "Policy Analysis and Congress," in *The Analysis and Evaluation of Public Expenditures: The P.P.B. System*, a compendium of Papers Submitted to the Subcommittee on Economy in Government of the Joint Economic Committee, Congress of the United States, vol. 3 (Washington, D.C.: Government Printing Office, 1969), pp. 943–52; "Strengthening Congress in National Policy Making," *Yale Review* 59 (June 1970), pp. 481–97; "Legislatures," in Fred I. Greenstein and Nelson W. Polsby, eds., *Handbook of Political Science*, vol. 5 (Reading, Mass: Addison-Wesley, 1975), pp. 257–319; "The 1896 Election and Congressional Modernization: An Appraisal of the Evidence," (with others) *Social Science History* 5 (Winter 1981), pp. 53–90; "Studying Congress through Time: A Comment on Joseph Cooper and David Brady, 'Toward a Diachronic Analysis of Congress,' " *American Political Science Review* 75 (December 1981), pp. 1010–12; "Some Landmarks in Modern Congressional-Presidential Relations," in Anthony King, ed., *Both Ends of the Avenue* (Washington, D.C.: American Enterprise Institute, 1983), pp. 1–25; "The Stabilization of the 20th Century Congress: New Evidence on Change in the American Political Universe," with A. Bogue, D. Brady, and J. Silbey, in *Annual Report, 1986, Center for Advanced Study in the Behavioral Sciences* (Stanford, Calif., 1986), pp. 57–69; "The Social Composition of Congress," in Uwe Thaysen, Roger H. Davidson, and Robert G. Livingston, eds., *The U.S. Congress and the German Bundestag* (Boulder, Colo: Westview, 1990), pp. 109–27; "Political Change and the Character of the Contemporary Congress," in Anthony King, ed., *The New American Political System*, second version (Washington, D.C.: American Enterprise Institute Press, 1990), pp. 29–46; "Congress Bashing for Beginners," *Public Interest* 100 (Summer 1990), pp. 15–23 (expanded version printed as "Congress Bashing through the Ages," *Roll Call Guide to Congress*, September 10, 1990, pp. 27–32); "The Making of the Modern Congress," in W. H. Robinson and C. H. Wellborn, eds., *Knowledge, Power and the Congress* (Washington, D.C.: Congressional Quarterly Press,

1991), pp. 80–90; "Restoration Comedy" (Review of George Will, *Restoration*), *Yale Law Journal* 102 (April 1993), pp. 1515–26; "Does Congress Work?" *Bulletin of the American Academy of Arts and Sciences* 79 (May 1993), pp. 30–45; and "Some Arguments Against Congressional Term Limitations," *Harvard Journal of Law & Public Policy* 16 (Winter 1993), pp. 101–7.

6. For a brief discussion of Ralph Huitt's influence on congressional studies, see Nelson W. Polsby and Eric Schickler, "Landmarks in the Study of Congress since 1945," *Annual Review of Political Science* V (Palo Alto, Calif.: June 2002), pp. 333–67.

7. David B. Truman, *The Congressional Party: A Case Study* (New York: Wiley, 1959); Stephen K. Bailey, *Congress Makes a Law: The Story Behind the Employment Act of 1946* (New York: Columbia University Press, 1960); Lewis Anthony Dexter, "Congressmen and the People They Listen To" (1956). This was later (1959) Dexter's doctoral dissertation at Columbia University and in 1963 a condensed version was published as part V of Raymond A. Bauer, Ithiel de Sola Pool, and Lewis Anthony Dexter, *American Business and Public Policy* (New York: Atherton: 1963).

8. Clem Miller, *Member of the House: Letters of a Congressman*, edited with additional text by John W. Baker (New York: Scribner, 1962).

9. Charles O. Jones, "Representation in Congress: The Case of the House Agriculture Committee," *American Political Science Review* 55 (June 1961), pp. 358–67. Nicholas A. Masters, "Committee Assignments in the House of Representatives," *American Political Science Review* 55 (June 1961), pp. 345–57. Ralph K. Huitt, "Democratic Party Leadership in the Senate," *American Political Science Review* 55 (June 1961), pp. 333–44.

10. The degree was finally awarded in 1983, a year before Mosher died, aged 78. See "Reinterpreting Congress and Its Works" by Charles Adams Mosher, a master's thesis submitted to the Department of Government, Oberlin College, 1983, revised July 1984.

11. As a party loyalist Mosher voted, for example, with his party leadership against the packing of the Rules Committee in January 1961, even though this was contrary to his views favoring civil rights. This was one of Mosher's very first votes as a freshman member, and it took place before Republican committee assignments had been made. See Mosher's column of January 19, 1961 in the *Oberlin News Tribune* "Change the Rules? Mr. Sam's Plan to 'Pack' House Committee is not a Reform, it is Cynical Expediency." He also wrote a letter to Minority Leader Charles Halleck apologizing for going off the reservation on foreign aid (August 17, 1961) on a teller vote.

A decade later, in the fall of 1971, Mosher was opposed in the Republican conference for advancement to ranking member of the Science and Technology Committee. He wrote:

As the second ranking in seniority, under the old rules I automatically would have succeeded [James G.] Fulton [R-Pa]; but the new reform [in the Republican conference] required that other committee members also be considered, that not seniority alone but any other qualifying factors should be considered as the entire minority party membership voted their choice.

It became a genuine test, because there developed strong opposition to choosing me. Many of my more conservative Republican colleagues charged I was too liberal, and too often independent of our party's leadership and party policy decisions in my voting record. They argued that only a more loyal, dependable partisan should be elected as ranking minority member of any committee, that the new anti-seniority rule was in part intended for the very purpose of applying sanctions to enforce party discipline (Mosher, "Reinterpreting Congress and Its Works," p. 62).

Mosher landed on the Science Committee when he first entered Congress in 1961, two years after the committee had been established in response to Sputnik. In his master's thesis he explains how it happened:

It seemed that I should request placement on the Education and Labor Committee, and there did exist a minority vacancy open there, a "natural" because my specialty had been education legislation as the Ohio Senate's Education Committee chairman. But I balked. My excuse was that I had become bored with education issues. But mainly I balked because of the labor aspect of the House committee's jurisdiction. I had won election with only 51.4 percent of the vote in an increasingly industrialized union-organized district, and I arrived in Washington trailed by the most virulent possible denunciations from labor union sources, knowing "They're out to get me next time." Though always officially opposed by organized labor, our relations had been usually congenial during my service in the Ohio Senate. It was mutually recognized that I could and did vote their way when convinced of their case, and that I always was available to hear their side. But in a special "lame duck" session of the Ohio General Assembly, following my November 1960 election to Congress, the highly emotional issue was SUB (supplementary unemployment benefits) legislation. The labor supported bill lost by one vote in the Ohio Senate. I voted against, and the unions urgently hoped, anticipated, I would vote for it. They denounced me in the bitterest of terms. I decided against becoming immediately embroiled in labor issues in a congressional committee. (Mosher, "Reinterpreting Congress and Its Works," p. 55.)

12. It was the week of July 10, 1961. This was a sufficiently unusual research method on Capitol Hill 40 years ago to rate an Associated Press story in Ohio newspapers. See Neil Gilbride "Mosher 'Shadowed,' but Likes It," *Fremont* (Ohio) *News Messenger*, July 17, 1961. Also Mosher's extension of remarks

in the *Congressional Record*, June 24, 1965, "The Study of Congress," pp. A 3329–30.

13. Scholars have no facility on Capitol Hill comparable to the jealously guarded press galleries to which journalists can gain accreditation. These provide space for work and ready access to the legislative chambers. See Norman C. Miller, "The 'Free' Press Makes Out Okay at Public Expense," *Wall Street Journal*, June 17, 1977. Scholars are herded about like tourists until they develop a relationship with a congressional office. Charles O. Jones, for example, notes in the preface of one of his books: "As he has done so often in the past, Congressman E. Y. Berry of South Dakota provided office space so that I could type interview data and make telephone calls. His secretary, Mrs. Mavis Daly arranged appointments with junior members and assisted in countless other ways" (*Party and Policy-Making: The House Republican Policy Committee* [New Brunswick, N.J.: Rutgers University Press, 1964], p. viii).

14. Nelson W. Polsby, "Two Strategies of Influence in the House of Representatives: Choosing a Majority Leader, 1961," in Robert L. Peabody and Nelson W. Polsby, eds., *New Perspectives on the House of Representatives* (Chicago: Rand McNally, 1964), pp. 237–70. I also wrote another article at that time, never published, about John McCormack's succession to the Speakership, "A Tacit Bargain in the House."

15. Richard Fenno describes one such set of occasions: "We met in the early 1960's, as members of a small group of young political scientists who came together to share the excitement of our budding research on Congress. We got a grant to get together periodically in Washington to take members of Congress to dinner and talk about how to study Congress. There were eight of us: Doug [Price], Chuck Jones, Nelson Polsby, Bob Peabody, Milt Cummings, Randall Ripley, Joe Cooper, and myself . . . 'The Boys of Congress.' " (Richard F. Fenno, Jr., "Introduction" to H. Douglas Price, *Explorations in the Evolution of Congress* [Berkeley: IGS Press, 1998] p. xiii).

16. Tip O'Neill, with William Novak, *Man of the House* (New York: St. Martins, 1987), p. 159.

17. O'Neill's biographer John A. Farrell writes:

Novak interviewed three dozen of O'Neill's family members, friends, and former colleagues and got him to talk for hours into a tape recorder that summer [1985] on the Cape. Novak combed O'Neill's well-kept scrapbooks, his fragmented diaries, Breslin's *How the Good Guys Finally Won* and *Tip*, a 1979 book by Paul Clancy and Shirley Elder, for material. After a shaky start, the ghost writer did a fine job capturing O'Neill's voice and cataloging anecdotes. (John A. Farrell, *Tip O'Neill and the American Century* [Boston: Little, Brown, 2001] p. 680.)

18. John Hohenberg gives an official version of what happened in committee in his book *The Pulitzer Prizes* (New York: Columbia University Press, 1974),

pp. 270–73. The biography jury for 1957 proposed Alpheus T. Mason, *Harlan Fiske Stone: Pillar of the Law* or James MacGregor Burns, *Roosevelt: The Lion and the Fox*. J. O. Ferguson, editor of the *Milwaukee Journal*, a member of the Advisory Board to whom the jury reported, recommended *Profiles* instead. He said that he "read [*Profiles*] aloud to my 12-year-old grandson . . . and the boy was absolutely fascinated." Hohenberg also says, rather cryptically, "In Washington, naturally, Arthur Krock was also beating the drums for his friend."

19. Hymel says,

The way it happened, I was to write down Tip's stories I had heard many, many times and we would assign a principle. Remember, Tip was a storyteller, not a story-writer. After I did the easy stories, he would usually call me on Monday morning and say, "I thought of two more stories during the sermon yesterday." I would write out a story, and he would expand on it and the editor would cut it back. One day he said, "Did you ever write a book?" I replied, "Tip, I never took a note." "That's what I like about you," he said. (Personal communication, April 8, 2002.)

20. Ronald M. Peters, Jr., *The Speaker: Leadership in the U.S. House of Representatives* (Washington, D.C.: Congressional Quarterly, 1995), p. ix.

21. Gary Hymel says, "Whenever I get nailed like this I say, 'That's what Tip would've said if he had thought about it' " (personal communication, April 8, 2002).

22. Christopher Madison, "A Man of the House," *National Journal*, March 18, 1989, p. 646.

23. Carl Elliott, Sr., with Michael D'Orso, *The Cost of Courage: The Journey of an American Congressman* (New York: Doubleday, 1992).

24. See Jeffrey R. Biggs, "Working with the Congressman: The Speaker as Co-Author," *Extension of Remarks: Legislative Studies Section Newsletter* (Washington, D.C.: American Political Science Association, January 2000), pp. 12–16.

25. Richard F. Fenno, Jr., *Watching Politicians: Essays on Participant Observation* (Berkeley: Institute of Governmental Studies Press, 1990).

26. E.g., interviews with Emilio Daddario (D-Conn.) on August 15, 1961, and James G. O'Hara (D-Mich.) on January 15, 1962.

27. Henry S. Reuss, *When Government Was Good*(Madison: University of Wisconsin Press, 1999), p. 102.

28. Nicholas Masters, "Committee Assignments in the House of Representatives," *American Political Science Review* 55 (June 1961), pp. 345–57. The quotation, with emphasis supplied, is from p. 346. See for the relevant rules of the House, *Cannon's Precedents* 8, sections 2179, 2195. Compare Floyd M. Riddick, *The United States Congress: Organization and Procedure* (Manassas, Va: National Capitol Publishers, 1949), pp. 164–68. Riddick says (p. 168):

If [new committee members] are freshmen congressmen or of equal seniority, the committee rank will be determined by drawing the names out of a box or alphabetically. Alphabetical order is constantly being violated. In the 86th Congress [1959], for example, the following freshmen were placed on the Post Office and Civil Service Committee, in order of rank: Shipley (IL), Levering, Dulski, Prokop, Foley, Irwin, Harmon, Alford. It seems, furthermore, highly unlikely that the findings reported are the result of random procedures.

29. It can be said in defense of McCormack's performance in this area that his roles as majority leader and as senior leader of the New England delegation were somewhat incompatible. As majority leader he presumably had to worry about the overall consequences for the Democratic program of the entire roster of new assignments and transfers, and hence his preferences could be expected to be governed by considerations of ideological balance (or intended imbalance), informal access for him to private committee activities, and a host of other factors. O'Brien, on the other hand, was relatively free to pursue single-mindedly the goal of advancing "his boys." This is an excellent illustration of circumstances under which leaders who specialize may have advantages over leaders who for one reason or another do not.

30. O'Brien's obituary in the *Chicago Tribune* said,

Unknown to many, O'Brien is credited by House veterans as being the person most responsible for putting Rayburn in line for the Speakership. In January, 1937, the House had to choose a new Majority Leader. John O'Connor (D-NY) . . . was the candidate of several Chicago Democrats in the House . . . some of whom, like O'Connor . . . were Catholics. At a dinner party in Chicago on the eve of the vote, O'Brien announced he was for Rayburn. The rest of the Illinois delegation swung behind O'Brien, and the vote of the delegation gave Rayburn the Democratic leadership. . . .

Mr. O'Brien liked lots of fresh air and sunshine, provided he could get it at a racetrack. He often boasted that he had never taken a drink of whiskey in his life. He did not smoke or play cards. He rarely ate a midday meal and he never ate butter. ("Rep. O'Brien, Democratic Leader, Dies," *Chicago Tribune*, April 15, 1964.)

See also Tom Littlewood, "How Powerful Uncle Tom O'Brien Landed Prison for Illinois," *Chicago Sun-Times*, July 26, 1959.

31. e.g., Ira Katznelson, Kim Geiger, and Daniel Kryder, "Limiting Liberalism: The Southern Veto in Congress, 1933–1950," *Political Science Quarterly* 108 Summer, 1993, pp. 283–306.

32. V. O. Key, Jr., with the assistance of Alexander Heard, *Southern Politics in State and Nation* (New York: A. A. Knopf, 1949).

33. T. M. Luhrmann, "Thick Description," in *International Encyclopedia of the Social and Behavioral Sciences*, vol. 23 (Amsterdam: Elsevier, 2001), p. 15666.

34. Obviously, I am alluding here to the very absorbing epistemological flap over Margaret Mead's work on Samoa touched off by the publication of Derek Freeman's book *Margaret Mead and Samoa: The Making and Unmaking of an Anthropological Myth* (Cambridge, Mass.: Harvard University Press, 1983).

35. Still, there is always room for skepticism. Here is a critical comment about John A. Farrell's thorough biography of Tip O'Neill:

> Farrell had no opportunity to interview O'Neill. Instead he has cobbled together from published sources and interviews with O'Neill's family members, staff, colleagues, cronies, adversaries, and observers a montage of O'Neill's life grounded in the faith that what respondents can agree on is what in fact occurred. (Ronald M. Peters, Jr., "Book Review," *Extensions: A Journal of the Carl Albert Congressional Research and Studies Center*, Spring, 2001, p. 28.)

36. For an extended discussion of the literature on Congress, see Nelson W. Polsby and Eric Schickler, "Landmarks in the Study of Congress Since 1945."

37. In particular, I commend to readers David W. Rohde's *Parties and Leaders in the Post-Reform House* (Chicago: University of Chicago Press, 1991).

38. Eric Schickler, *Disjointed Pluralism: Institutional Innovation and the Development of the U.S. Congress* (Princeton, N.J.: Princeton University Press, 2001).

# INDEX